HELPING SOCIALLY WITHDRAWN AND ISOLATED CHILDREN
AND ADOLESCENTS

COLLEGE LIBRARY

**Please return this book by the date stamped below
- if recalled, the loan is reduced to 10 days**

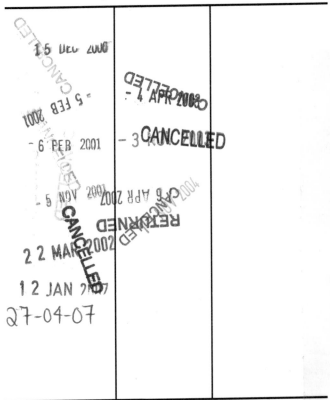

Fines are payable for late return

Also available from Cassell:

Dr Ved Varma (ed.): *Coping with Unhappy Children*
Susan Hart and Dennis Mongon: *Improving Classroom Behaviour*
Brenda Robson: *Pre-School Provision for Children with Special Needs*
Beta Copley and Barbara Forryan: *Therapeutic Work with Children and Young People*
Dr Garry Hornby: *Working with Parents of Children with Special Needs*

Helping Socially Withdrawn and Isolated Children and Adolescents

Maurice Chazan, Alice F. Laing, Diane Davies and
Rob Phillips

CASSELL

Cassell
Wellington House
125 Strand
London WC2R 0BB

PO Box 605,
Herndon,
Virginia 20172

First published 1998

British Library Cataloguing-in-Publication Data

A catalogue record for this book is available from the British Library.

ISBN 0-304-33969-5 (hardback)
    0-304-33970-9 (paperback)

Typeset by Textype Typesetters, Cambridge
Printed and bound in Great Britain by Biddles Ltd, Guildford and King's Lynn

Contents

Authors' Note   vi
Abbreviations   vii

1. Introduction   1
2. The Development of Social Relationships in Childhood and   14
    Adolescence
3. Withdrawn and Isolated Children: Patterns of Behaviour   30
4. Techniques for Assessing Withdrawn and Isolated Behaviour   49
5. Causes of Withdrawal and Isolation   70
6. Consequences of Withdrawal and Isolation   88
7. How Schools and Teachers Can Help   104
8. The Role of Parents and Peers in Helping Withdrawn Children   121
9. Specialized Help   133
10. Conclusion   153

References   165
Index of Case Histories of Children   205
Name Index   206
Subject Index   212

Authors' Note

The names of individuals in the case histories are all fictitious.

The authors would like to thank Ms Karen Glover for her helpful secretarial assistance in the preparation of this book.

Abbreviations

AS	Abiding Self (Elkind and Bowen)
BCL	Behaviour Check List (Richman)
BSAG	Bristol Social Adjustment Guides
BSQ	Behaviour Screening Questionnaire (Richman *et al.*)
CBL, TRF	Child Behaviour Checklist, Teachers' Report Form (Achenbach and Edelbrock)
CCAQ	Children's Cognitive Assessment Questionnaire (Zatz and Chassin)
CDI	Children's Depression Inventory (Kovacs)
DES	Department of Education and Science
DFE	Department for Education
DISC	Diagnostic Interview Schedule for Children (Costello *et al.*)
EBDs	Emotional and Behavioural Difficulties
FSSC-R	Fear Survey Schedule for Children, Revised (Ollendick)
HSS	High Social (sociometric) Status
IAS	Imaginary Audience Scale (Elkind and Bowen)
ICPS	Interpersonal Cognitive Problem-Solving
ILEA	Inner London Education Authority
LEA	Local Education Authority
LSS	Low Social (sociometric) Status
PBQ	Prosocial Behaviour Questionnaire (Weir and Duveen)
PE	Physical Education
PNID	Peer Nomination Inventory of Depression (Lefkowitz and Tesiny)

PSE	Personal and Social Education
RBPC	Revised Behaviour Problem Checklist (Quay and Peterson)
RCMAS	Revised Children's Manifest Anxiety Scale (Reynolds and Richmond)
RE	Religious Education
SATs	Standard Assessment Tests
SI	Social Impact (Dygdon and Conger)
SST	Social Skills Training
TS	Transient Self (Elkind and Bowen)
YSR	Youth Self Report (Achenbach and Edelbrock)
Y1, 2 etc	Year 1 (age range 5 to 6+), Year 2 (age range 6 to 7+), and so on

Chapter 1

Introduction

IMPORTANCE OF SOCIAL RELATIONSHIPS

It has been increasingly recognized in recent years that the development of children and adolescents cannot be understood without taking into account the social context in which it occurs. Within the family, the analysis of mother–child or parent–child interaction has widened its scope to encompass a much wider set of kinship relations (Dunn, 1986; Richards, 1986). Further, perspectives on the study of social and emotional development from early childhood have broadened greatly from a focus on the attachments within the family to a concern also with children's relationships with other children outside the family – in school, playground and neighbourhood. As Malik and Furman (1993) assert, children's relationships with other children become very important to them, even at a young age. Peers are playmates, confidants and sources of support in times of stress. Children can be powerful socializing agents for each other, facilitating their social and emotional growth. Stocker (1994) underlines the importance of children's relationships for the development of self-worth and adequacy, social and academic skills, and general adjustment.

The social context in which children develop is a combination of a variety of factors (see, for example, McGurk, 1992; Erwin, 1993; Forman, Minick and Stone, 1993; and Jackson, 1993). These factors include (Evans and McCandless, 1978):

- the socioeconomic conditions in which children grow up – financial and educational opportunities or the disadvantages of low income and poor housing;

- family structure – nuclear, extended or communal;
- the attitudes of parents and teachers;
- contacts with peers – e.g. those influencing children and adolescents to refrain from, or indulge in, drugs and substance abuse;
- the mass media, providing many different models of how people interact;
- the national cultural heritage, including the general values, beliefs and social customs of the time; and
- the current world circumstances – e.g. of peace or war, depression or prosperity.

The development of social relationships in childhood and adolescence is discussed in more detail in Chapter 2 of this book.

EXTENT AND SIGNIFICANCE OF SOCIAL WITHDRAWAL AND ISOLATION

Perceptions of seriousness of inhibited behaviour

The aim of this book is to increase the general understanding of the nature and significance of failure in social relationships during childhood and adolescence, particularly that characterized by withdrawal and isolation. After a period of relative neglect, more attention is now being given by teachers, clinicians and researchers to children who are socially inhibited or isolated in the peer group, whether at school or in the community. It is not surprising if 'externalized' emotional and behaviour difficulties (EBDs), such as anti-social, restless and overactive conduct, tend to arouse more concern than 'internalized' EBDs, in the form of anxiety and timidity as well as withdrawal from everyday group activities. Adults feel much more threatened by children who are aggressive, destructive or disruptive than by those who seek to distance themselves from social contact. Further, the desire to be on one's own and away from social distractions is a common and normal experience in the case of both children and adolescents, and indeed temporary social withdrawal is often necessary to enable work or leisure pursuits to be carried out. It is not, therefore, easy to distinguish between such 'normal' withdrawal and social detachment indicating an emotional problem.

Moses (1982) considers that teachers do appear to be aware of the problems of withdrawn children and to make a clear distinction between behaviour that is problematical to the child and that which creates difficulties over discipline for the teachers. Laing and Chazan (1987), too, report that teachers would include 'withdrawal' in a list of behaviour that causes them concern. However, some teachers consider that reserved or shy children tend to be 'model' pupils and can be helped in class without recourse to outside help. The quiet, withdrawn child who is well-behaved in class but suffering emotionally may be overlooked to a greater extent than pupils with overt difficulties (Herbert, 1974).

In a study in Israel, Ziv (1970) found that a sample of teachers ranked cruelty, dishonesty, aggressiveness, stealing and temper tantrums as among the most serious problems presented by children and adolescents. There was a significant correlation between the rankings made by these teachers and those of a sample of clinical and educational psychologists, but the psychologists put more emphasis than the teachers on the serious nature of depression, shyness and dependency. Kauffman, Lloyd and McGee (1989) found that teachers in the USA were more concerned about breaches of discipline than internalized behaviour problems. Safran and Safran (1987), too, report that socially withdrawn children in the USA tend not to be given priority for special assistance in either mainstream or special classes. However, Safran (1989) points out that a number of American studies of how teachers cope with the management of classes have found, surprisingly, that internally-directed (e.g. withdrawn) behaviour is harder to handle than negative aggressive behaviour. In his study conducted in Australia, Safran found that, although teachers were particularly intolerant in regard to acting-out behaviour, they rated behaviour associated with a lack of communication (isolation, social withdrawal) as just as difficult to manage as anti-social conduct disorder. Nevertheless, pupils exhibiting withdrawn behaviour were not generally perceived as challenging the teacher's authority or requiring immediate attention, even if the teachers were sympathetic and saw some hope for improvement in the long-term. In general, the specialist services are less likely to be called upon in the case of internalized forms of EBDs than when aggression and disruption are at issue. For example, in one educational psychology service in England, 81 cases of withdrawn behaviour were referred in one year as compared with 269 for aggressive behaviour (Kurtz, Thornes and Wolkind, 1996).

Extent of problem of inhibited behaviour

It is not possible to give a precise estimate of the extent of social withdrawal and isolation in childhood and adolescence. As will be shown in Chapter 3, such behaviour takes many forms and may be defined in different ways in different studies. Withdrawal may, as stated above, be temporary and constructive, or it may be associated with a variety of other EBDs, both externalized and internalized, or even with serious mental illness. Furthermore, attempts to estimate any kind of emotional and behavioural difficulties are affected by many factors. These include the age of the children being rated; the methods employed by researchers to arrive at an estimate; who does the rating (teachers, parents or others); and the location of the sample in terms, say, of the nature of the catchment area of a school. A study by McGuire and Richman (1986) of the behaviour of 637 2- to 4-year-olds attending three types of pre-school group setting (day nurseries, playgroups and nursery classes) illustrates the importance of context in estimates of the prevalence of EBDs. Most of the difficult behaviours (including conduct problems, poor attention and emotional reactions) were found to be much more common in the day nursery group than in the other two settings. However, surprisingly, this was not so in the case of passive and withdrawn behaviour (reluctance to talk to peers or staff; extreme inactivity). McGuire and Richman suggest that day-nursery staff, having to cope with a substantial amount of disruptive behaviour, may be less able to give attention to withdrawn or isolated children; or that, in the absence of severe difficulties, teachers may be able to focus more on the development of children's social skills.

There may also be differences between different countries in the ways in which behaviour of various kinds is perceived. For example, Vikan (1985) found that far more children were rated by teachers, parents and health nurses in Norway as having internalized or 'neurotic' problems than externalized or 'conduct' disorders, which is not usually the case in other countries. Matsuura *et al.* (1993) report that deviance of the anti-social type was more frequent than the neurotic type (e.g. worried, miserable, timid) in Japan and China, whereas both types were almost equally frequent in Korea. Weisz *et al.* (1989), in a study comparing Thai and American children aged 6–11 years, found that Thai children were rated higher on both over-controlled and under-controlled behaviour, and had significantly more over-controlled than under-controlled problems such as shyness and depression. The authors explain that Thai children are taught to be peaceful, polite and deferential, and to strive for an attitude of self-effacement and humbleness that aims to avoid disturbing others. Thai children are also encouraged to inhibit and control the expression of anger and other strong emotions. Such Thai customs may foster not only politeness and non-aggression, but also inhibition and anxiety. Although cultural effects may be strong, Weisz *et al.* warn that it is simplistic to discuss the impact of a particular culture on children's problem behaviour without taking account of the intracultural setting (e.g. home or school) in which behaviour is studied, and also who does the rating (e.g. parents or teachers).

In the light of obstacles in the way of arriving at a reasonably firm estimate of the prevalence of withdrawal and isolation in children and adolescence, any figures cited should be regarded as applicable only to the specific samples used to generate data, in their particular contexts. Here, examples of studies providing data about the problem of withdrawal as a general concept will be given; the prevalence of different kinds of withdrawn behaviour and isolation will be discussed in Chapter 3.

Agreement among informants

As teachers see children in a variety of group settings and situations, and are usually readily accessible to researchers, most of the estimates of the extent of problems of withdrawal in children are obtained from schools, though a number of studies have used ratings by parents and, to an increasing extent in recent years, by pupils themselves.

Parents may be just as perceptive as teachers in recognizing 'internalized' or 'neurotic' behaviour in a child, but agreement between parents and teachers tends to be low on specific items of such behaviour relating to a particular child, such as being solitary, fearful or miserable (Rutter, Tizard and Whitmore, 1970). Verhulst and Akkerhuis (1989), for example, using the Achenbach Child Behaviour Checklist (Achenbach and Edelbrock, 1983) with a sample of 1,161 children aged 4–12 years from the general population in Holland, found low to moderate agreement between parents' and teachers' ratings of behaviour problems. However, agreement was lower for internalized difficulties than for externalized problems, as Kolko and Kazdin (1993) also report. As Verhulst and Akkerhuis state, parents are familiar with their child's functioning across time and across many situations, but teachers have the opportunity to compare children in groups of peers.

Self-reports from children can be a useful supplement to ratings from teachers and parents and may provide insights into the feelings of the child to which teachers and parents do not have access. Edelbrock *et al.* (1986) found low to moderate agreement between parents and child on symptoms of emotional and behavioural difficulties. Thompson *et al.* (1993) report low mother–child concordance for internalizing problems and moderate agreement for externalizing problems, both for clinical populations and non-referred children in the USA (see also Hodges, Gordon and Lennon, 1990). Verhulst and van der Ende (1992), comparing parents' reports and adolescents' self-reports of problem behaviour in 883 Dutch 11- to 19-year-olds, found that agreement between the parents and the adolescents themselves was moderately high. For the syndrome 'social problems', reflecting difficulties in peer relationships, adolescents reported slightly more problems than their parents did about them. The authors conclude that adolescents, especially as they grow older, are indispensable informants about their own problem behaviours.

Estimates by teachers, parents and others at different stages of development

Early childhood

Withdrawal is identified in children as young as 3 years, though it is especially difficult to judge the significance of inhibited behaviour in children between 3 and 5 years of age. At this stage of development, most children do love the company of others, not least other children of roughly similar age. As mothers of 4-year-olds in a study carried out in South Wales (Chazan, Laing and Jackson, 1971) commented:

'. . . he loves people and children.'

'. . . any size group – it does not matter.'

'. . . any child, any time, any amount [of social play].'

Yet at times children of this age also enjoy playing on their own. In make-believe play, they find their toys good company and endow some of them with life, conversing with them and involving them in dramatic situations. Such solitary play is found in children who are very active socially. The picture is, therefore, one of variable behaviour with regard to shyness and withdrawal rather than of general inhibition.

In a two-stage screening survey of 7,320 4-year-olds in two LEAs in England and Wales (Chazan *et al.*, 1980), nursery and reception class teachers and playgroup leaders, and in some cases health visitors, were asked to rate 1,145 children in the sample on a 5-point scale in response to the questions 'Is the child at all shy or timid? How does the child get on with strangers or other children when he/she first meets them?' The 1,145 children had previously been identified as having 'definitely' or 'possibly' one or more problems adversely affecting their development. 374 of this sample were rated as having 'mild' problems relating to withdrawal, and 95 as having 'severe' problems of this kind. The 469 children having a 'mild' problem ('does not easily relate to other children . . . but can be encouraged to co-operate with others') or a 'severe' problem ('very shy and/or withdrawn . . . avoids contact with others . . . lives in a world of his/her own') represented 6.4 per cent of the full sample of 7,320 4-year-olds, with 1.3 per cent of the total sample exhibiting severely withdrawn behaviour.

Osborn, Butler and Morris (1984), with the aid of health visitors interviewing parents at home, carried out a survey of all 5-year-old children who had been born in England, Wales and Scotland during a single week in April 1970; the total sample amounted to over 13,000. The behaviour scales used as part of the study, based on the Rutter Child Behaviour Scale (Rutter, 1967; Rutter, Tizard and Whitmore, 1970), included the item 'tends to do things on his own – rather solitary'. Parents thought that this statement applied 'somewhat' in the case of 35.3 per cent of the sample, and 'certainly applied' to 9.1 per cent of the children. On the basis of parental statements and ratings in a study of a representative sample of 98 children in an Outer London suburb, Richman, Stevenson and Graham (1982) reported that 4 per cent at 3 years, 6 per cent at 4 years and 8 per cent at 8 years had problems in their relationships with their peers.

Hughes, Pinkerton and Plewis (1979) studied a sample of 260 Inner London children when they had been in infant school for about half a term. Between 12 and 18 per cent of the children were rated by their teachers as having difficulties with social relationships. Some of these difficulties were short-lived, but they did not disappear in all cases. In a study of behaviour problems in 5-year-olds in infant schools in a number of areas in England and Wales (367 boys, 359 girls), Chazan and Jackson (1971, 1974) used the six Stott Adjustment Pointers (Stott, 1963, 1981), which included the question 'Is the child exceptionally quiet, timid or withdrawn?' Teachers responded with 'yes' in the case of 35 boys (9.54 per cent) and 33 girls (9.19 per cent). A similar picture was found in a follow-up at 7 years of age, but the children rated as withdrawn at that age were not necessarily the same as those previously rated in this way. Headteachers and teachers both ranked 'shyness' high in listing the frequency of different types of EBDs in school. No sex differences relating to 'withdrawal' emerged at either 5 or 7 years of age.

Middle childhood

Merrett and Wheldall (1984), who surveyed 119 teachers of junior (7–11 years) classes in 19 schools in the Midlands (UK), reported that about 6 per cent were rated as 'withdrawn' (i.e. seldom responding to general questions, non-participant, over-shy, with few friends), as opposed to about 11 per cent considered to be 'disruptive'. Rather more girls than boys were described as withdrawn. In a survey of 216 8-year-old German children, randomly selected, 7.4 per cent of 108 boys and 4.6 per cent of 108 girls (i.e. 6 per cent of the total sample) were rated by parents and teachers as having neurotic and emotional disorders (Esser, Schmidt and Woerner, 1990). However, in a predominantly rural area in Wales, Baker, Davies and Stallard (1985) report that only 2.8 per cent of 8,948 pupils aged 4–11 years were said by their teachers to be 'exceptionally quiet, lethargic, depressed, very variable in energy'.

John and Elizabeth Newson (1976), studying about 700 7-year-olds in their home environment, included questions about social relationships in their guided interview schedule with the mothers of these children. In response to the questions

● How does he manage in new situations? Does he enjoy them, or is he bothered by what he isn't used to?

- How about new people? Is he shy?
- In general, how would you say he gets on with other children? Does he make friends easily?

the Newsons concluded that about 30 per cent of the sample had problems either with new people or with new situations, with a further 11 per cent experiencing difficulty with both. 19 per cent of the children were said not to make friends easily. This group included some children who were withdrawn and inward-looking, but also some who were too overbearing and bossy for others to tolerate, or who were 'odd' in various ways.

The Newsons found no significant sex differences in respect of problems with new people, new situations or making friends in the 7-year-olds studied. This is in keeping with the findings of many other studies, to the effect that, although by the age of about seven a clear-cut difference emerges in the prevalence of 'anti-social' deviance, with more boys presenting externalized EBDs than girls, no significant sex difference is usually reported in the case of internalized problems. However, some studies report more girls than boys being rated as having such problems (Rutter, Tizard and Whitmore, 1970; Rutter *et al.*, 1975; McGee, Silva and Williams, 1984; Merrett and Wheldall, 1984). A typical pattern is illustrated by Stevenson, Richman and Graham (1985), who, using the Rutter Teachers' Child Behaviour Scale with a representative sample of 535 8-year-olds (270 boys, 265 girls) in London, reported 17 per cent of the boys as presenting anti-social deviance as compared to 5 per cent of the girls. In the case of 'neurotic' deviance (internalized EBDs), however, there was little difference in prevalence between the sexes (11 per cent of the boys, 10 per cent of the girls).

Adolescence

With the child's entry into puberty and adolescence, it becomes increasingly difficult to assess the significance of withdrawal. Apart from the necessity to be on one's own to cope with the demands of homework or pursue a hobby which does not require others to participate, most adolescents have moods during which they seem to want to shun company, particularly at home. These are usually temporary and leave no lasting impact if they are tactfully handled. However, withdrawal and prolonged self-isolation may be an indication of a serious mental health problem such as depression or schizophrenia. Rutter *et al.* (1976), on the basis of an epidemiological study of 14- to 15-year olds in the Isle of Wight (UK), conclude that inner turmoil, as represented by feelings of misery and self-depreciation, is quite frequent at this age. However, psychiatric disorders during adolescence were only slightly more common in their sample than in middle childhood, though the pattern of disorders changed in terms of an increase in depression and school refusal. A rise in depressive disorders in adolescence has also been reported in a number of other studies, with about twice as many females as males suffering from serious depression. Cohen *et al.* (1993), in a study of children and adolescents aged 10–20 in New York State, found that major depression showed a sharp rise in post-pubertal girls, though not in boys (see also Hops and Lewinsohn, 1995).

Erwin (1993), reviewing relevant studies, asserts that early adolescence is a crucial time for the experience of shyness, while loneliness peaks in adolescence and is among the most frequent problems mentioned by the adolescent. This is not surprising seeing that adolescents have to face new social challenges, including expectations about popularity with both sexes and scholastic success, without necessarily having the experience or skills required to maintain relationships (Marcoen and Goosens, 1993). The transition from primary to secondary school often involves having a different status in the group, and may well bring about some degree of isolation, imposed by the self or by others. In the German study by Esser, Schmidt and Woerner (1990), mentioned above, 28.2 per cent of 191 13-year-olds had moderate problems in connection with peer relationships and 6.2 per cent had severe problems of this kind, with far more boys than girls experiencing difficulties with peers.

Information from self-reports on the sources of distress experienced by adolescents comes from studies by Ostrov and Offer (1978) and McGee and Stanton (1992). Ostrov and Offer, in a study of a large group of adolescents in a mid-western city in the USA, report that about 20 per cent of younger adolescents (aged 12–15 years) and about 13 per cent of older adolescents (16 to 20 years) admitted to feeling very lonely. The authors found far more serious loneliness among a group of disturbed adolescents who had been admitted to a psychiatric treatment centre (36.2 per cent of 166 boys; 55.1 per cent of 74 girls) – see also Kimmel (1985). McGee and Stanton (1992), reporting on a study of a New Zealand sample, state that 10 per cent of 489 boys, and 17 per cent of 456 girls aged 15 years, said that they 'felt left out of things' at least 'sometimes', the level of distress being quite high in many of these cases.

In summary, up to 30–40 per cent of children and adolescents seem to have at least a moderate problem with regard to withdrawal, isolation or feelings of loneliness, and up to about 10 per cent have serious difficulties in these respects. However, as already stated, these are only very general estimates, and it is necessary to specify the kind and level of withdrawn behaviour in order to make estimates of prevalence more meaningful; this is done in Chapter 3.

MAIN DIRECTIONS OF RELEVANT RESEARCH

The findings of numerous research studies relating to peer relationships and social withdrawal will be referred to in the ensuing chapters of this book. Here it will suffice to highlight the emphasis and main directions of recent and current research of relevance to the topics discussed in this volume.

Dunn and McGuire (1992), in an overview of research into sibling and peer relationships in children, point out that the surge of research interest in children's relationships with other children has several sources, but two in particular stand out. These are, first, the argument that the interaction between children has a special significance in many aspects of children's development; and, second, the growing evidence that there are associations between troubled peer relationships and adjustment problems (see also Williams and Gilmour, 1994). Dunn and McGuire see the following as areas which have attracted attention from researchers: the associations between peer or sibling interaction and the child's sociocognitive development and sense of self; developmental changes in peer relationships; and intervention studies focused on the role of peers in educational settings.

Defining relationships

Researchers have been at pains to attempt to describe and define relationships as precisely as possible. Hinde (1976; 1979) has pointed to the need to study the complex qualities, diversity and dynamic properties of social interactions, stressing that each participant in a relationship is enmeshed in a network of other relationships (see also Malik and Furman, 1993, who comment on the importance of studying the associations between family and peer relationships). Scarlett (1980) asserts that terms such as shy, withdrawn, passive and dependent have been used to describe isolated children, but without adequately specifying the behaviour of these children in detail. Crozier and Burnham (1990), too, draw attention to the necessity of distinguishing between different forms of shyness. The uncertainty over the exact meaning of such much-used terms as 'anxiety' and 'depression' – conditions often associated with social withdrawal – and the increasing trend to conceptualize both anxiety and depression as multifaceted and multidimensional phenomena are emphasized by Craig and Dobson (1995).

Assessment

The need to describe and categorize peer relationships has led to an interest in devising instruments for identifying and assessing such relationships (see Chapter 4). The past two decades or so have seen a revival of interest in the study of sociometric status in children (Ollendick *et al.*, 1991; Williams and

Gilmour, 1994). Ollendick *et al.* assert that many of the complex issues associated with this field of inquiry have become better understood, including the preferred strategies for identifying children at risk for social dysfunction. The value of obtaining fuller information on peer relationships by including children's self-perceptions and the perceptions of other children has been recognized by a number of researchers (Mitchell, 1990; Cheek and Briggs, 1990; Stocker, 1994). Crozier (1995), for example, points out that self-reported shyness may not necessarily find expression in behaviour, and that inhibited behaviour may reflect introversion rather than shyness.

The difficulties in the way of determining the causal direction of associations between peer relationships and adjustment have also been acknowledged in recent research (Dunn and McGuire, 1992). As Stocker (1994) observes, causal direction cannot be assumed solely on the basis of correlational analyses.

Children with disabilities

The increasing trend to integrate children with physical and learning disabilities into mainstream schools makes research on the peer relationships of these children particularly necessary. However, the development of disabled children's difficulties with their peers remains relatively under-explored (Dunn and McGuire, 1992). Research in this area has focused on the effects of mainstreaming on disabled children's relationships with their non-disabled peers, and has tended to show that children with even minor disabilities are at risk of rejection by their peers. Waldrop, Bell and Goering (1976), for example, found that the presence of minor physical anomalies was significantly related to inhibited and socially ill-at-ease behaviour in elementary school girls in the USA; and Nabuzoka and Smith (1993) showed that, in a sample of children aged 8–12 years in mainstream schools in an English city, those with learning difficulties tended to experience more dissatisfaction and anxiety about their peer relations than their normally-developing classmates (see also Taylor, Asher and Williams, 1987; Lewis and Lewis, 1988; Guralnick, 1990).

Friendship

Research on friendship has added to the understanding of peer relationships in childhood and adolescence. Dunn and McGuire (1992) see this area of inquiry as especially important in view of the significance of supportive close relationships in adulthood, and welcome recent developments in research on friendship. These include increased interest in how children's behaviour with friends and others differs, the variation in types and stability of friendships, the relation of family experiences to the quality of friendships, and the relation of friendship to adjustment and self-esteem.

Cairns *et al.* (1995) assert that there is much greater fluidity in peer bonds than has been generally recognized. Hartup (1996) stresses that the developmental implications of friendship cannot be specified without distinguishing between having friends, the identity of one's friends and the quality of friendships. To date, children are usually differentiated from one another in diagnosis and research only according to whether or not they have friends. However, Hartup argues, predicting developmental outcome also requires knowing about the behavioural characteristics and attitudes of children's friends as well as qualitative features of these relationships.

Peer collaboration

Foot, Morgan and Shute (1990) underline the importance of research on peer tutoring and collaboration. They show that research in these areas has been mainly concerned with peer-helping relationships in educational settings, but point out that an interest is emerging in studying helping relationships between siblings at home, and in other contexts outside the home such as clinics and hospitals. Peer tutoring and how peers can help peers at home and in the community are discussed in Chapters 7 and 8 of this book.

Intervention strategies

Malik and Furman (1993) discuss a number of different approaches which have been developed for improving children's peer relationships, including social skills training, social cognitive training and co-operative group programmes. Community intervention programmes aimed at reducing bullying and victimization have also been designed (Olweus, 1993; Smith and Sharp, 1994; Sharp and Smith, 1994). Malik and Furman stress that problems with peers are often associated with other difficulties that require treatment, for example by attention to learning difficulties or by clinic-based therapy. The wide range of intervention strategies available to help withdrawn and isolated children is discussed in detail in Chapters 7, 8 and 9.

THE SCOPE OF THIS BOOK

This introductory chapter has emphasized the importance of social relationships in the general development of children and adolescents, and discussed the extent and significance of failure in relationships characterized by withdrawal and isolation. It has also highlighted the main directions of recent relevant research.

In Chapter 2, the development of social relationships is outlined, with particular reference to interaction with siblings and peers. The many factors affecting social relationships are considered, such as gender, stability over time, social class and cultural diversity.

In Chapter 3 patterns of withdrawn and isolated behaviour are described and discussed, and the connection between withdrawal and other problems of adjustment (e.g. aggression, anxiety, depression and psychiatric behaviour) is explored. Chapter 4 considers a wide range of techniques for assessing withdrawn and isolated behaviour in childhood and adolescence, including sociometric techniques, observation, questionnaires and inventories, and interviews.

Chapter 5 examines various possible causes of withdrawn behaviour, relating to the individual, the home and community, and the school. These include temperament, child-rearing practices, opportunities for social relationships, membership of minority groups and being disabled. Chapter 6 looks at the short-term and long-term consequences of withdrawal and isolation in regard to later adjustment and achievement.

Chapter 7 suggests how schools and teachers can help withdrawn and isolated pupils. Ways of preventing and managing such pupils include the development of whole-school policies, making adequate counselling provision, ensuring that the curriculum caters for personal and social education, and the use of group work and peer tutoring. Chapter 8 considers the role of parents and peers in helping withdrawn children, the responses of parents when their children are in conflict with siblings or peers, and how peers can help their fellows at home and in the community.

Chapter 9 discusses how the specialized support services can help, for example in providing expert counselling. Behaviour modification strategies and social skills training are examined, as well as the application of psychotherapeutic approaches.

In the final chapter, an overview of the book is provided and suggestions for future research and action are made.

Chapter 2

The Development of Social Relationships in Childhood and Adolescence

The emphasis in this book is on social development, especially the development of social relationships. However, the acquisition of social skills in children and young people cannot be considered in isolation from their cognitive and emotional development. The interplay between cognitive, emotional and social aspects of development, with one now dominating and then another, lies at the root of an individual's behaviour. While this chapter will look at how social relationships develop between individuals and how socialization in this sense evolves, it is useful to give some attention at the beginning to cognitive and emotional development. Gender, social class and cultural diversity must also be considered, as they too affect interactional performance. All of these related topics are weighty ones and so can only be dealt with briefly here. Some references will, however, be given so that further investigation can be undertaken.

FACTORS AFFECTING SOCIAL RELATIONSHIPS

Cognitive Development

It is difficult, and not very helpful, to try to separate cognitive development in general from social development. As children begin to form a concept of themselves as separate from – and different from – others around them, they take the first steps in relating to those others in their environment. To begin with, these relationships are structured in a highly egocentric (self-centred) way, with self-interest predominating. Infants want immediate satisfaction of their needs. But, surprisingly quickly, children learn the effects of their demands on others and how to maximize these effects to their advantage. The process is not solely one-way. Children learn and adapt, structuring their future reactions to some extent on the observed reactions of those who are important to them. Prosocial behaviour, that is behaviour which shows concern for others and a willingness to put them in the centre of the picture, is something which appears a little later but still at a very early age.

Growing awareness of self and others, which is central to children's social relationships, is influenced by, and influences, cognitive development. A sense of self is also influenced by children's growing physical abilities, their ever-widening range of contacts and their developing language skills. All of these feed into children's understanding in a highly complex way, and widening understanding leads to behavioural changes, including behaviour towards others. 'Driving self concern', so evident in young children, begins to give way in some degree to 'a new sense of themselves and an increased capacity to plan and achieve goals' (Dunn, 1988, p. 176).

Cognition is involved, therefore, from the earliest social relationships and, indeed, becomes more dominant as children grow older. Early spontaneous responses are brought under cognitive control or receive cognitive scrutiny, although they may remain influential in determining behaviour. Establishing social relationships is part of social competence and competence is inherently cognitive. In its turn, according to Piaget (see, for example, Flavell, 1963, or Phillips, 1975), cognition adapts to the new information coming from the environment. Understanding is restructured and elaborated in order to accommodate what is perceived to be supportive or contradictory evidence (Brown and Desforges, 1979). Other writers may not fully agree with Piaget's point of view (e.g. Cohen, 1983) but most accept the importance of social input in cognitive development. Thus Case (1985) sees three processes as fundamental to the essentially cognitive function of problem-solving in children, namely an urge to explore, a tendency to imitate, and an ability to work with and adapt to other people. All of these are also social activities.

A discussion of the various theories which seek to explain how cognition develops can be found in Meadows (1993). The link between cognitive and social development can be well demonstrated by looking at play and informal activities (see later in this chapter). For the moment, however, it may be appropriate to indicate how the growth of social relationships is linked to another aspect of the development of the individual, namely emotional development.

Emotional Development and Social Relationships

'In social exchange between individuals, feelings of obligation, gratitude and trust play an important role' (Mays, 1982, p. 32). 'Emotions are embedded in social relationships' (Woodhead *et al.*, 1995, p. 139). The feelings of those involved in social interactions influence the extent to which such interactions will be pursued, the interpretation of the on-going interaction, and the effects the interactions have on those involved in them. Thus children in the playground may be eager to make relationships with other children, feel happy and at ease in their company and look back on what happened with satisfaction. Their eagerness for subsequent encounters may well be even greater than it was because of these feelings. They realize the advantages of social 'give and take' and are confident that they have a position in a relationship that they can build on.

Of course, the above description is a rather idealized one. Interactions are not always satisfying; children do not always fulfil the expectations that others have of them. Disappointment, anger, fear or loss of self-esteem may replace satisfaction and, in their turn, colour future relationships. Temperamental differences between children help determine how flexible children will be with regard to the vicissitudes of interpersonal actions and reactions (Thomas and Chess, 1977). Whereas some children may retain positive feelings towards others despite occasional setbacks, others may withdraw from contacts if they feel in any way rebuffed.

Dunn (1988) stresses the importance of very early adult–child interaction in encouraging the development of social understanding. The carer's emotional reactions to the child's behaviour indicate to the child what emotion is appropriate and how it should be expressed when it is acceptable, or repressed when not. As children acquire these affective strategies, so they also acquire elements of social competence in a framework of rules for social interaction. If this social learning does not take place smoothly, the children may find it difficult to establish or maintain social relationships. Their behaviour may not fall within the parameters of their own or others' expectations. More will be said later in this chapter about changes over time in social relationships but for the moment the point to stress is the extent to which emotion colours these relationships from the very beginning. It is within the family that children lay the foundations of how effective they will be in relating to others, how they will feel about these relationships, and how they will understand them and their own reactions at a later time. If, for whatever reason (see discussion in Chapters 3 and 5), relationships are not established effectively, there is a danger of persisting distortion as children grow.

Competence in establishing relations is closely linked with the concepts of empathy and sympathy. The former implies the ability to take on another's perspective, to see things from another's point of view; the latter implies concern for another individual and the recognition that one's own feelings, good or bad, are not necessarily shared by others who bring their own social, cognitive and emotional history to bear on events. At times of high concern about personal needs, such as the very early years or the adolescent years, individuals may find personal interests dominating. Their social behaviour puts themselves at the forefront, and the high emotionality they exhibit when thwarted overwhelms both empathy and sympathy, as adults who are close to them know to their cost. The development of social relationships is not, however, a simple, inevitable progression disrupted by stress in some unfortunate cases. Dunn (1988) and Meadows (1993) both suggest that environmental challenges not only help to determine the direction of growth but are essential in promoting that growth. Meadows (1993) says of cognitive development: 'what may be important about cognitive "complexity" is the availability of a range of alternative strategies and the ability to select between them as appropriate to the particular situation' (p. 366). This statement would also seem to be apposite to emotional development and, of course, social development.

Gender

Gender, that is, the way in which males and females come to see themselves in society, is still highly important in any consideration of social interactions despite current antipathy towards anything that could be considered sexist. In recent years (see Hutt, 1978), what were firm beliefs about differences in development between the sexes have been challenged, and there is now far less certainty in this area. Nevertheless, sex stereotypes continue to intrude into our everyday thinking, and questions about a baby's sex are still among the first asked. From the moment the baby is identified as a boy or a girl, different expectations for behaviour, temperament and growth exist, whether or not they are openly expressed.

Biological and physiological differences between the sexes inevitably ensure that the two sexes cannot be treated as the same. What other gender differences can be identified in the establishment of social relationships? If these differences are generally found in Western societies, then argument as to whether they are innate or culturally induced does not add much to our understanding, at least at the moment. Five areas will be looked at briefly, although each is of itself wide-ranging. Some of these points are discussed further in Delamont, 1980; Henshall and McGuire, 1986; Barnes, 1995.

Language

Conventional belief has been, although not now always supported, that girls are more verbally proficient than boys, beginning to talk earlier and making more use of language than boys (see discussion in Hutt, 1978; Tough, 1984). How far these differences, where they exist, arise from child-rearing practices in the early years is difficult to determine. It does seem, however, that girls come to make use of verbal and facial expression, whereas boys are encouraged towards competitive physical activities where noise may replace speech.

Size of group

Perhaps because of girls' preference for quieter, verbally-based play, their groups tend to be smaller than those of boys. The latter are often happy in rough-and-tumble activities, running and chasing, where fairly large groups are an advantage. Differences in group size, however brought about (cultural expectations clearly have a part to play), are especially marked at adolescence, when girls favour small groups of two or three close friends, whereas boys retain their preference for larger groups, both for games with rules and for 'fooling about'.

Identification with adults

In many cases, the main carer is female and so initial relationships with the girl in the family may be more easily developed than with the boy. It has been shown (see Hutt, 1978) that 'by eighteen months of age the impact of the same-sex parent was greater than that of the opposite-sex parent' (p. 186). Cultural pressures are towards the boy moving away from a close early relationship with a female carer but the girl remaining quite appropriately in that relationship.

Dependency and autonomy

As has just been noted, girls are encouraged to retain close identification with the mother, whereas this is discouraged in boys. Boys are expected to become independent, self-reliant, out-going and even aggressive; girls are expected to be much more biddable, shy, fearful and even clinging. Tears are appropriate for girls, not for boys. Somewhere in these expectations may lie some of the reasons why girls seem to prefer smaller groups.

Sex roles

By identifying with adults who are significant to them, carrying out the behaviour expected of them, challenging accepted norms and observing the reactions of others, and hearing and seeing all around them examples of what is taken to be gender-appropriate behaviour, children develop roles in society, that is, behaviour which is fairly congruent with how they see themselves. In most cases, the role played reflects the gender identity which the individual has internalized but, in children, both identity and role are open to a degree of change. Boys show less flexibility in changing their role than girls. Girls can show behaviour more typical of boys and it will be accepted, even admired, by other girls and on occasion by boys. But the same is not true of boys (Archer, 1992). There is little latitude in the role expected of them. What is judged to be 'feminine' behaviour is likely to mean exclusion from the masculine group. As Archer points out, more girls want to join boys' groups than boys want to join girls' groups, an indication of the higher status of boys' groups in this culture.

The extent to which gender colours the views individuals hold of themselves as members of a society is clear from the above discussion. With regard to social relationships, from the very early years up to and beyond adolescence, gender influences the range of interactions available, the size and status of the group and even how autonomous the individual is allowed to be in establishing social contacts.

Social Class

Jahoda (1959) has shown, in a small study in Scotland, that by the age of six years children are aware of the societal concept of class. Although this knowledge is important in social development, it may not, however, be as important as the unconscious effect that social class has had on their attitudes, feelings and general understanding since birth. There may be reluctance to acknowledge that social class still has considerable influence today, yet parents and carers continue to perpetuate different practices in child-rearing which retain some class differences. The work of the Newsons (1963; 1968; 1976) illustrates how cultural and local expectations affect development in a wide variety of ways, including the extent of freedom offered to children within and outside the home, the quality of language used and the amount of negotiation permitted, as well as the areas which are open to negotiation. When the expectations of home and school are congruent, children can adapt with ease to the demands and opportunities of a learning environment; when they do not match, withdrawal or frustration may well result. At the same time, 'home is by no means an inferior substitute for school' (Tizard and Hughes, 1984). Unless totally without stimulation, a child's home usually offers a great many learning opportunities in small group situations, with a fair amount of self-selection and decision-taking.

Homes which disadvantage children have their effect on social development. This is particularly true of homes in which there is linguistic deprivation.

Children who are less verbally outgoing than others give the impression of being unresponsive and so may well not be viewed with favour by their teachers and their peers (Chazan *et al.*, 1977). This effect can be found at school entry (ibid.) and in the junior school (Croll and Moses, 1985). Research in the ILEA (Inner London Education Authority) has shown that primary schools have an effect on non-cognitive as well as cognitive outcomes, with some schools coping much more effectively with potential behaviour problems than others (Mortimore, 1986). Such a differential effect is an important finding, which has also been shown at the secondary stage (Rutter *et al.*, 1979). The conclusion would appear to be that social class differences still exist to some extent, but that schools which are prepared to work with their pupils, instead of confronting them or expecting from them responses of which they have little experience, can change behavioural (including social) outcomes.

Cultural Diversity

Child-rearing practices also differ between cultural groups, especially where parents and carers are close to their ethnic origins. Cultural conditioning, that is the pressure from within any culture for its members to conform to that culture, remains a powerful determinant of behaviour. It may be a source of discord when children find themselves part of a culture clash between their ethnic group and the culture into which they have been born. A further difficulty lies in the value system adopted by a culture with regard to women if that system depreciates their work and abilities so that discrimination results. It is impossible to discuss all the implications of cultural diversity here but reference could be made to a few publications in this field: Tomlinson, 1980 and 1983; Willey, 1984; DES, 1985 (The Swann Report); Verma, 1989.

It is not surprising that links have been found between ethnic background and behaviour. Mortimore, in the ILEA study (1986) mentioned earlier, found a higher incidence of behaviour difficulties amongst Caribbean pupils, but this appeared to be largely related, at the secondary stage, to their lower attainments. Expectations on the part of teachers, parents and the pupils themselves would also have affected performance and behaviour (Bushell, 1996).

Children themselves construct a cultural system which is appropriate to their level of development and based on their social interactions. In 'pretend' play, children not only come to realize their own self-identity more clearly but also extend their social competence and knowledge of societal roles (Faulkner, 1995). They are thereby promoting their cultural identity by assuming in some form the language and concerns of those they see around them. This is also the case in fantasy play which has a shared theme, inasmuch as children create their own worlds into which others are allowed in order to enrich the experience. Dunn (1988) points out that children engage in this type of play at a surprisingly early age (from 18 months onwards), if older siblings or friends are involved.

Cross-cultural studies (Curry and Arnaud, 1984) reveal very clearly the cultural content of many forms of socio-dramatic play. While young children the world over may play at being someone else who is important to them, changing this role at will to take on another one or adapting it to incorporate others who become involved, the scenario and the plot vary according to the culture in which they are being reared. It follows, therefore, that observed and accepted behaviours will be the mainstay of such play as children try to come to terms with what they see around them, impose their will on their experiences, and find out the limits of their powers. They seldom invent completely new interactions (although they may be new to them) but utilize the information they have acquired from people around them and the media. Different environments will provide sources for different acculturation. In a shrinking world this remains true, although the differences between cultures may not be so marked as previously and what they have in common may be more pronounced.

As noted at the beginning of this chapter, the development of social relationships cannot be considered in isolation from many other aspects which impinge on it. Some of these have now been looked at briefly, but there is one further point. Social interactions may be prosocial or antisocial, that is, concern and care for others may be shown in the interaction or there may be aggression, even bullying. Furthermore, interactions are not one-way. By definition, an interaction implies the involvement of at least one other. There may therefore be a lack of coherence in interactions, so that one person involved might be concerned, another hostile and yet another largely neutral. Again, if those involved in the interaction change their behaviour for any reason, the whole essence of the interchange alters. It is, therefore, unwise to think of children's social behaviour as being fixed and inevitable, changing only as they grow older. It is nearer the mark to think of social interactions as changing according to who is involved, the mood of the various participants, the place in which the interaction occurs (e.g. playground, classroom, home, a new venue), as well as the sex and age of those interacting. Finally, children may on occasion show less well-developed behaviour than they are capable of displaying, or even act beyond their years if with older children or in a crisis.

THE DEVELOPMENT OF SOCIAL RELATIONSHIPS

It is convenient, when considering the interactions of children with those in close contact with them, to begin in the early years. This is not, however, to take up a rigidly developmental perspective and imply that what happens in the very early years is bound to have an effect on later behaviour. Nor is it intended to endorse a 'stage' theory of development in which children are seen as making a universal and fairly uniform progression towards social understanding. The intention is rather to suggest that early interactions may lead to expectations about social relationships which persist because they are, on the whole, unchallenged. Carers and children, for example, are striving to set up a routine which is as satisfactory as possible to all concerned. Circumstances change, of course, as children get older, but unless there is considerable social upheaval involving complete change in established relationships, there is likely to be an underlying consistency. Flexibility in interactions and modifiability in behaviour remain, however, important considerations.

Relationships with adults

Two concepts have been seen as particularly important in early relationships between children and their adult carers. These are attachment (Bowlby, 1969, 1973, 1980) and maternal deprivation (Bowlby, 1953). When infants are cared for by their natural mothers, it would be surprising if they did not form a strong attachment to them. But the role of the mother can be successfully taken over by another carer altogether or can be shared, provided that the infant's psychological welfare is ensured (Rutter, 1972; Schaffer, 1977; Cowie, 1995). Feelings of security and trust in adults (White, 1979) encourage young children to tackle new experiences with a degree of confidence and growing competence (Richards, 1974).

As Dunn (1988) points out, children in their early years face many problems in social relationships. She sees such problems as growth points in developing knowledge of self and others. Sensitivity on the part of the carer (Ainsworth, Bell and Stayton, 1974) helps growth, as do consistency and warmth, and the absence of these qualities is indeed deprivation. Can early deprivation be compensated for? The answer to this question is complex. Early gains have been shown when programmes aimed at reducing disadvantage have been tried (see, for example, Bronfenbrenner, 1974). Children have benefited but the programmes need to be well organized, of a reasonable duration, and fully supported by those close to the children concerned. The same could be said about day care in the early years, another topic over which there is disagreement (Pilling and Pringle, 1978; Clarke-Stewart, 1982; Melhuish *et al.*, 1990a; 1990b).

As children get older, they become involved with more adults: in the neighbourhood, as visitors and, of course, when they go to school. These relationships are also two-way, inasmuch as children are active participants, not passive receivers, in interactions with adults, just as in the very early years. The widening range of adult contacts which children experience through the middle years of childhood enables them to develop self-awareness and the ability to adapt their social behaviour in reaction to how they perceive other people behaving. Adopting the roles of others, usually adults, allows them in their play to imitate older people and stand in their shoes (Light, 1979). Children's interpretations of the roles of others may not, of course, be realistic. But if they are meaningful to the children concerned, they will influence the relationships they establish. At adolescence, too, young people are still keenly aware of how others around them are behaving, both in their own environment and in the media, and incorporate what they admire into what they themselves do.

Social relationships are the product of a number of social interactions in which quality is certainly as important as quantity. Taking on social roles is only one aspect of the development of social relationships, although it may well be an important part. Relationships with siblings and friends and interactions with peers must also be considered.

Relationship with siblings

'Driving self concern characterizes much of children's behaviour toward other family members in this age period [i.e. early childhood] as they develop a new sense of themselves and increased capacity to plan and achieve goals' (Dunn, 1988, p. 176). To any adult in contact with young children, this is a familiar picture. It sometimes seems that the concept of fairness (often meaning 'what I want') is the first one the infant grasps. There is mutual help between siblings, and perhaps shared activities, but there is also 'mutual antagonism, jealousy and aggression' (Meadows, 1986, p. 189).

In their research on a large number of Swiss children, Ernst and Angst (1983) often found little support for popular beliefs about birth order and size of families, once other factors such as social class or parental education were controlled. For example, they claim that:

● they found no evidence for a 'first-born personality' or a 'single child personality';
● in their study, single children were slightly more extroverted and slightly higher achievers than those with siblings;
● first-born children had closer relationships with their parents than those born later.

This last finding is not really surprising, bearing in mind that the first-born child (who may or may not be a singleton in the long run) has sole call on his or her parents' attention and affection, however successful he or she may be in gaining this. The consensus of opinion on birth order would appear to be that differences between and within families in the ways that family members interact, produce wide variations which make stereotypes of 'the only child' or 'one of a large family' unhelpful.

The close proximity of siblings does, however, lead to intense emotions:

> each child knows well what the other particularly likes and dislikes, especially if they are close in age. This closeness of interests . . . means that young children probably have less difficulty in understanding how to annoy, comfort or anticipate the moods and responses of their siblings than those of their parents. (Dunn, 1988, p. 46)

It could be suggested that such knowledge is retained at adolescence and throughout life.

Because of the differences in family circumstances, it may be more useful to give a specific illustration rather than generalize.

> *Jamie* was a much-wanted child who, when he finally came, was the centre of his parents' attention at all times. Rather unexpectedly a second child, *Jessica*, was born when Jamie was just over two years of age. She was a sunny, relaxed child whereas Jamie was inclined to be over-sensitive, anxious and dependent. Jamie did not particularly welcome his new sister and, as she grew, preferred to exclude her from his play as much as possible. Jessica treated his rebuffs with equanimity, only occasionally crying if pushed away too vigorously. She liked to have the same toys to play with as Jamie but, if they had to be shared, Jamie allocated her the oldest or broken ones while he carefully gathered all the others into his corner and defended his possessions. He frequently manipulated Jessica into doing what he wanted, although if she had a good idea for playing he would appropriate it. When, at just over two years of age, Jessica had an imaginary companion, Jamie also took it over. Certainly the presence of a sibling has affected both children's social development and it is interesting to speculate how their relationship will develop over the years. It can be said that Jamie, on going to play-group and nursery class, is to be seen collecting anything he might want to play with and exhibiting considerable reluctance to share equitably. Jessica, on the other hand, as she gets older, is beginning to stand up to Jamie and demand her rights, although she shows a much more caring attitude to her brother than he does towards her.

The reactions siblings display towards one another in their own home are not necessarily, of course, those they show outside. Siblings who quarrel frequently in the family setting may be protective of one another when others are involved, or may collude to present to others a picture of a united family. It is also the case that siblings may deliberately try to be quite different from each other, especially if they are made aware of others' expectations of them. If teachers or relatives expect academic prowess or creative excellence, there may be reluctance even to attempt to shine in these areas. Unfortunately, if little is expected of a pupil because of difficulties with an older sibling, such an expectation is only too likely to be fulfilled (Hargreaves, Hestor and Mellor, 1975; King, 1978; Rogers, 1982).

Hinde (1979) distinguishes between 'complementary' activities (where the activities of those interacting complement each other) and 'reciprocal' activities (where those involved take turns in the interaction or combine in it). Where there is a fairly wide age gap between siblings, complementary interactions may be more common, with older siblings making allowances for younger ones and helping or comforting them. Children who are closer in age are more likely to imitate each other, to get on well with their peers (Hartup, 1978) and to have common interests, although the latter can also be a cause of friction. Individual differences in temperament, physique and family history complicate this taxonomy, however, as do sex differences, that is, whether those interacting are of the same or different sex.

At adolescence, siblings may be supportive of one another, showing responsibility and offering advice. But they may also avoid sibling contacts and be jealous of their possessions or interfere in their sibling's growing independence. Surface changes in relationships often occur in these years and it is difficult to predict how permanent these changes will be or what will cause some family members to come closer together and others to drift further and further apart in adulthood.

Relationships with friends

As children grow, the scope for establishing social relationships outside the family widens, as do the opportunities for prosocial behaviour, that is, 'voluntary actions that are intended to help or benefit another individual or group of individuals' (Eisenberg and Mussen, 1989, p. 3). Some consideration has to be given to prosocial behaviour because, in Western society, it is still seen as on the whole desirable, within the limits of safety and self-preservation (Hay, 1994). Very young children seem to be naturally prosocial but this declines with age. On school entry, self-interest and self-assertion may replace concern for others, at least to begin with (Hay, ibid.). At the junior school stage and at adolescence, children will show prosocial behaviour when they feel competent in the situation, when they are with friends and when the cost to themselves of the action is low (Eisenberg and Mussen, 1989). The absence of prosocial behaviour at this stage or at adolescence is likely to lead to difficulties in establishing friendships and to lack of ease in group situations.

The concept of friendship is an interesting one (Hartup, 1992). Even quite young children appear to have preferred companions, although the reasons for their choice may be no more than that they come together fairly frequently (e.g. meeting with relatives, near neighbours, children of their mother's friends, members of the same toddler group). By the time children are four or five years of age, close relationships begin to emerge, although they may not be sustained for any length of time. At the primary stage, there are many more opportunities for choice as children grow in independence and come up against others not just in class or playground but in a number of different settings (e.g. church, leisure activities, organized groups). Some friendships flourish and fade; others last throughout life. Again, it is not easy to explain why this should be so.

Friendships serve a number of functions (Hartup, 1992) inasmuch as they provide opportunities to try out a range of social skills and to practise those that seem appropriate; they may provide information about how to behave and about how others might interpret behaviour; they can help individuals to cope with emotions and stresses; and they can help those involved to appreciate the benefits of close, supportive relationships as they move towards establishing adult relationships. These functions are particularly important at adolescence when young people are liable to be unsure of their behaviour at a time of considerable personal change and emotional upheaval.

Morris (1968) distinguishes between social knowledge (that is, an understanding of society and its organization) and effectiveness in social relationships. Both areas concern adolescents and are of such complexity that it is understandable why close friendships are so important to both sexes at this stage of development. They offer 'the provision of a sense of solidarity, protection in an unfamiliar social environment, the provision of guidelines which are continually revised to meet changing circumstances, and the opportunity to experiment at moderate risk' (Morris, 1968, p. 380). It must also be said, of course, that these positive outcomes are not inevitable. Reliance on close friendship groups can lead individuals into behaviour, attitudes and even prejudices which run counter to the norms of the majority of society.

Inter-ethnic friendship groupings have not been found to occur often, even with primary-age pupils (Jelinek and Brittan, 1975). It may be, of course, that these findings are now out of date. Schools today have a wide ethnic mix, with many of their pupils coming from families well-established in this country. On the one hand, this would appear to suggest that factors other than ethnic origin now determine friendships. On the other hand, it may be that if real or imagined racial discrimination is detected, certain groups coalesce to maintain their position, thereby increasing the likelihood of alienation and antagonism towards other ethnic groups.

The reasons why friendships are established between pupils are many

(Wood, 1981). The benefits to the individuals concerned are, undoubtedly, considerable. While the mainstays of the relationship are co-operation, communication, reciprocity and shared interests, there exists also the ability to cope with disagreements, even though these may be fairly frequent in some cases, especially at the junior school stage (Hartup, 1992). Girls tend to have rather fewer friends than boys but to be more intensely involved with their friends. For example, girls spend more time with their friends than boys do and, at adolescence in particular, prefer conversing in small groups to engaging in more extensive groupings and varied activities. Friendships, however, are not the only groups in which children and young people are involved.

Relationships with peer groups

When the span of development from birth to adulthood is considered, more time is probably spent by the growing individual in interactions with contemporaries than with adults (see e.g. Hartup, 1983). Usually these interactions are in the course of play, although it is notoriously difficult to separate 'play' from 'work' because so much learning takes place in play.

In the early years, play offers children stimulation, companionship, a release of surplus energy and the opportunity to interpret experience and explore new ideas and activities, as well as encouraging them to use language effectively. Play is at the same time relaxing, challenging and therapeutic. Small wonder then that play has been considered by many writers as essential for children's cognitive, emotional and social development (see e.g. Piaget, 1951; Bruner, Jolly and Sylva, 1976; Smith, 1984). Bruner (1974) suggests that play, which for very young infants has been largely 'means–end matching' (p. 176), that is, mastering a whole variety of ways through which an objective can be achieved, develops symbolic features in late infancy when objects are taken to have different properties or a variety of roles is assumed. Symbolic, dramatic play, which frequently involves considerable verbalizing so that the intention of the play can be elaborated or changed, is important for cognitive development (Smilansky, 1968) and social development in the early years. Joint involvement in play episodes (Schaffer, 1992) encourages children to raise their levels of performance, an effect which led Vygotsky (1976) to claim that 'in play it is as though the child were a head taller than himself'.

By seven years of age, changes can be seen in children's play. Rule-governed games are favoured, often requiring fairly large groups, and play fighting, pushing and chasing are common. Children seem to be trying to assess their physical prowess and also to establish how far they can go in interactions which are basically confrontational. Even at adolescence, similar activities can be observed, especially in groups of boys. Also at adolescence, the peer group becomes the most important reference point for acceptable behaviour (Sherif and Sherif, 1964), solidarity with it being seen as indicative of independence from adult support. Groups develop their own norms, conformity to which ensures inclusion, and they pointedly exclude those who, for whatever reason, are seen as outsiders. There is potential danger in such a situation if the group norms are aggressive or incorporate violence seen in the media (Eisenberg and Mussen, 1989).

In the playground, pupils are freed from the support or supervision of adults and can reveal how they function with their peers. Boulton (1995), for example, looks at the playground behaviour of boys aged 8–10 years who have been identified as bullies or victims by their peers. He found that both bullies and victims had similar 'social networks' (i.e. the number of different children with whom they interacted), and that these were much the same as for those who were neither bullies nor victims. The victims, however, were found to spend less time in rule games than the others, more time in approaching others and also more time on their own. These findings suggest a pattern of failure to establish real involvement with others and a tendency 'to wait and hover on the periphery' so that victims 'were often ignored and left out' (op. cit., p. 173). Not being part of a group which might come to their aid made victims more vulnerable to aggressive approaches from others.

As has been stressed throughout this chapter, it is in social interaction that children and young people come to perceive themselves as having certain characteristics and to develop expectations about how others will behave towards them. Those who are seen by others as likeable and are welcomed into any group have acquired the prosocial skills of interest in those around them, willingness to adapt to what others want to do and sympathy with how they feel, without losing the ability to contribute from their own resources and hold a point of view of their own. Where group entry skills are poor or individuals want only to dominate others or cannot sustain behaviour which leads to an end which is satisfactory to the rest of the group, there is difficulty in establishing the relationships necessary for social well-being, a point which will be looked at in greater detail in Chapter 5.

CONCLUSION

The pre-school and school years see the refinement of social interactions and the widening of social relationships. Whereas very young children use interactions to satisfy their immediate needs and develop a relationship with those to whom they are attached, older infants observe and to some extent interpret the actions and reactions of those around them. Going to school makes far more interactive experiences available. Children grow in self-perception, in the realization that others have a point of view, and in their skills as group members. By adolescence, friendships and ease in joining in with others are of major importance.

Social contexts are always changing. The people in them behave differently towards one another because of changes in the membership of the group, temporary changes of mood, or changes in circumstances. Carers may behave differently towards their child when, for example, another adult or child is present, they have just had an argument with a partner, or they have lost someone close to them. Children find their expectations of others have to change. In a similar way, the expectations others have of them may change if they themselves experiment with different ways of behaving. It is probably through these changes and inconsistencies, however, that a more elaborated understanding emerges, creating a more robust social being than would be the case if there were no challenges to make the individual think.

Children and young people need security, affection and status if they are to be involved in interactions which are positive for all concerned. Unproductive interactions change the interpretations which are put upon the actions of others, the subsequent behaviour displayed by the individual and, in turn, the reactions of others towards that individual. If repeated, negative outcomes may put any relationship 'at risk'. In making generalized statements, however, it must always be remembered that there is a wide spectrum of individual differences in social behaviour and that what people want to get out of social interactions, or actually do get out of them, is very varied. What might be perceived as rejection by some may be seen in quite a different light by others. On the other hand, some may feel themselves popular with others when they are in fact only just tolerated. The next chapter will look at those who, for various reasons, do not establish successful social relationships or do not feel that they do so.

Chapter 3

Withdrawn and Isolated Children: Patterns of Behaviour

As pointed out in Chapter 1, there are different degrees of social withdrawal in childhood and adolescence, and the patterns of behaviour shown by withdrawn and isolated children are very varied. These patterns will be discussed in this chapter, which will also consider the links between withdrawal and emotional and behavioural disturbance such as aggression, anxiety states, depression, autism and schizophrenia.

TYPES OF WITHDRAWN AND ISOLATED CHILDREN

Socially withdrawn and isolated children and adolescents cannot easily be categorized, and delineated 'types' of children exhibiting withdrawal tend to present an over-generalized picture. For the sake of convenience, however, different kinds of withdrawn behaviour will be discussed here under the following headings, though there may well be some degree of overlap between the categories used:

- 'reserved' children
- inhibition in new entrants to school
- 'shy' children
- social neglect and isolation
- 'rejected' children
- children of 'controversial' sociometric status
- severe withdrawal associated with:

- fearful behaviour
- depression
- pervasive developmental disorders
- schizophrenia
- selective mutism.

'Reserved' children

Some children may fall into the category of being 'reserved' or 'socially neutral'. Such children are of an introverted temperament and spend most of their time in their own company. They may be relatively inactive socially but not necessarily altogether withdrawn, as they do not shun social activities if pressed to participate. They are not unhappy and do not show signs of emotional disturbance. Because they have few social distractions, they are likely to do well at school, perhaps developing a strong interest in reading or other hobbies which can be pursued without company. They may not be entirely without friends or companions.

> *Tina*, a girl aged 9, has no particular friends but is seldom entirely alone. She joins the fringes of groups, especially those involved playing games such as skipping or netball where conversation is minimal. She accepts overtures from staff and will run errands, but she does not seek attention. She is not perceived by the school as being or having a major problem. Although she has had some learning difficulties, she will work quietly at a given task. Tina cannot participate in out-of-school activities because of her family commitments, being in a one-parent family with responsibility for looking after younger siblings when her mother is on shift-work, so that she cannot cement friendships in the same way as other children of her age.

> *Helen*, a girl of 15, gets on normally with her younger brother and sister at home. Throughout her school years, she has always been very quiet, reserved and self-contained, rarely speaking to her teachers or most of her class-mates. Yet she is a happy girl and satisfied with having one or two close friends outside school, to whom she relates normally. While she does not go out of her way to take part in group activities, she does not refuse to participate in those that are required in school. Helen is of high intelligence and is making very good progress with her school work. She has a strong interest in reading, particularly books relating to science.

Whether or not such children as described above need special attention will depend on the circumstances of each individual. For example, Tina's situation will need to be monitored from the point of view of her home circumstances and her learning difficulties, particularly as friendship groups become more important, with the accompanying risk of Tina feeling left-out and isolated. All Helen needs is a sensitive understanding of her temperament and personality on the part of all those in contact with her.

Inhibition in new entrants to school

It is not surprising that inhibited behaviour is seen in otherwise normally-functioning children on entering school for the first time, transferring to a different school, or changing from primary to secondary stage, when (as mentioned in Chapter 1) a change of social status may be involved (see case study *Claire*, p. 36).

McGrew (1972) found a number of behaviours, which he termed 'hovering', to be characteristic of new children entering a nursery school. These included having a sad face, crying, chewing lips, grinding teeth, sucking fingers, hovering at a distance, shuffling, standing immobile, and whining. Elizur (1986) points out that school entry constitutes a period of stress for a number of children and their families: the child has to adjust to the new rules of the school environment and to develop the emotional, cognitive and social skills needed for coping with the new demands. Hughes, Pinkerton and Plewis (1979) suggest that young children who join an already established class may be particularly vulnerable to difficulties on starting infant school, especially if the class is large. From the child's point of view, it may well be harder to join an existing group of children, with an established social order, than to start with a group who are all equally new. The teacher's task is harder, too, when she has a small number of new children to integrate than when all the class have started together (see also Chapter 1, pp. 6–7).

New entrants to school usually show only short-lived withdrawal behaviour, if this occurs at all, but attention needs to be given to inhibited children to ensure that they do not feel isolated in the classroom or playground. Schools can help in the way they organize new intakes of pupils, and by their sensitive reception of pupils joining school for the first time. Parents as well as teachers may be able to support particularly vulnerable children in the way in which they manage separation from the home into the school environment.

By the time children move from the primary or elementary stage of school to a secondary school, they are better able to cope with the demands of changed social situations than they were at a younger age. However, as Marcoen and Goosens (1993) state, the transition to secondary school involves a move into a different school context and may be seen as increasing rather than decreasing feelings of peer-related loneliness as adjustment to a new group takes place. Pupils who have been the oldest in the primary school become the youngest in the secondary school, and even those who have been used to leadership positions may have to accept a lowly status, for a time at least, in their new school. Further, close friends may be separated at this stage.

Ewan is an 8-year-old boy who has recently transferred from a mainstream infant school to a special class in a primary school 4 miles from his home. He has low all-round ability and specific literacy problems of a severe type. He is now in a class of eight pupils, but the only child of similar age is a girl, and the rest of the class is made up of much older pupils who get on very well together. Ewan is of small stature and quietly spoken. The class is accompanied at playtime by a supervisory assistant who encourages the children to participate in group activities. Without her help, Ewan would have been isolated, especially in the early days after his transfer. In his previous school he was bullied by some pupils, who mocked the nature of his learning difficulties. No such bullying occurs now, but Ewan does not seem to have the social skills to join in easily.

Ewan has little contact with other children out of school. While he does not appear unhappy, he has not established a friendship group and his special-class status cuts down on the opportunities for social contact.

'Shy' children

Definitions of shyness

Shyness is probably the form of inhibited behaviour with which parents and teachers are most familiar. Shyness is characterized by anxiety in social settings, awkwardness in relations with others and a tendency to withdraw in the face of unfamiliar situations (Asendorpf, 1991, 1993). Arkin, Lake and Baumgardner (1986) view the shy person as consistently doubting his or her ability to make a favourable impression, and therefore motivated by the desire to avoid negative outcomes (e.g. disapproval) rather than the desire to gain positive outcomes (e.g. attention, recognition). Whereas non-shy people engage in behaviour designed to achieve positive results, the shy individual adopts self-protective strategies to deflect attention and possible criticism.

Crozier (1995) found that shyness in children aged 9–12 years was significantly correlated with measures of global self-esteem: shy children tend to doubt their ability to contribute effectively to social encounters. Shyness, in the view of the children themselves, was associated with feeling scared, hiding, being embarrassed, not speaking, sadness and being nervous. Situations arousing these feelings included being involved in novel encounters with teachers, other adults and other children; having to perform in front of the class; being told off; and going to a party.

The concept of 'unforthcomingness', which is a core syndrome in the diagnostic category of 'under-reaction' (as opposed to 'over-reaction') in the Bristol Social Adjustment Guides (Stott and Marston, 1971), discussed further in Chapter 4, is similar to that of 'shyness'. The 'unforthcoming' child fears new tasks or strange situations and is timid with people while maintaining a need for affection. As a relief from anxiety about school learning, the child may accept the role of being dull. Stott and Marston distinguish 'unforthcomingness' from 'withdrawal', which covers various types of social unresponsiveness – indifference to affection and human attachments, or a defensiveness against them arising from bad experiences. This is a narrower definition of 'withdrawal' than is used in the present book, where 'withdrawal' is considered as a generic term. As Stott and Marston suggest, shy children usually do want to be liked and to participate normally in social activities. This desire to be less shy and unforthcoming is helpful to those seeking to change the perceptions and actions of children hovering on the fringes of groups. Asendorpf (1986) also points out that shyness is an 'ambient affective state', representing attraction to interaction patterns and yet a wariness of them.

Forms of shyness

Lazarus (1982) emphasizes that shyness is an ambiguous concept which spans a wide behavioural–emotional continuum: it can range from bashfulness through timidity to a chronic fear of people. It should be borne in mind, too, that it is possible for an individual to label him or herself as shy but behave in a non-shy manner.

Crozier and Burnham (1990) found support for the hypothesis that *fearful* shyness would be developed prior to *self-conscious* shyness (Buss, 1984, 1986), with the transition between the two forms taking place at around 7–8 years. On the basis of interviews with children aged 5–11 years, they report a clear tendency for references to self-consciousness and embarrassment (rare at 5–6 years) to increase with age; references to fearful shyness were frequent throughout the age group.

Alden, Bieling and Meleshko (1995) refer to the frequent distinctions made in the literature on social anxiety between *skilled* and *unskilled* shy, anxious or socially phobic individuals. In the case of *unskilled* shy persons, signs of behavioural awkwardness, poor social skills and inhibition are seen. The *skilled* shy individual, however, is characterized primarily by negative cognition, that is, he or she generally processes social information in a way that accentuates negative views of the self and the responses of others to the self.

Elkind and Bowen (1979) used an Imaginary Audience Scale (IAS) with 697 students at various stages of their school career. This scale assesses young people's willingness to reveal different facets of themselves to an audience, and consists of two subscales – Transient Self (TS) and Abiding Self (AS). TS items refer to momentary appearances and behaviours, whereas AS items are concerned with long-lived characteristics such as personality traits (the IAS is discussed further in Chapter 4, p. 57). Elkind and Bowen found that 8th-graders (13-year-olds, young adolescents) were significantly less willing than older adolescents or younger subjects to reveal their transient and abiding selves to an audience. Self-consciousness was particularly marked at this stage of adolescence, with girls tending to be more reluctant than boys to reveal themselves to an audience.

Prevalence of shyness

Shyness in some degree is very common: many individuals – children, adolescents and adults – feel shy in some social situations. Asendorpf (1986) found that pre-school teachers rated 16.8 per cent of their pupils as 'shy-inhibited', whereas Zimbardo and Radl (1981) report that 30 per cent of pre-school children showed shyness, according to parents and teachers. Lazarus (1982) studied the incidence of shyness in children aged 10–11 years in Florida. When the children were asked to rate themselves on a seven-point scale ranging from never being shy to being shy all the time, 28 per cent of the sample felt that they were shy at least half the time; 5 per cent thought of themselves as almost always shy; and 2 per cent felt that they were shy all the time. Lazarus found that elementary school teachers were much more likely to nominate girls than boys as shy, suggesting that shyness is possibly seen as more appropriate and acceptable in girls. 26 per cent of the boys and 49 per cent of the girls in the Florida sample applied the 'shy' label to themselves. Zimbardo, Pilkonis and Norwood (1975) report findings similar to those of Lazarus in the case of young adults.

Daisy is a girl aged 6 years, of very pleasant appearance. Her eyes are a distinctive feature, especially as they frequently have a 'longing' look about them. Daisy is frequently described as 'timid'. She will actually hide physically behind other children if given the chance. She does mix with other pupils, but is always a meek follower.

Daisy uses gesture to replace speech at times, using nods and shakes of the head for 'yes' and 'no' unless she is pressed. She still has some of the mannerisms of a younger child such as thumb-sucking and hair-twisting. These mannerisms are considerably more noticeable in situations which she finds stressful.

Daisy waits to be invited to join in games and activities, but because she is so willing to be directed, is rarely left out entirely. Hanging back and looking on longingly is actually proving quite an effective method of becoming included. She blushes easily and is very self-conscious, appearing ill-at-ease even when comments made about her are positive. She has to be actively encouraged to call attention to herself: in class prayers and school productions she can be persuaded to take the stage only as part of a group.

At home, Daisy is said by her mother to be strong-willed and prone to attempting to get her own way through temper-tantrums and tears. The mother is amazed that Daisy's behaviour at school is so different from that at home.

Although, as Erwin (1993) states, a degree of shyness is normal and adaptive to the extent that it allows situations to be assessed before an individual commits him or herself, both shy behaviour and feelings of shyness are likely to have adverse consequences (Lazarus, 1982).

> *Claire* is an 11-year-old girl in the first year at secondary school, one of the youngest pupils in her year group. She is the middle one of five sisters, reported by her parents to be overlooked by both older and younger sisters, thought the older sisters tend to be very protective of her. Claire is of a very shy and timid nature, a passive observer both in class and in the playground. She has no close friends in her new class. Her teachers sense that she does not enjoy her existence on the fringes of the social group and would prefer to be more actively involved, but she does not possess the social skills necessary to gain admission to the group. Her primary teachers reported that Claire tended to wait to be invited to participate in various games and activities, and at that time such invitations were forthcoming. However, this is not the case at her new secondary school, and she now spends long periods of time as a spectator.
>
> In the third term of her first year, Claire continues to be very self-conscious, blushing very easily at any approaches by the teacher or, on rare occasions, by other pupils. However, in reality she would very much like to respond more effectively to such approaches and become a part of the group.

Social neglect and isolation

Identifying neglected and isolated children

In sociometric terms, 'neglected' children ('neglectees') are those who make very little impact as members of a classroom or other group. These children are not nominated as particularly liked or disliked by their peers. Typically, in sociometric tests requiring children in a class to say whom they would like or not like to sit next to, work with or play with, neglectees would receive very few, if any, positive or negative choices.

Dygdon and Conger (1990) compared two methods for identifying 'neglected' members of a group: (1) using *social impact* (SI) scores formed from sums of nominations to Like and Dislike dimensions, and (2) asking in a private interview for *direct nominations* to categories of Like, Dislike and Neglect. Direct nominations to the category of Neglect would be obtained by saying, 'Now sometimes in a group this big, some children are just forgotten. I want you to show me someone to whom your classmates don't pay very much attention.' Dygdon and Conger concluded that, while both social impact measures and direct nominations tapped social dysfunction, direct nominations seemed better suited to identifying 'socially neglected' members of a group.

Neglect, isolation and rejection

Neglectees may be isolates and spend most of their time in solitary activities; their isolation may be largely self-imposed, or inflicted on them by their peers (rejected children are discussed in the next section of this chapter, pp. 39–41). However, according to Malik and Furman (1993), neglect is not to be equated with social withdrawal or low rates of actual interaction with peers. Neglected children are not necessarily actively rejected by their peers. They tend to be less aggressive and less sociable than others (Coie, Dodge and Kupersmidt, 1990), but such behavioural differences are not very large or consistent (Newcomb, Bukowski and Pattee, 1993). Isolates, however, do show behavioural differences from others, usually marked.

Scarlett (1980) carried out an intensive study of 11 isolates (6 boys and 5 girls), of normal intelligence and emotional stability, chosen from 6 different pre-schools in the USA, the age range being 42–59 months. The results of the study supported the expectation that pre-school children who interact infrequently with their peers share a pattern of behaving – a pattern not depicted by any simple label such as shy or apathetic. In particular, these children differ from their peers by

- spending less time playing with and more time watching peers;
- rarely trying to influence or structure how their peers behave, even when interacting with them;
- spending less class-time in imaginative–dramatic play;
- being more likely to interact with peers when in more structured and smaller groups.

Scarlett asserts that isolates at the pre-school stage contribute to their own isolation, particularly by playing less than others: young children's attempts to structure one another are especially important in developing peer relations. Social isolation from age-mates may be fostered by the isolates' own behaviour, the treatment of isolates in school, and situational variables.

In studies with elementary school children, Dodge, Coie and Brakke (1982) also found that neglected children approached their peers relatively infrequently in social situations, and met with frequent rebuffs when they did make overtures to their classmates. However, unlike actively rejected children, they showed relatively few task-inappropriate and aggressive behaviours.

Forms of isolation

Gottman (1977) observes that there are two separate definitions of social isolation in the literature, one based on low frequencies of peer interaction and the other based on low levels of peer acceptance using sociometric measures. In his own work with children aged 3–5 years, Gottman found no relationship between peer acceptance and relative frequency of peer interaction, and he suggests that these two measures of social isolation do not tap the same dimension. He highlights a group of children who were frequently 'tuned-out' or off-task when alone. These children had the lowest mean scores in regard to peer acceptance, and were high on a set of shy, anxious and fearful behaviours called 'hovering' by McGrew (1972) – see above, p. 32. This group seemed to fit best the construct of the shy, socially anxious child who is also neither accepted nor rejected but rather ignored by his or her peers.

Rubin and Mills (1988) distinguish between *passive-anxious* and *active-immature* types of social isolation among children aged 7–10+ years. *Passive-anxious* isolation involves largely quiet, sedentary, solitary, constructive or exploratory behaviour on the part of children who are given the chance to engage in free play, but who continue to be on their own without reference to the peer group. This form of isolation is consistently related in this age group to internalized difficulties and negative social self-perceptions, and might lead to depression and loneliness by the age of 10 or 11 years. *Active-immature* isolation is infrequent and unstable, and more often associated with aggression and other externalized difficulties than with internalized problems, though not predictive of substantial disturbance by the age of 10 or 11 years.

Feelings of loneliness

Distressing feelings of loneliness in childhood are very common, but in most cases are situationally determined and short-lived (Marcoen and Goosens, 1993). It is during adolescence that feelings of loneliness can be particularly disturbing (Kimmel, 1985). At this stage, new pressures may be expressed in regard to position in the social group and relationships with peers of the same and opposite sex. Adolescents may not yet have enough social skills to maintain relationships, and loneliness may be felt keenly when an intimate friendship breaks down. In a survey of a large group of adolescents in a mid-western city in the USA, Ostrov and Offer (1978) found that 20 per cent of the younger (12- to 15-year-olds) and 13 per cent of the older (16- to 20-year-olds) adolescents reported feeling very lonely. As would be expected, far more serious loneliness was found among a group of disturbed adolescents who had been admitted to a psychiatric treatment centre (36.2 per cent of 166 boys; 55.1 per cent of 74 girls).

> ***Robin*** is an intelligent 11-year-old boy in the second term of his first year in a comprehensive secondary school. He is quite tall for his age and always very smart in his appearance. When he started at the comprehensive school, he came with a record

of being quiet and retiring. The school took pains to put him in the same class as his only friend in the primary school from which both boys came. However, his friend soon abandoned him and Robin was left isolated. At first this did not seem to have an adverse effect on the boy, who resisted attempts by his form tutor to encourage him to form new friendships and retreated into more solitary pursuits, continually asking to stay in class to read a book or complete a project, rather than going into the playground.

By the end of the first term, however, it was clear that Robin's work was deteriorating in quality. When his parents were contacted, they amazed the form tutor by revealing that for the five to six weeks leading up to the end of term Robin had protested strongly against coming to school, feigning illness, crying bitterly and finally resorting to severe temper tantrums. At a series of family discussions, Robin had indicated that he felt desperately lonely, claiming that the other boys in his class were hostile towards him. This was not in fact the case: members of staff commented that, in general, Robin's classmates were oblivious to him, demonstrating no real feelings of any kind towards him. Some staff felt that Robin's isolation was largely self-imposed.

Reluctantly Robin brought himself to discuss his situation with his form tutor, agreeing that he had not been harassed by his classmates, but saying that he had interpreted their ambivalence towards him as hostility. Robin confided that he particularly feared break times and lunch times, since these were periods when his isolation was most highlighted and made him feel most vulnerable.

Rejected children

Identifying rejected children

Rejected children are those actively disliked by many of their peers and positively nominated by few or none of them on sociometric measures (Malik and Furman, 1993). On the basis of a review of the literature, Williams and Gilmour (1994) estimate that between 10 and 20 per cent of children are rejected by their peers, aggression being the single most important correlate of rejection. Rejected children tend to be aggressive, highly impulsive, disruptive and unco-operative (Cillessen *et al.*, 1992). According to Coie, Dodge and Kupersmidt (1990), rejected children engage less often in positive interaction than their socially accepted mates, engage more often in negative interactions (especially fighting and arguing), and experience many rebuffs. They spend some of their time in inappropriate solitary activities, such as clowning, daydreaming or wandering aimlessly around the classroom (Dodge, Coie and Brakke, 1982).

Types of rejected children

However, rejected children are not all aggressive, and they seem to form a heterogeneous group. Parkhurst and Asher (1992) found that, particularly in adolescence, a rejected/withdrawn group can be distinguished from rejected/aggressive children. In their study of pupils in early adolescence, they report that most of the rejected individuals were aggressive or submissive, but it was the combination of aggression or submission with low levels of prosocial behaviour that was associated with peer rejection. Submissive-rejected subjects reported high levels of loneliness and worry about social relationships, but aggressive-rejected pupils did not differ from average-status adolescents in those dimensions.

Cillessen *et al.* (1992) suggest that about 40–50 per cent of rejected children are perceived as aggressive by their peers, a further 10–20 per cent are shy and socially withdrawn, and up to 40 per cent differ little from average status children. Dodge and Feldman (1990) consider that it is in certain key situations, such as responding to provocation, trying to resolve conflicts, or attempting to acquire a peer's possessions, that rejected children display incompetent and aversive behaviour; most of the time they behave adaptively and constructively. Unpopular children, according to Dodge and Feldman, are less skilful in interpreting cues, are biased in their attributions of others and blame social failures on internal causes. Frederickson (1991), too, asserts that rejected children are less likely to be proficient in generating a range of possible responses and evaluating the probable consequences of responses in social situations.

Laura is an 8-year-old girl in foster care. Initially she gave the impression in school of being a confident, self-assured and mature child, but this view of her has proved erroneous. Laura is seriously lacking in self-confidence, but can put on a very plausible front. She has few, if any, strategies for making and keeping friends. She is a bad loser and hits out at those who beat her even in simple playground games. Laura seems incapable of playing by the rules and has been rejected as a playmate. She imposes herself upon children in the playground, but is only accepted by those who fear the consequences if they do not allow her to join in. Even these groups find ways of avoiding her, and Laura is constantly moving from group to group. There are frequent complaints from pupils who are required to sit next to her in class, as she demands access to their work. She has good oral skills, but can be disruptive when listening is called for. Laura is frequently out of her seat without cause and is prone to being off-task.

Laura's rejection at school is compounded by rejection in her foster-home, where she is described as a compulsive liar, aggressive and destructive.

James is a 13-year-old boy who is overweight and suffers from asthma. He is the subject of a statement of special educational needs, as he has long-standing learning difficulties, not helped over the years by irregular attendance and a tendency to tear up his exercise books and weep when frustrated in his attempts to complete classroom tasks. James has a fiery temperament and is easily upset by even the most innocuous things his peers say to him. From the early days at secondary school, James has been teased about his weight and shape. Whenever he is taunted, his face contorts into a mask of rage, he screams and swears and generally abuses his tormentors; then he takes out his frustrations upon innocent bystanders (usually smaller, younger pupils) who are unfortunate enough to be close to the scene. Such behaviour inevitably ends with James being in trouble with staff.

James is very unpopular within his year group. In various activities such as PE and games, the other boys in his year group frequently protest at having him in their team. His fearful temper tends to disrupt such games as football and basketball. As a consequence of his aggressive and disruptive behaviour, advances made by James towards establishing friendships are met with rejection. James's peers tend to regard him with a mixture of fear and contempt, and have made him something of a scapegoat figure.

James is also often in conflict with members of staff, and has a disturbed home background.

Children of 'controversial' social status

Sociometric tests show up a small number of children who receive both high negative and high positive nominations. Such children have been termed of 'controversial' status. They are often disruptive and aggressive, arousing feelings of dislike, but can also acquire a certain popularity because they may possess leadership qualities, even if these are not used in the right direction. 'Controversial' children may, for example, be disliked by some peers for bullying, but be leaders of a group of classmates and have a high impact in their peer group (Williams and Gilmour, 1994).

Dodge (1983), observing the development of sociometric status over time in groups of 7-year-old boys, found that 'controversial' children engaged in high frequencies of both prosocial and antisocial behaviour. They showed a good deal of skilled interpersonal behaviour, but also played aggressively, made hostile statements, and indulged in irritating behaviour such as making meaningless noises. In the case of older elementary schools pupils and adolescents, too, Coie, Dodge and Coppotelli (1982) found individuals who engaged in actively anti-social behaviour associated with rejection and yet were viewed as leaders and not seen as shy: they were perceived as neither highly co-operative nor as unco-operative, and gave rise to considerable feelings of ambivalence on the part of their peers. Coie, Dodge and Coppotelli, while acknowledging that negative-choice sociometric questions should be used with caution, underline the importance of using both positive and negative sociometric-choice questions. Only in this way can a more differentiated picture be obtained of both the dimensions of social status that can be found among these groups.

Cairns *et al.* (1988) studied social networks and aggressive behaviour in school in two cohorts of boys and girls, one with a mean age of 10.2 years and the other with a mean age of 13.4 years. They found that aggressive subjects tended to affiliate with aggressive peers, and that peer social clusters might provide mutual support for aggressive behaviour as new social units emerge in adolescence. Highly aggressive boys and girls, while less popular than others in the social network at large, were usually solid members of peer clusters and typically had a network of friends. Thus failure to achieve broad-based popularity should not be taken as evidence of complete social rejection.

Harry is a 9-year-old boy who looks and acts 'tough'. He is like a magnet to younger pupils with behaviour problems. These boys are not really close friends of his, but he is popular with them, and they join him in trouble-making in school. Harry is actively avoided by most pupils, who know that sooner or later he and his gang will be in trouble. In his home neighbourhood, too, he is often involved, as a leader of a gang, in acts of vandalism.

Joe is a 15-year-old secondary school pupil of unkempt appearance and with poor standards of hygiene. Until the previous year, he was a shy, timid and rather withdrawn boy, very much an isolate in relation to the other boys in his year group. He was unpopular in this group for no particular reason, though bullying during the early stages of his secondary school career had made him rather nervous and ill-at-ease with other pupils and deeply unhappy over most aspects of school life.

Coincident with a growth spurt at about 14 years of age, which made him considerably taller and stronger than previously, Joe became more self-confident, outgoing and gregarious than previously. He now has a considerable influence on younger pupils at the school and has formed friendships with some of these. He has assumed a leadership role with these pupils and often leads them into trouble, as he himself has become increasingly disaffected with school. This newly-found status receives no recognition from pupils of his own age, who are scornful of him and occasionally bully him.

Joe is now perceived in different ways by different people. His teachers and the parents of younger boys who form his friendship group view him as a trouble-maker. Pupils in school of his own age despise him and let him know this at every opportunity, whilst the group of boys inside his friendship group view him as an extremely popular figure.

Severe withdrawal associated with emotional/behavioural disturbance

Severe withdrawal from school, out-of-school and/or family activities is usually associated with emotional and behavioural disturbance, personality disorder or mental illness. In this section, the links between severe withdrawal and fearful or phobic behaviour, depression, pervasive developmental disorders, schizophrenia and selective mutism will be discussed briefly.

Withdrawal and fearful or phobic behaviour

Fearful behaviour is central not only to normal development but also to the development of anxiety disorders. To preserve health and life, children are deliberately taught to fear certain things – for example, strangers or aggressive children – and to avoid and withdraw from dangerous situations. It is not easy to find out what children are afraid of, especially as observed approach/withdrawal behaviour is not always correlated with fears reported by parents or children (Stevenson-Hinde and Shouldice, 1995).

Shy children are often fearful children, and withdrawn children may be highly anxious. Many childhood fears cause major distress to the individual: highly fearful children tend to feel less good about themselves and their abilities to control events around them (Ollendick, Yule and Ollier, 1991). Studying fear in American and Australian children aged 7–16 years, Ollendick, King and Frary (1989) found five clusters of fear: of failure and criticism; of the unknown; of injury and small animals; of danger and death; and of medical concerns.

Extreme fears or phobias can greatly interfere with normal functioning and may involve serious withdrawal from school or social activities, disrupting the child's daily life. Children may have a persistent fear of one or more situations involving scrutiny by others because of the possibility of doing something embarrassing. In some cases, the individual has only one such social phobia (e.g. having to speak publicly in class or meeting unfamiliar people), but often he or she fears several social situations or even most social events (see Kendall and Brady, 1995).

School phobia illustrates extreme fear which is most disruptive for the individual affected. Characteristically, the child suffering from school phobia shows signs of extreme anxiety or panic when the time for going to school arrives, or even when going to school is discussed at home; he or she is unable to leave home and may complain of stomach pains or other ailments. The child may not only withdraw from school, but from social contact with other children. However, in some cases the withdrawal may be related solely to the specific school situation. School phobia affects boys and girls equally and may occur at any stage of schooling, though it is found particularly at the ages of 5–6, 11–12 and 13–14 years (Hersov and Berg, 1980; Kahn, Nursten and Carroll, 1981; Blagg, 1987).

Susan is a 15-year-old girl who is painfully thin and ill-looking. She is an intelligent pupil with considerable academic potential, but her secondary-school career has been adversely affected by her two interacting phobias – one about school, and another about food. In the early stages at secondary school, she possessed a pleasant, outgoing personality and engaged the company of a number of friends. However, in her third year at the school, Susan's size and shape suddenly became a major issue for her and her friends. The girls in Susan's friendship circle seemed to become adolescents in every sense of the word, beginning to wear fashionable clothes and dating boys, whereas Susan, who had always tended to be overweight, failed to keep up with her peers. She became isolated within her group, largely through her appearance, and was taunted about her size and her lack of boyfriends. Susan reacted by opting out of school altogether for a period of time which has now exceeded 18 months, and refusing food to the extent of becoming ill and very weak.

Withdrawal and depression

As Kazdin (1990) states, depression can refer to different characteristics. Some depressive symptoms, such as sadness and fatigue, are common and normal in an appropriate context. However, depression as a syndrome or disorder is serious and requires expert attention. Withdrawal from social contacts and activities is a typical feature of depressive states, in which weepiness, unhappiness, feelings of worthlessness or guilt, impaired concentration and thoughts relating to death may also be found (Pearce, 1977; Kennedy, Spence and Hensley, 1989; Kendall and Brady, 1995). Interpersonal difficulties and low academic achievement may also feature in cases of depression in childhood or adolescence. At home, there may be sleeping and eating disturbances, irritability and complaints about aches and pains, as well as a tendency to withdraw from the family group, perhaps to the child's bedroom for long periods (see Goodyer, 1995 for a comprehensive account of depression in childhood and adolescence).

In a study by Kent, Vostanis and Feehan (1995) of 45 schoolchildren in Birmingham, England (mean age 12.4 years, age range 7–16 years), referred for depression to psychiatric units over a two-year period, teachers described these children as quiet, lacking in self-confidence, likeable, sensitive and anxious. The most commonly selected items on the Rutter Child Scale B (Rutter, 1967) included: 'not much liked by other children'; 'tends to do things on own'; 'tends to be fearful of new things or new situations', and 'often worried/worries about many things' – although these items were not applicable in all cases.

Lynne, aged 13 years, was referred to a psychiatric clinic during her second year at secondary school. In spite of her intelligence, she had difficulty in concentrating in school and her work was deteriorating. She showed persistent anxiety and a lack of self-confidence. She began to shrink from contact with the outside world and could not face the thought of going out by bus or going to school. At home, where there was poverty and overcrowding, she was very moody and dispirited, ate badly and had difficulty in sleeping. Lynne's symptoms were exaggerated following the death of her father, to whom she had been closely attached.

After psychiatric treatment and a prolonged period away from school, Lynne showed a marked improvement in her emotional state. She also made better progress at a new school, a change of school having been arranged to give her the opportunity for a fresh start.

Estimates of the prevalence of depression vary according to the criteria used and the method of assessment. In the USA Cohen *et al.* (1993) estimated that 2.3 per cent of a sample of girls and 1.8 per cent of boys aged 10–13 years suffered from major depression. At ages 14–16, 7.6 per cent of girls and 1.6 per cent of boys were diagnosed as very depressed, with 2.7 per cent of both boys and girls aged 17–20 fitting into this category. In the study of a sample of 8-year-olds in Germany carried out by Esser, Schmidt and Woerner (1990), 0.9 per cent of boys showed severe symptoms of depression; at age 13, 2 per cent of boys were severely depressed, some of them showing suicidal tendencies. No girls were identified as severely depressed in this survey, at either age. Lefkowitz and Tesiny (1985) found severe depression in 5.2 per cent of a sample of over 3,000 8- to 11-year-olds in the USA. Figures are much higher when moderate symptoms of depression are under consideration, especially when self-reports are asked for. Esser, Schmidt and Woerner (1990), for example, report that as many as 25 per cent of the boys and 35 per cent of the girls in their sample showed moderate symptoms of depressed mood at the age of 13 years, while Rutter *et al.* (1976) found that, at the age of 14–15 years, over 40 per cent of the adolescents in the Isle of Wight survey admitted to feelings of misery and depression.

Withdrawal and pervasive developmental disorders

Withdrawn behaviour is a key feature of pervasive developmental disorders such as autism and Asperger's syndrome. These are relatively rare disorders, but they have received a good deal of attention from clinicians and researchers.

Autism As Bailey, Phillips and Rutter (1996) put it, the syndrome of autism is defined by social abnormalities accompanied by deviant language development and stereotyped repetitive patterns of behaviour. The main social abnormalities seen in autistic individuals include a general failure to use smiling, gesture or physical contact in a normal way to respond to, or signal, social intent; a lack of eye contact, a lack of interest in sharing feelings with others, even a lack of awareness of others; and a failure to use speech for communication (Howlin and Rutter, 1987; Bailey, Phillips and Rutter, 1996).

Lorna Wing and her collaborators (Wing and Gould, 1979; Wing and Attwood, 1987; Wing, 1988) have proposed the following three sub-types of autism based on the quality of social interactions occurring in the spectrum of this disorder:

- an *aloof* group – most cut off from social contact; these children often avoid close proximity to others and reject physical and social contact;
- a *passive* group – such children make social approaches only to satisfy their needs, although they may accept approaches from others;
- an *active-but-odd* group – these children approach others in a way that is one-sided, repetitive and even bizarre, e.g. repeatedly asking inappropriate questions.

Symptoms of autism may be shown in the first year of life and serious social difficulties may persist into adult life, even if some improvement is shown in relationships with others. Autism is much more common in males, and occurs in about 4 or 5 in every 10,000 children (Lord, 1984; Howlin, 1986).

> **Stanley** is an 11-year-old boy at primary school who exhibits autistic tendencies. He attended a mainstream nursery and reception class, but was moved to a special class at the age of 5. At that time, he could read simple words and phrases and copy writing, speaking in short, stylized sentences. Over the next few years his progress slowed, stopped and then deteriorated. He does not make eye contact with adults, but will get their attention by touching them. He makes no attempt to pay attention to other children unless they invade his space or try to take away any of his possessions. When interfered with, he lashes out with arms or legs. Stanley's day must have a fixed routine, as changes in routine cause him trauma. An example of his obsessional behaviour is that he recites lists, and if interrupted will go back to the beginning and recite the list again. He carries two books with him at all times – they even accompany him to the dining room and bathroom – and 'reads' these to himself.

Asperger's syndrome   Asperger (1944, 1979) has distinguished a group of children with autistic-like features, particularly social impairments, but typically intelligent and able to use language fluently if often strangely. The validity of the so-called Asperger's syndrome has been much debated (Gillberg and Gillberg, 1989; Szatmari, Brenner and Nagy, 1989). Tantam (1988) considers that the concept should be reserved as a descriptive term for autistic children who

- use language freely but fail to adjust to different social contexts or the needs of different listeners;
- wish to be sociable but fail to make relationships with peers;
- are conspicuously clumsy;
- develop idiosyncratic but engrossing interests;
- have marked impairments of non-verbal expressiveness which affect tone of voice, facial expression, gesture, gaze and posture.

Ehlers and Gillberg (1993), on the basis of a total population study of 1,519 children aged 7–16 years in an outer borough of Göteborg, Sweden, estimate that the prevalence figure for Asperger's syndrome (definite, suspected and possible cases combined) is 0.71 per cent (0.97 per cent of all boys and 0.44 per cent of all girls).

Schizophrenia

Withdrawal from reality is a feature often found in schizophrenia, which occurs in about 1–2 per cent of the population and is rare before adolescence. Schizophrenia is a generic name for a group of disorders characterized by a progressive disintegration of the personality and its relationship with the world (Stafford-Clark and Smith, 1983). Key features are disorders of thinking, including delusions; feelings of passivity and hallucinations; disorders of emotions; and bizarre movements and behaviour. The individual affected may show indifference to other people and external events, lose any motivation to look after him or herself, and lack warmth of feeling.

In the youngest age group and adolescents, the presence of schizophrenia is characterized by high levels of anxiety; incoherent speech; bizarre actions such as grimacing or stereotyped movements; intense preoccupation with inner thoughts; poor emotional control with unpredictable aggressive outbursts; and maintenance of social distance (Steinberg, 1985).

Schizophrenic children and adolescents are likely to need hospital in-patient treatment, perhaps over a considerable period (see Chapter 6 for a discussion of the outcome of schizophrenia in childhood and adolescence).

Henry, aged 12 years, began to stay away from school during his first year at secondary school. He complained of feeling 'far away' at times while in class, and of other children 'getting at' him, though there was little evidence that this was the case. He was afraid to be away from home and shunned the company of others. Even at home Henry often abruptly withdrew from the family circle and remained in his room for long periods, often doing nothing. He was uncommunicative most of the time, and when he did speak, his utterances were often bizarre and incomprehensible. Members of his family found it difficult to have a reasoned discussion with him.

There were no adverse material circumstances and Henry did not experience any serious educational difficulties at the primary stage. Henry was treated in hospital, but made little progress and could not be persuaded to return to school.

Selective mutism

'Selective' or 'elective' mutism is found in a small number of children, fewer than 1 in 1,000. Children exhibiting this condition are able to talk, but choose to communicate only to a small group of individuals. Most are moderately or severely withdrawn, negative and moody. Selective mutism is more likely to occur in school than at home, and withdrawn behaviour tends to be shown more frequently in relation to peers than adults. Selective mutism usually develops between the ages of 3 and 5 years after a period of speech development, and affects boys and girls equally (Kolvin and Fundudis, 1981; Cantwell and Baker, 1985).

CONCLUSION

This chapter has highlighted the many different patterns of behaviour in childhood and adolescence subsumed under the terms 'withdrawal' and 'isolation'. These patterns range from normal reserve in well-adjusted children to behaviour that is associated with, and indicative of, serious emotional and behavioural disturbance, especially in adolescence. Within each of the categories considered in this chapter, individual variations and sub-groups may be found. Withdrawal is not necessarily persistent or consistently shown by any individual, and a child's social behaviour may not be the same in different groups, such as the classroom, home and neighbourhood. Changing circumstances, too, may alter a child's status in the group. Even relatively short periods of isolation from the group are likely to cause distressing feelings of loneliness or rejection.

Chapter 4

Techniques for Assessing Withdrawn and Isolated Behaviour

Teachers, educational and clinical psychologists, psychiatrists, and other professional workers such as counsellors and researchers have an interest in identifying and assessing children and adolescents who are withdrawn or isolated. In seeking to do so, they are likely to request information from parents and others in close contact with the individual concerned in order to obtain as full a picture as possible. Personality and behaviour checklists and schedules, peer-referenced assessment, systematic observation, interviews and self-monitoring may be used to collect data about withdrawn and isolated behaviour. As information from one source is often different from that gained from another source (see Chapter 1, pp. 3–4), it is desirable to get to know the perspectives of the school, parents, child and support services where appropriate.

Apart from describing in as precise terms as possible both the nature of the child's difficulties and the various contexts (e.g. classroom, playground, home and neighbourhood) in which these difficulties do or do not occur, it is important to draw up a profile of the child's general development and scholastic progress, highlighting strengths as well as weaknesses. It is also essential to discover, as far as possible, relevant details of the child's background and to pinpoint those factors which seem to be particularly associated with the child's behaviour. The purpose of any assessment should always be kept in mind. Apart from assessment used in research projects, enquiries about a child should focus on information likely to help in hypothesizing his or her needs and planning a programme of action that will bring about desired changes. The assessment of emotional and behavioural difficulties is always a matter for team-work, whether based primarily in school or clinic (DFE, 1994).

This chapter will discuss the varied techniques available for the assessment of withdrawn and isolated behaviour under the following headings, which do overlap somewhat:

- personality and behaviour checklists and inventories (for teachers, parents and self)
- peer-referenced assessment
- systematic observation
- interviews
- self-monitoring
- assessment for social skills training
- general assessment.

There is such a plethora of techniques which fall into the above categories, particularly checklists and inventories, that it is not feasible to provide a comprehensive coverage in this chapter. However, examples will be given of a wide range of approaches, especially those in common use (for a good coverage of assessment techniques used with children and adolescents, see Ollendick and Hersen, 1993).

Apart from the approaches to assessment listed above, psychologists may also use repertory grid techniques, designed to elicit the personal constructs of the individual (that is, how he or she interprets his or her world and seeks to anticipate events), or projective techniques, aimed at uncovering hidden or complex feelings. These approaches will not be discussed in this chapter, but discussions of repertory grid techniques will be found in Bannister and Fransella, 1986; Beail, 1985; and Winter, 1994. Projective techniques are discussed in Pervin, 1980; Semeonoff, 1981; and Finch and Belter, 1993.

PERSONALITY AND BEHAVIOUR CHECKLISTS AND INVENTORIES

Over the years many different checklists and inventories have been designed for completion by teachers and parents and in self-reporting. These provide helpful information, though teachers, psychologists, counsellors and psychiatrists are likely to be more interested in the qualitative aspects of this form of assessment and its use as a basis for further exploration than in the scores obtained, which may be of concern to researchers. Colmar (1988), while acknowledging that a behaviour checklist may function as a useful guide to making a general assessment, in that it samples the individual's behaviour or repertoire of skills in a given area, emphasizes that checklists have very real limitations. In particular, the aspects of behaviour sampled are not always described clearly with reference to their context, nor are they always relevant to intervention. Checklists, therefore, should be regarded as making only a partial contribution to a comprehensive assessment.

Checklists for use by teachers

Teachers rarely have sufficient time or opportunity to observe a child systematically in a variety of contexts, though they may be able to do this with the help of an educational psychologist (see below, pp. 62–4). However, the use of a schedule or checklist may help teachers to systematize their thoughts and observations of pupils' behaviour. Two such instruments in common use in Britain are the Bristol Social Adjustment Guide and the Rutter Child Behaviour Scale.

The Bristol Social Adjustment Guide (BSAG) (Stott and Marston, 1971; Stott, 1963; 1974)

The BSAG (Child in School) is intended for use by teachers with pupils aged 5–16 years in day school. It provides a comprehensive variety of phrases (both positive and negative) describing a child's behaviour; the teacher has to underline those phrases which most nearly describe that behaviour.

A diagnostic form is provided for recording those underlined phrases which indicate 'under-reactive' or 'over-reactive' behaviour, and for scoring 'core syndromes'. The scores on the BSAG form the basis for identifying children with varying degrees of 'under-reactive' or 'over-reactive' behaviour, in terms of categories ranging from 'stability' to 'severe maladjustment' (Stott, 1974). 'Over-reaction' refers to inconsequential and aggressive behaviour, while 'under-reactive' core syndromes cover 'unforthcomingness' (timidity, fear of new tasks or strange situations), 'withdrawal' (various types of social unresponsiveness) and 'depression' (lack of response to stimuli).

Examples of items which relate to socially withdrawn or isolated children are as follows.

Unforthcomingness   Wants adult interest but can't put himself forward / shy but would like to be friendly / likes sympathy but reluctant to ask / has to be encouraged to take part.

Withdrawal   Avoids contact both with teacher and other children / distant, ignores others / never makes any sort of social relationship, good or bad / remains aloof in a world of his own.

Depression   Too lethargic to be troublesome / apathetic, 'just sits' / unmotivated, has no energy / couldn't care whether teacher sees his work or not.

The BSAG, while somewhat idiosyncratic in its structure and use of terminology, has proved a useful schedule in surveys and the classroom, especially as a basis for discussion with a psychologist. A strong point in its favour lies in the fact that the negative items are intermingled with positive ones, thus avoiding a possible negative stance on the part of the rater using the Guide.

Rutter Child Behaviour Scale B (Rutter, 1967; Rutter, Tizard and Whitmore, 1970)

The version of this scale designed for use with 7- to 11-year-olds has been widely used in schools, clinics and research projects, mainly as a screening instrument for emotional and behavioural difficulties. It consists of 26 statements of possible behaviour problems, the rater having to check whether 'certainly applies', 'applies somewhat' or 'doesn't apply' is appropriate in each case for the pupil concerned. It is easy to complete, though its simplicity means that the Scale should be used with caution in allocating children to particular categories such as 'neurotic' or 'anti-social' (Venables *et al.*, 1983). Examples of those items which refer to socially withdrawn children are

– not much liked by other children;
– tends to do things on his own – rather solitary;
– tends to be fearful or afraid of new things or new situations;
– often appears miserable, unhappy, tearful or distressed.

The format of the Rutter Scale, containing as it does only items about undesirable traits and tendencies, may lead the rater to adopt a negative attitude towards particular children (Fitton, 1972) and is often disconcerting to respondents, who want to identify a child's strengths. Goodman (1994) added items referring to 'prosocial' (desirable) behaviour to the original Rutter Scale for teachers, using the twenty items of the Prosocial Behaviour Questionnaire (PBQ) developed by Weir and Duveen (1981). Goodman suggests that the focus on strengths as well as weaknesses is likely to increase the acceptability and attractiveness of the scale to respondents and increase their motivation to complete the questionnaire.

There is a slightly modified form of the Scale for infant school pupils (aged 5–7+ years), and Behar and Stringfield (1974) in the USA have produced a modification of the original questionnaire for 3- to 6-year-olds, which provides information on Anxious-Fearful children in addition to those who are Hostile-Aggressive and Hyperactive-Distractible (see also Behar, 1977).

In the USA, two questionnaires for teachers which are considered to have reasonably good validity and reliability (see Ollendick, 1995) are the Child Behaviour Checklist (Achenbach and Edelbrock, 1983) and the Revised Behaviour Problem Checklist (Quay and Peterson, 1987).

Child Behaviour Checklist (Teachers' Report Form) (CBCL, TRF)
(Achenbach and Edelbrock, 1986; Achenbach, 1991)

This checklist, for use by teachers of pupils aged 6–16, contains 118 specific problems, scored 0 as 'not true' of the child, 1 as 'somewhat or sometimes true' or 2 as 'very true or often true', on the basis of observations over two months. The syndromes derived from the completed questionnaire include those designated

– 'uncommunicative': e.g. won't talk, secretive;
– 'social withdrawal' (ages 6–11): e.g. poor relations, likes to be alone;
– 'hostile withdrawal' (ages 12–16): e.g. lonely, destroys own things;
– 'depressed' (6–11 years only): e.g. feels unloved, sad, worrying;
– 'schizoid' (12–16 years only): e.g. fears own impulses, hears things.

Harris, Tyre and Wilkinson (1993), on the basis of a study carried out in Wales, have confirmed that the Child Behaviour Checklist is a reasonably valid scale for use in Britain.

Revised Behaviour Problem Checklist (RBPC) (Quay and Peterson, 1979,
1987)

The RBPC (covering childhood and adolescence) has 77 scorable items, rated 0 (not at all), 1 (mild problem) or 2 (severe problem) and 12 items not scored. Work on the checklist has produced six factors, including personality problems and inadequacy–immaturity (see Boyle and Jones, 1985; Ollendick, 1995).

Other checklists for teachers devised in the USA include the Conners Teachers Rating Scale (Conners, 1969; Taylor and Sandberg, 1984), the Comprehensive Behaviour Rating Scale for Children (Neeper and Lahey, 1988); and the Teacher–Child Rating Scale (Hightower *et al.*, 1986).

Checklists for use with parents

A number of checklists for use by teachers are accompanied by questionnaires to be completed by parents. This is useful because it enables data to be collected from the two sources in easily comparable form. There is, for example, a parent version to accompany the Rutter Child Behaviour Scale which has 31 items seeking information about health problems, habits and possible behaviour difficulties (see Rutter, Tizard and Whitmore, 1970). Parent versions are also available for the Behar and Stringfield (1974) *Preschool Behaviour Questionnaire* and the Achenbach and Edelbrock *Child Behaviour Checklist* (see Achenbach and Edelbrock, 1983; also Weisz *et al.*, 1991 and Sawyer, Baghurst and Mathias, 1992). Other schedules for parents devised in the USA include the *Screening Inventory* (Langner *et al.*, 1976), which aims to assess psychiatric impairment in 6- to 18-year-olds, and covers seven factors, including isolation; and the *Louisville Behaviour Checklist* for males aged 6–12 years, covering eight factors including social withdrawal, anxiety and immaturity (Miller, 1967).

Richman (1977) has devised a Behaviour Check List (BCL) for self-completion by parents of pre-school children. In the BCL, three statements are made about each of 21 areas of behaviour, and the parent is asked to mark which applies best to the child, e.g.,

11.   Not clinging, can easily be left with people he/she knows
       Gets upset if away from mother but gets over it
       Very clinging, can't be left with others . . .
19.   Gets on well with other children
       Some difficulties playing with other children
       Finds it very difficult to play with other children

Richman, Stevenson and Graham (1982) suggest that the BCL can be regarded as a useful and inexpensive screening device for behaviour and emotional disorders, although its use would result in missing a significant number of disorders, especially those of mild severity. More effective in screening is the *Behaviour Screening Questionnaire* (BSQ), used in a semi-structured interview (see below, p. 66).

Self-reports: personality and behaviour

It is an important part of the assessment of behaviour problems to seek information from the child him or herself, as long as he or she is mature enough to respond to relevant questions. Well-structured questionnaires enable the enquirer, who should be trained in the use of such instruments, to gain insight into thoughts and feelings which are inaccessible through other sources. Even if self-reports may be liable to greater distortion than reports from parents and teachers, they can provide a basis for discussion and exploration in counselling and therapy. Here, examples will be given of personality questionnaires and self-report checklists and inventories relating to general adjustment, shyness, loneliness, fears and anxiety, and depression.

Personality

Personality questionnaires aim to give a picture of the main dimensions of personality. Much work on the construction of such questionnaires has been carried out by Hans and Sybil Eysenck in Britain and by Cattell and his colleagues in the USA. The frequent changes in the format of personality inventories from these sources over the years tend to cause some confusion amongst users.

The Eysencks see the main dimensions of personality to be extraversion/introversion, neuroticism and psychoticism (Eysenck, 1970). The typical 'extravert' is friendly, sociable and easygoing; the 'introvert' is quiet, retiring, introspective and reserved. The 'neurotic' individual is anxious, worrying, moody and prone to depression. In the case of children, high scorers on 'psychoticism' are odd, isolated, insensitive, aggressive and hostile. The *Eysenck Personality Questionnaire* (Junior Version: Eysenck and Eysenck, 1975), which Kline (1993) considers to be a reliable and valid instrument, provides norms for the three dimensions of personality for children aged 7+ to 15+ years. Respondents are required to answer 'Yes' or 'No' to 81 items, such as:

– Would you rather be alone, instead of meeting other children? (Extraversion/Introversion Scale)
– Do you ever feel 'just miserable' for no good reason? (Neuroticism Scale)
– Do you enjoy hurting people you like? (Psychoticism Scale)

Cattell and his colleagues view personality in terms of sixteen primary bipolar factors, including

– reserved, detached vs outgoing, warmhearted
– humble, mild vs assertive, dominant
– shy, timid vs venturesome, uninhibited
– group dependent vs self-sufficient

The *16 Personality Factor Test* (for older adolescents and adults: Cattell, Eber and Tatsuoka, 1970) aims to present a personality profile of an individual in terms of the 16 primary factors. There are versions for children of different age groups, including the Child's Personality Questionnaire, for children aged 8–12 years (Porter and Cattell, 1968). This questionnaire contains 70 questions in a forced-choice format, e.g.,

Would you like to play with mechanical toys ☐ or ☐ with friends?

Does almost everyone like you ☐ or ☐ only some people?

The Cattell inventories have been widely used, though some doubts have been raised about their reliability and validity (Swanson and Watson, 1982; Kline, 1993).

Personality questionnaires are mainly useful in research, although they have a limited role to play in clinical practice, in screening, diagnosis and as a possible starting-point for discussions between client and therapist.

General adjustment

Achenbach and Edelbrock (1987) have compiled a *Youth Self Report* (YSR) to complement the Child Behaviour Checklists for teachers and parents described above (pp. 53–4). The YSR has, for example, been used in a study by Sawyer, Baghurst and Mathias (1992), comparing reports of childhood emotional and behavioural disorders obtained from different sources in the case of children aged 10–16 years.

The *Mooney Problem Check Lists* (Mooney and Gordon, 1950) are very simple to complete and yet cover much ground. There are forms for different age-ranges at the secondary-school stage and beyond, consisting of a long list of problems to be underlined if applicable to the subject. Any problem causing particular concern to the respondent is circled and there are also some open-ended questions. The Mooney checklists are not meant to be tests of personality or adjustment, but merely provide a preliminary basis for understanding a pupil's problems and for counselling.

The *Rogers Personal Adjustment Inventory* (Rogers, 1961), for children aged 9–13 years, aims to assess the extent to which a child is satisfactorily adjusted to his or her fellows, family and self, and also to provide information about the ways in which he or she meets difficulties. Four diagnostic scores are obtained from the responses: (1) personal inferiority; (2) social maladjustment; (3) family maladjustment; and (4) daydreaming (fantasy life). This inventory has been updated and anglicized by Jeffrey (1984). It is particularly useful for educational psychologists and counsellors in their work with shy or withdrawn children. Examples of the kind of items used are:

(Boys)   Suppose you could have just 3 of the wishes below, which would you want to come true? (a list of 12 wishes follows)

(Girls)   Jean is better at sports than any other girl in the class. Are you like her? Do you want to be like her? (Yes/in between/no)

(Boys)   Steven always has a wonderful time at parties. Are you like him? Do you want to be like him? (Yes/in between/no)

(Girls)   How many friends would you like to have? (None/a few good friends/many friends/hundreds of friends)

Shyness

Crozier (1995) has devised the *Children's Shyness Questionnaire*, containing 26 items to which the respondent answers 'Yes', 'No' or 'Don't know', e.g.

- I find it hard to talk to someone I don't know.
- I feel shy when I have to read aloud in class.
- I am usually shy in a group of people.

Items for this questionnaire were based on concepts of shyness elicited from primary school children. Crozier has used it with children aged 8–12 years and found it to have satisfactory internal consistency, although as a new scale it needs to be used more widely to establish its reliability and validity. Significantly, shyness measured by this questionnaire was negatively correlated with global self-esteem measured by the *Coopersmith Self-Esteem Inventory* (Coopersmith, 1967); external locus of control (the tendency to attribute events to external causes such as luck or powerful others) assessed by the Nowicki and Strickland (1973) *Locus of Control Scale*; and perceived competence on the basis of the Harter (1985) *Self-Perception Profile for Children*, which assesses Global Self-Worth and perceived competence in five domains: scholastic, social acceptance, athletic, physical appearance and behavioural conduct.

Lawrence and Bennett (1992) used self-report measures based on Pilkonis (1977), Zimbardo (1977) and Cheek and Buss (1979) in a study of the relationship between shyness, social class and personality variables in adolescents. As mentioned in Chapter 3 (pp. 34–5), Elkind and Bowen (1979) compiled the *Imaginary Audience Scale* (IAS), which consists of two subscales, the Transient Self (TS) and Abiding Self (AS) subscales. The Abiding Self Scale (with six items) assesses long-lived characteristics such as mental ability and personality traits, e.g.,

'If you were asked to get up in front of the class and talk a little bit about your hobby . . .'
- I wouldn't be nervous at all
- I would be a little nervous
- I would be very nervous.

The Transient Self Scale (also with 6 items) covers momentary appearances and behaviours, such as a bad haircut or inadvertent words or acts, not regarded by the individual as indicating his or her true self.

Loneliness

The *Loneliness Scale* devised by Asher, Hymel and Renshaw (1984) contains 16 items about children's feelings of loneliness in relation to peers and 8 filler items about hobbies and interests. Responses to each item are given on a three-point scale (yes, sometimes, or no). The scale seems to have a satisfactory internal consistency and to correlate well with peers' reports of sociometric status (see Stocker, 1994). It is suitable for children aged 9+ to 12+ years. Examples of the items are:

- I have nobody to talk to
- It's hard for me to make friends
- It's hard to get other kids to like me.

Research on loneliness is discussed by Perlman and Peplau (1981), Peplau and Perlman (1982) and Marcoen and Goosens (1993); see also Chapter 3, pp. 38–9.

Fears and anxiety

Ollendick (1995) provides a wide-ranging review of approaches and techniques used in the assessment of anxiety and phobic disorders in children. As he states, a variety of self-report instruments are available, mainly lists of fear-evoking and anxiety-arousing stimuli and situations.

An example of a self-report instrument in common use is the *Fear Survey Schedule for Children* (FSSC-R: Ollendick, 1983). This is suitable for children and adolescents between 7 and 18 years of age and requires respondents to rate their fear of 80 items on a three-point scale by answering 'none', 'some' or 'a lot'. Satisfactory reliability and validity are claimed for this schedule. Examples of the items used in the schedule are:

- getting lost in a strange place
- having to go to school
- not being able to breathe.

The FSSC-R provides information about five factors – fear of failure and criticism, fear of the unknown, fear of injury and small animals, fear of danger and death, and medical fear.

The Revised Children's Manifest Anxiety Scale (RCMAS) (Reynolds and Richmond, 1978, 1983) – the 'What I Think and Feel Test' – is a revision of Taylor's (1951) *Children's Manifest Anxiety Scale*. The RCMAS has been used frequently to obtain information about what children feel in anxiety-provoking situations. It is intended for children between 6 and 18 years, and has 37 anxiety and 11 lie items. The scale yields three anxiety factors: Worry/Over-sensitivity, Concentration, and Physiological. Examples of the items used (to which the child has to respond 'true' or 'false') are:

- I worry a lot of the time
- My hands feel sweaty
- It is hard for me to keep my mind on my school work.

Depression

Kazdin (1990) has reviewed the great variety of self-report measures available for the assessment of childhood and adolescent depression. As he states, self-reporting has been much used, as key symptoms such as sadness, feelings of worthlessness and loss of interest in activities reflect subjective feelings and self-perceptions. Examples of self-report measures are the *Children's Depression Inventory* (CDI: Kovacs, 1985) and the *Children's Depression Scale* (Lang and Tisher, 1978, 1983).

The Kovacs Children's Depression Inventory contains 27 items about children's feelings and behaviours. Children choose from three responses to each question indicating the frequency and severity of depressive feelings and behaviours during the previous two weeks. Scores on all items are summed to give a total depressive mood score. The scale can be used with children in the age range 7–17 years. An example of an item in the scale is:

    a) I am sad once in a while (score 0)
    b) I am sad many times (1)
    c) I am sad all the time (2).

The Kovacs Inventory is widely used and has been well researched; it seems to have high internal consistency and moderate test–test reliability (Knight, Hensley and Waters, 1988; Kazdin, 1990; Stocker, 1994).

The *Lang and Tisher Children's Depression Scale* has 66 items, each on a card (48 depressive, 18 positive items). The cards are sorted in boxes reflecting a one-to-five point scale. The scale is suitable for the age range 9–16 years, and seems to be reasonably valid and consistent internally (Knight, Hensley and Waters, 1988). It provides a total depression score, a total pleasure score and scores for each of the six subscales (affective responses, social problems, self-esteem, preoccupation with sickness and death, guilt, and pleasure).

PEER-REFERENCED ASSESSMENT

Peer-referenced assessment is a rich source of information about an individual's status and behaviour in groups, especially as the views of a relatively large number of peers are sought. Such assessment has to be interpreted sensitively and cautiously, as the stability of assessments by peers is difficult to establish. Group status and behaviour may be affected by changes in circumstances such as alterations in the composition of a group, as well as by developmental changes. Frederickson (1991) has emphasized the need to take account of interactions between children in different situations. Further, different methods may tap different aspects of peer relations (Asher and Hymel, 1981); and the specific strategy adopted for judging status within a group will have a bearing on the outcome, as Musun-Miller (1990) has shown. Nevertheless, a moderate degree of stability has been found in the categorization of children as popular, average, neglected, rejected or controversial by their peers (Coie, Dodge and Coppotelli, 1982; Coie and Dodge, 1983). Peer-referenced assessment has certainly added to our understanding of children who do not fit easily into a group and it can contribute much to the selection of individuals for appropriate intervention (Hartup, 1989; Ollendick *et al.*, 1991; Malik and Furman, 1993).

In considering peer-referenced assessment, a distinction has been made between sociometric assessment and peer assessment of behaviour, although there is much overlap between them (Asher and Hymel, 1981; Gresham and Little, 1993). Sociometric techniques measure the degree to which children are liked or disliked by peers, whereas peer assessment is used to obtain ratings of behaviour in a group.

Sociometric techniques

Williams and Gilmour (1994) have reviewed the range of sociometric techniques in use. The most common method employed to establish sociometric status in a school class or other group is peer nomination. Typically, children are asked to name three members of the group with whom they would most like to undertake certain activities (e.g. play with or sit next to) and three with whom they would most dislike to associate. In the case of younger children, photographs of members of the group may be used to facilitate responses (McCandless and Marshall, 1957), as well as pictures representing the concepts of like and dislike (Frederickson, 1991). Scores derived from peer nominations may be used, usually after standardization, to form sociometric status categories (Newcomb, Bukowski and Pattee, 1993), and a sociogram depicting the structure of the group may be drawn, using arrows to indicate the directions of choices between group members on a particular criterion.

A method used less often than peer nominations is that of obtaining ratings of each other member of a classroom or other group from each child. This is usually done with the aid of a Lickert-type five-point or seven-point scale, enabling the respondent to rate his or her peers on choices ranging from 'most liked' to 'least liked' (see Asher and Dodge, 1986; Ollendick *et al.*, 1991).

Williams and Gilmour (1994) point out that this approach has several advantages: it is less pejorative, avoids forcing children to nominate disliked children directly, provides information on how children feel about all their mates, and avoids children nominating only their best friends. However, it is time-consuming and may not be as effective as the nomination method in identifying children neglected by their peers. As mentioned in Chapter 3, Dygdon and Conger (1990) found that direct nominations in a private interview to the categories of 'Like', 'Dislike' and 'Neglect' were particularly successful.

Many practitioners and researchers are unhappy with the use of negative nominations, that is, asking children to suggest whom they would *not* like to play with, and so on. These objections are put forward mainly on the grounds that participation in sociometric assessment using negative nominations could worsen the position of children already rejected or isolated. However, the use of positive nominations alone tends to produce more limited information about the sociometric structure of a group. The general practice, therefore, in recent years has been to use negative as well as positive nominations in order to obtain as complete a picture of the group as possible, but to strive to do so with care and sensitivity. On balance, this approach seems justified, provided that the understanding of neglected and rejected children is increased and, whenever possible, positive action follows from sociometric findings.

Peer assessment of behaviour

Peer assessment of behaviour is a useful adjunct to peer ratings of popularity. In their research studies, Coie, Dodge and Coppotelli (1982) asked children to nominate three of their peers who best filled each of six behavioural descriptions: co-operates, disrupts, shy, fights, seeks help and leaders, e.g.,

> *Shy*: This person acts very shy with other kids, seems always to play or work by themselves. It's hard to get to know this person.

Lefkowitz and Tesiny used their *Peer Nomination Inventory of Depression* (PNID: Lefkowitz and Tesiny, 1985) in a survey of elementary school children in New York. Peers nominate children in response to such questions as

- Who often looks sad?
- Who often plays alone?
- Who doesn't play?
- Who thinks others don't like them?

Others have used a version of the 'class play' approach originally devised by Lambert and Bower (1961). In this approach, each child is asked to act as the director of a play and cast the members of the class into a variety of positive and negative roles, e.g.,

- someone who could play the part of a true friend
- some girl who could play the part of a mean, bossy sister.

Masten, Morison and Pellegrini (1985) designed a revised class play to improve the assessment of social competence as well as the psychiatric properties of the method. They derived three dimensions from a factorial analysis of the results: sociability-leadership; aggressive-disruptive; and sensitive-isolated. Shapiro and Sobel (1981) devised the *Shapiro Sociometric Role Assignment Test*, a variation of the class play approach. In this procedure, class members produce descriptions of classmates, sort them into positive, neutral and negative categories and then choose a classmate who fits each description (see Gresham and Little, 1993).

SYSTEMATIC OBSERVATION

Observation in school

Systematic observation of children, requiring the use of a coding system or observation schedule, needs time and resources. As mentioned earlier in this chapter (p. 51), teachers tend to find that they have little opportunity to carry out planned observation of an individual child or small group, although with the aid of a psychologist, systematic naturalistic observation may prove practicable (see below, pp. 63–4). The use of schedules such as the *Bristol Social Adjustment Guide* or the *Rutter Child Behaviour Scale* may help to structure the daily observations of teachers in the course of their normal work.

It is helpful for the teacher to note exactly how a child about whom there is concern behaves in specific circumstances in a variety of contexts. Attempting to answer precise questions is useful. For example, a teacher might want to know, in the case of a timid, inhibited child:

- In what particular circumstances is the child especially timid, shy or withdrawn?
- What does the child do in the face of stress? (e.g. covering face, sucking thumb, refusing to answer)
- When does the child behave normally and positively?
- With which children (if any) does the child play co-operatively (in class, in the playground)?

Teachers may find that detailed recording of 'initial' or significant incidents is helpful in monitoring a child's behaviour over a period of time, e.g. when a child bursts into tears, suddenly withdraws from group activities, or makes no attempt to pursue a task (Laing and Chazan, 1987). Discussions about observation in school may be found in Wragg, 1994 and Fawcett, 1996.

Observation in clinical practice and research

Direct observation of children has been used widely in clinical practice and research. Clinicians may set up their own systems to observe children before, during and after treatment, or employ an existing behavioural observation system (Ollendick, 1995); and researchers have contributed much to the compiling of coding systems or schedules to be used in systematic observation. A child may be observed in naturalistic situations or in specially designed and controlled conditions. Examples of these two approaches will be given here.

Naturalistic observation

Scarlett (1980) observed children aged 42–49 months during nursery school free play sessions as well as in specially arranged small group sessions. The main aims of Scarlett's study were to describe how isolates as compared to non-isolates behave during nursery school free play sessions, how they are treated by peers and teachers, and how isolates and non-isolates react to changes in group size and structure. Categories used for describing the children's behaviour were based mainly on these constructed by Parten (1932), and a second judge helped the author of the study to test the reliability of these categories. The results of the project provided useful information about social isolation in nursery school children. However, Scarlett emphasizes that information derived from direct observation needs to be supplemented by data on how isolates and non-isolates view their peers as well as by information on the home background of children who are isolated in the peer group.

Dodge, Coie and Brakke (1982) used naturalistic observation to obtain information on the actual behaviour of popular, average, rejected and neglected 8- to 9- and 10- to 11-year-olds selected by sociometric peer nominations. They observed these children in their usual classrooms as well as in the playground.

Systematic observation of behaviour in natural situations is particularly important if behaviour modification strategies are to be employed. This enables precise targets for desired changes to be set up and progress over time to be charted. Chazan *et al.* (1983) give an example of the use of systematic observation in school, involving a teacher working with an educational psychologist.

> *Jane* was a withdrawn, dependent child aged 4 years. Observation showed that Jane avoided contact and play with other children in a variety of settings; she was difficult to make contact with; shrank from strangers even before any approach was made;

and withdrew from any physical contact. She was reluctant to take an adult's hand, be lifted or helped physically. The class teacher began a Behaviour Modification programme with a time-sample recording of observation periods of thirty minutes each day for six days. Then an intervention programme began, with Jane being rewarded whenever she remained at an activity when another child approached, and later when she began to join in activities spontaneously. Further time-sample recording four months later showed considerable improvement in Jane's social behaviour.

Observation in experimental situations

Rubin and Mills (1988) demonstrate how observation in specially arranged situations can be used as a part of the study of different forms of social isolation in children. They observed 7-year-old children in free play sessions, each child being invited to play with three children of the same sex and age for four 15-minute sessions in a laboratory playroom. The children's playmates differed in each session (i.e. twelve different playmates were involved). The children were observed from behind one-way mirrors, following prepared observation procedures, and solitary, parallel and group activities were noted. Each individual was scored for social behaviour, solitary-passive activity, and solitary-active play.

Dodge (1983) drew attention to the differences between studying children with established sociometric status (e.g. in a school class) and studying them in settings where the children do not know each other at the start. In a study of the behavioural antecedents of peer social status, he brought together 48 previously unacquainted 7- to 8-year-olds in six playgroups of eight boys each. The groups met under supervision for one hour at a time for eight sessions. Observations were recorded using a complex event-recording system and the sessions were also videotaped. At the end of the final session, each subject was interviewed sociometrically and status groups of popular, rejected, neglected, controversial and average boys were identified.

As part of a study of fears and worries in a sample of children aged 4.5–7 years, Stevenson-Hinde and Shouldice (1995) arranged an experimental situation to assess approach/withdrawal behaviour. The mother and child were taken to a room with chairs, a small table and toys. Various events were planned over about an hour, including mother and child being alone for a few minutes and the introduction of a stranger. The child's initial responses to unfamiliar people, places or things were rated by the mother, and the experimenters' direct observations were recorded on a nine-point scale, ranging from 1 (relaxed/responsive) to 4 (normal for age) to 9 (high tension/no verbal response). The value of direct observation is indicated by the finding that, in this study, no relationship was found between observed approach/withdrawal behaviour and fears and worries reported by either mothers or children.

INTERVIEWING

Ollendick (1995) emphasizes that the behavioural interview is an important first step in the assessment process. The purposes of the interview are threefold: (1) to establish rapport with child and family; (2) to obtain information as to the nature of the behaviour over which there is concern; and (3) to determine the broader socio-cultural context in which the behaviour occurs. Interviewing may take place at school, in the clinic for diagnostic purposes, or as part of research projects. Discussions of interviewing techniques and instruments can be found in Breakwell (1990) and Hodges and Zeman (1993).

Interviewing at school

Headteachers and teachers usually interview the parents of any child about whom they are concerned at an early stage, and professionals in the support services rely greatly on information provided by schools as a starting point for conducting their own interviews with parents. School staff normally interview parents in an informal way, but it is useful for them to have a clear idea of what kinds of information they are seeking, though they need to be sensitive to the possible reluctance of parents to disclose details of family life, particularly in an initial interview. The information sought from parents might include basic details of family background and relationships; the health, behaviour and social competence of the child; peer relationships and out-of-school activities; and the child's attitude to school and scholastic work (for relevant schedule and record forms see Chazan *et al.*, 1983; Blagg, 1987).

Interviewing for diagnostic and research purposes

Interviews for diagnostic or research purposes may be carried out in a highly structured or semi-structured format. Highly structured interviews are particularly suitable in research, as they enable direct comparisons to be made, for example between different respondents such as parents and child; they can be used by trained lay interviewers; and they maximize reliability (Herjanic and Reich, 1982). Semi-structured interviews tend to be more flexible, allow for freer communication between interviewer and respondent, and be more interesting for the interviewee. Examples of the two approaches will be given here (for a further discussion of structured interviews, see Hodges, 1993).

Highly structured interviews

Highly structured interview schedules tend to include a large number of standardized questions to which a simple answer is required (for example, 'Yes', 'Somewhat' or 'Sometimes', or 'No'). The *Diagnostic Interview*

Schedule for Children (DISC: Costello *et al.*, 1984) was used by Edelbrock *et al.* (1986) to study parent–child agreement on child psychiatric symptoms. The DISC has parallel formats for children (aged 6–18 years) and parents, employs direct questioning and provides specific codes for recording responses (see Shaffer, 1994 and Hodges, 1993; 1994 for a discussion of the DISC).

Herjanic and Reich (1982) also studied parent–child agreement using their *Diagnostic Interview for Children and Adolescents*, which has versions for children aged 7–17 years as well as parents and can be used to diagnose common psychiatric disorders. This schedule was used by Burbach, Kashani and Rosenberg (1989) in a study of depressive disorders in adolescents. Herjanic and Reich stress that the highest agreement between parents and children is obtained on questions about symptoms which are concrete, observable, severe and unambiguous.

Semi-structured interviews

Semi-structured interview schedules also provide standard questions, but these are less rigid than in highly structured schedules and can be added to if necessary. Richman, Stevenson and Graham (1982) used a semi-structured interview – the *Behaviour Screening Questionnaire* (BSQ) – with parents of children aged 3 and 4 years. During the interview, the parent is asked for actual concrete descriptions of behaviour rather than for his or her attitude or opinions about the behaviour of the child. When the interviewer has obtained sufficient information to make a rating, the item is coded according to pre-established criteria. Twelve types of behaviour are covered, including relationships with other children, mood, worries and fears, by questions such as (in the case of relationships):

- How has X got on with brothers/sisters in the past 4 weeks? Do they squabble much? How much is playing together affected? What about other children?

The responses to the questions in this section are coded:

– Trivial or no difficulties	0	
– Some difficulties, play disrupted or prevented most times but only for short periods	1	a) Siblings ☐
– Marked difficulties: play disrupted or prevented most of the time	2	b) Peers ☐
– No siblings/no opportunity to play with others	3	

Rutter and Graham (1968) developed semi-structured interview procedures for 10- and 11-year-old children and their parents (see also Graham and Rutter,

1968). Other semi-structured interview schedules include the *Kovacs Interview Schedule for Children* (Kovacs, 1978) and the *Hodges Child Assessment Schedule* (Hodges *et al.*, 1982).

SELF-MONITORING

The assessment of disorders such as phobias or depression may be helped by self-monitoring. Self-monitoring requires the child to record specific behaviour and thoughts as they occur, rather than recalling those experienced at an earlier stage (Beidel, Neal and Lederer, 1991). Forms may be provided for this purpose and completed by both parent and child at the same time. Self-monitoring tests may be used following participation in, for example, a simulated or real-life situation. A list of statements is provided to help the child to record what he or she was thinking during the task (Stefanek *et al.*, 1987; Ollendick, 1995). For example, Zatz and Chassin (1983), in a study of test-anxiety, asked 11- and 12-year-old children to complete tasks such as the Coding-B sub-test of the Wechsler Intelligence Scale for Children and an anagram test. Then the children were given their *Children's Cognitive Assessment Questionnaire* (CCAQ), which contains 40 yes/no items, with four subscales covering negative evaluations (I'm doing poorly), positive evaluations (I do well on tests like this), off-task thoughts (I wish this was over), and on-task thoughts (I have a plan to solve this).

ASSESSMENT FOR SOCIAL SKILLS TRAINING

Withdrawn and isolated children are often deficient in social skills and need specific training to improve their competence in relating to others. Assessment in relation to social skills training is, therefore, of considerable relevance to meeting the needs of these children. Shepherd (1983), in an account of such assessment, explains that the adult concerned may begin by discussing with the client the kinds of social situations with which he or she has difficulties, e.g. meeting new people. Clients may have to complete various questionnaires covering their social anxieties and the range and frequency of their social contacts.

Spence (1980) has devised the *Social Behaviour at School Questionnaire*, to be completed by teachers, which aims to measure a child's interpersonal skills. Nabuzoka and Smith (1993) used this questionnaire in a study of sociometric status and social behaviour in children with learning difficulties. In addition to questionnaires, Frosh (1983) advocates the use of sociometry, observations of behaviour, role-play and problem-solving tasks in the assessment of social competence. Frosh has designed an observational system applicable in infant schools, in which the observer records various aspects of the child's social behaviour, including constructive solitary activity and 'zonking out' (dreaming, staring aimlessly, or passively watching others) (see Frosh and Callias, 1980). Cognitive tasks may be based on the work carried out in the USA by Spivack and Shure, 1974 (see also Spivack, Platt and Shure, 1976).

GENERAL ASSESSMENT

In the case of any child with social, emotional or behavioural difficulties, it is important that assessment should lead to a profile which highlights strengths as well as weaknesses in various facets of school and out-of-school life. The DFE (1994b) *Code of Practice on the Identification and Assessment of Special Educational Needs* stresses that the school should provide information on a child being assessed derived from class records, National Curriculum attainments and standardized test results, in addition to observations about the child's behaviour. Parents, the child him or herself, and others involved should be encouraged to be positive in their reports, wherever this is appropriate.

Scherer's (1988) *School Skills Checklist* (see Scherer, Gersch and Fry, 1990) can make a contribution to providing a comprehensive view of a child. This checklist has a positive format, and includes peer interaction skills in class, social interaction in and out of class, and the expression of feelings, as well as sections on several aspects of the child's approach to classwork. Scherer suggests how the schedule can be used to formulate goals for action to meet the pupil's needs.

CONCLUSION

This chapter has discussed the wide range of instruments and techniques that are available for the assessment of children and adolescents who are socially withdrawn or isolated. It advocates that information should be sought from a variety of sources, including school, parents and professionals in the support services. If the child is mature enough, it is essential to obtain his or her views and gain insight with sensitivity into his or her feelings. Examples of approaches to assessment adopted in school, clinic and research are given, including checklists and schedules, peer-referenced assessment, systematic observation and interviewing. It is stressed that it is important to focus on the positive as well as the negative aspects of the child's development, behaviour and school progress. The purpose of assessment should always be borne in mind, namely that it should lead to a better understanding of the child's needs and how to meet these needs.

Chapter 5

Causes of Withdrawal and Isolation

At the heart of withdrawal often lies an inability on the part of an individual to relate to others. It might be considered that this inability is always present but it must be remembered that there are individuals who are quite capable of joining in adequately but prefer not to do so. They show withdrawn behaviour (and may, indeed, become isolated) but they could, if they wished, be more sociable. These individuals will not be considered in the present chapter, although they may have some of the characteristics or experiences of those whose withdrawal, to whatever degree, reveals a lack of ability in establishing the kind of social interactions they desire.

The causes of withdrawal and isolation in any one person are difficult to disentangle. What might be thought of as an individual's 'map of experience' (Burnham and Harris, 1996) has evolved over the years from specific events which have been interpreted in the light of previous experience and in the context in which they occur at that particular time. Thus, similar experiences will be interpreted very differently by different people and even by the same person depending on where they happen, who is present and when they take place. The social demands inherent in any potential interaction are therefore complex, and attempts to separate out various elements in reactions to situations suffer from the disadvantage that the 'parts' seldom tell the 'whole' story.

Daisy (see Chapter 3, p. 35) is only 6 years old but her behaviour is already difficult to understand. Her teachers and her mother see her as a different person. In school, she is meek and biddable, communicating largely through body language (standing on the fringe of the group and looking longingly at the main organizers). At home, she is self-willed and emotionally volatile, determined to have her own way. Both behaviour patterns do show a degree of immaturity but to say that her social development is slow only begs the question as to why this should be. Why has she not learned the social skills which would enable her to interact with peers and adults in a way appropriate to her age group? Has something happened in her earlier history so that her 'map of experience' offers her little help in establishing satisfying (to her) relationships? Had she been born into a different family or gone to a different school would she still behave in the same way? These questions (and there are others which could be posed) demonstrate that the causes of withdrawal and isolation are far from simple.

This chapter will look at the personal characteristics and environmental factors which have been associated with withdrawn behaviour. It should always be borne in mind, however, that individuals vary widely in the ways in which they react to situations (Hetherington, Reiss and Plomin, 1994). While a certain set of circumstances may lead some to withdraw from social interaction, others may be unaffected by similar circumstances or may turn to aggressive, 'acting out' behaviour or even vary between aggression and withdrawal.

PERSONALITY CHARACTERISTICS

Temperamental differences

Differences in individual social development have already been discussed in Chapter 2 and the variety of ways in which children and adolescents may display withdrawn or isolated behaviour are considered in Chapter 3. Interactions between children and their main carer lead to characteristics being developed in young children which are likely to become typical reactions to new social demands. While children do change their behaviour according to circumstances and as they grow and develop, there often remains a degree of consistency in their reactions which carers, and the children themselves, come to expect. Research on young children showing behavioural difficulties, for example, has found a tendency for those considered to have problems at three years of age to be still causing concern five years later (Richman, Stevenson and Graham, 1982). Are some children, then, born to become socially maladroit?

Cattell (1946; 1965) and Eysenck (1970) have both presented evidence of temperamental characteristics which they believe shape the individual's behaviour through life. In Eysenck's classification (see Chapter 4), a bias towards introversion would lead to quiet, retiring, controlled behaviour where impulse is distrusted and self-sufficiency preferred to social support (Eysenck and Eysenck, 1963). Another major personality dimension suggested by Eysenck's work is that of neuroticism or emotional instability, seen as characterized by 'depression, nervousness, hypersensitivity, inferiority feelings, overcriticalness, quarrelsomeness, introspectiveness and social shyness' (Warburton, 1969). It is, of course, really impossible to say how much of this behaviour is genetic in origin and how much the result of environmental interaction. Mothers will argue that their children have different temperaments from birth, but it is also the case that they probably react to the new-born according to these perceived differences, so that one child may be cuddled more than another or handled in a more relaxed fashion. Visitors also will say of new-born twins, 'This is the smiling one', or 'This is the one who is always yelling her head off', and expectations specific to individual children are formed. Thus the development of personality characteristics is essentially a two-way process. Past and present environmental demands and expectations are also highly involved in any behavioural outcome, whatever the child's temperament.

Anxiety

Wolff (1981) has emphasized that children who score highly on measures of neuroticism, as those who are withdrawn and isolated may well do, tend also to be highly anxious. She sees anxiety as having different sources at different ages. Thus, in very young children it springs first from a fear that immediate physical needs will not be met, and then that the main carer will disappear. By two years of age, anxiety is more likely to be aroused by feelings of inadequacy or inability to meet expected standards, which will bring about disapproval from others. Yet older children exhibit anxiety over possible threats to their self-esteem or demands on their developing sense of right and wrong. As adolescence approaches, anxiety flares up in relation to how individual performances will be viewed by peers even more than by adults. Whatever the age, anxiety will tend to disrupt performance in the immediate and longer term.

Response to the environment

Lack of consonance between the organism and the environment (Thomas and Chess, 1977) is particularly anxiety-provoking. Thus, children who have difficulty in adapting to new demands may well be 'at risk' in their social development. These children were categorized by Thomas and Chess as 'slow-to-warm up', that is, they show mildly negative reactions to social demands, becoming more positive if given both time and opportunity to succeed. Other children were considered to be either 'easy' or 'difficult' to handle, the latter also being slow to adapt to change but showing intense negative moods which carers found very trying. Whilst it should be remembered that about a third of the sample studied did not fit into any of these groups, the temperamental characteristics described are recognizable and may help to explain the varying reactions children show to similar social opportunities, particularly with regard to anxiety and hostility.

Sarason *et al.* (1960), writing of children aged 8–11 years, pointed out that anxiety leads to 'heightened self-awareness' (p. 161) which can distort how individuals view a situation, especially any situation where evaluation of performance occurs. Highly anxious children are, therefore, at a disadvantage in tests and examinations, especially when the format, venue and even the invigilator may be unknown to them. The writers go on to suggest that reactions to evaluative test situations may reflect the children's experience of evaluation in the home, perhaps before and after school entry. Parents who repeatedly comment on their child's performance in a negative, critical way arouse in the child conflicting feelings of aggression and guilt, leaving him or her with the belief that others are in control of the situation and thus encouraging him or her to withdraw from it. Sarason *et al.* also noted that highly anxious children, in contrast to those who were low in anxiety, had experienced 'more unfavourable events, situations and relationships' at home (p. 225).

At adolescence, when anxiety over peer evaluation is strong and school pressures on young people to produce acceptable work increase, those whose self-image is poor as a result of constant derogatory remarks may find themselves in real difficulties. The case of *Susan* (see Chapter 3, pp. 43–4) is a good example of how her tendency to be overweight generated such self-consciousness that she became anorexic to a markedly debilitating extent. Individual characteristics which predispose the pupil to be less forthcoming in social relationships exacerbate feelings of low self-esteem (Brooks-Gunn and Paikoff, 1992), especially when accompanied by feelings of loneliness and depression (see Chapter 3). Maccoby (1980), however, points out that where parents are low in their demands, children's behaviour will reflect this also, resulting in high aggression, undercontrol of impulse and immaturity.

EARLY PARENTING EXPERIENCES

Maternal depression

Parents differ in their personal characteristics just as much as children and adolescents. The temperament and mood of the main carer have, therefore, a marked effect on all aspects of children's development, illustrated clearly in the effect of maternal depression on children's social expertise. Depressed mothers

(Webster-Stratton and Herbert, 1994) seem to be particularly given to making critical remarks to their children about what are seen as shortcomings in performance and also, depending on the extent of their depression, to issuing a high number of commands. The latter are often not enforced as the mothers do not have the energy to follow them up, and so the children learn non-compliance and avoidance, strategies which are not looked on with favour in school. Depressed mothers themselves are often isolated in the community, seeing contact with relatives, friends or helping agencies as unproductive and unsupportive. They withdraw into themselves and show little interest in or warmth towards their family.

Post-natal depression inhibits the mother's reactions to her newborn child's demands (Cox *et al.*, 1987). Indeed, she may be so preoccupied with her own feelings that she fails to respond to her child's needs or demands (Murray, 1992). She is 'psychologically unavailable' (Wasserman and Allen, 1985), a reaction which can be seen also in mothers' responses to the birth of a severely handicapped child (see later in this chapter). With non-handicapped infants, the effect of post-natal maternal depression on their subsequent development cannot be accurately predicted as it is only one (although an important one) of many factors which impinge on the child in the very early years, including gender, cognitive level, degree of anxiety induced, severity of the mother's condition and the quality of the support available to both mother and child. From the point of view of social development, the dangers would seem to be that the behavioural reactions seen in some infants with depressed mothers, especially sleep problems, temper tantrums or low response to stimulation, may generalize to interactions with other adults as well as to subsequent transactions with their mothers. Non-depressed adults in their turn may then alter their behaviour in relation to these infants (Field *et al.*, 1988).

Maternal depression in the child's first year of life would seem to have a greater influence on subsequent development (especially for boys) than later onset depression (Sharp *et al.*, 1995). The effect has been seen in intellectual as well as social development, although further research is needed in such a complex area (see Cummings and Davies, 1994). It is too simple to attribute to unresponsive mothers the difficulties which some children have in forming attachments. 'Irritable' children, for example, by which is meant children who do not respond as expected or who resist the establishment of an acceptable (to both parties) routine, provoke less responsive care and show insecure attachment (Crockenberg, 1981), particularly when support from others is low. Again the importance of support from others (partners, neighbours, relatives, people in the community) must be stressed. Too much emphasis may have been put on the mother–child dyad, which does not exist in isolation from other influences (Barnes, 1995).

Child-rearing practices

Much has been written about the effects of different child-rearing practices on all aspects of development (Sears, Maccoby and Levin, 1957; Baumrind, 1971; Maccoby, 1980). Grouping family styles of parenting into a few broad categories, however, does not quite match the reality of the situation. Parents change their style in different settings and at different times; children in the same family are treated differently; adults involved in bringing the children up may not agree over how authoritarian or democratic they would like to be; and children themselves make a significant contribution to the parenting process (White and Woollett, 1992). Where the parenting style tends towards the autocratic, it has been suggested that children may well become fearful and timid, unhappy in their relationships with others and uncertain as to how better relationships could be established. Lack of maternal warmth and marital discord in the home may, however, play a more important part in children's social development than the style of parenting which seems to be preferred.

Family adversity

Children whose main carers are somewhat lacking in warmth towards them (reserved and usually cool rather than hostile or rejecting), may show withdrawn behaviour, that is, a generally sad mood and inadequate strategies for approaching others and, perhaps because of these, have few friends (Maccoby, 1980). Maternal depression exacerbates this situation, as do problems in marital relationships (Puckering *et al.*, 1995). Parental discord often leads to the children being viewed more negatively by at least one of the parents or used as a pawn in the adults' bickering. There may be less time available for the child, so that the parenting style becomes more authoritarian, while incidents of aggressive behaviour may increase in the adults and a 'spiralling negative cycle' of depression and moodiness leads to the disruption of the family home (Webster-Stratton and Herbert, 1994).

Most families have within them potentialities for violence (Bolton and Bolton, 1987) which show in the various discords which inevitably arise. What is important is how the discord, and any consequences which may arise (for example, reconciliation, separation or divorce), are handled by those involved and those who come to know about what is happening. Also important are the number and combination of adverse life-events which stress the family as a whole or particular members of it (Johnson, 1986; White and Woollett, 1992). Finally, the breakdown of one family with its approach to child-rearing may lead to the creation of another family, where the balance of power and the intra-familial relationships may have changed. 'Despite the wide-spread belief that remarriage will provide a solution . . . the reality is much more complicated' (Burgoyne, Ormrod and Richards, 1987, p. 105).

The case of **Peter** provides a link between this section and the next one. Peter, who is nearly ten years of age, has a brother a year older than himself, Mark. They also have a young half-sister, Elizabeth, the child of their mother's second marriage. Up to the age of seven, Peter was a cheerful, co-operative boy with a wide circle of friends. His older brother, however, was abused by his natural father and developed acute behaviour problems; he took to stealing and vandalism and showed considerable aggression towards adults and other children. The marriage broke up and Peter's mother remarried. This proved to be a disaster for Peter and, indeed, his mother. Both were abused by Peter's stepfather and for a time his mother took both boys and left home. Elizabeth remained with her father and Social Services were involved. Subsequently, the second family reunited with help from Social Services.

Peter's behaviour in school completely changed after these marital upheavals. He now avoids any close contact with adults and pupils alike. He is reluctant to make eye-to-eye contact and rarely smiles. His work in school has not suffered as Mark's did when his relationship with his natural father broke down. Staff are concerned about Peter but are uncertain what to do. Social Services assure the school that all is going reasonably well at home and that Peter will be removed from their 'At Risk' register. But Peter remains a changed child with no real friends and a lack of meaningful contact with peers or staff.

NEGLECT AND ABUSE

Neglect

Where parents are hostile towards their children or reject them, children may react by showing aggression and defiance or become passive and withdrawn (see Chapter 3). Children who are neglected, however, may come to see themselves as not worthy of attention or affection; they may make few demands on peers or adults and the lack of care of their person adds to the likelihood that others will overlook them, if not actively avoid them.

Wayne is of average height and weight for his fourteen years but presents a very neglected appearance. Lengthy periods of time pass before his clothes are changed and his hair, face and hands seem to be seldom washed. He has two older members of the family in the same school but they pay as little attention to him as he does to them. He shows indifference towards social relationships whether with family, peers or teaching staff. He is of average ability but uninterested in school work and so has been placed in classes with pupils of less ability than himself. He lacks any motivation to succeed, causing his teachers considerable frustration. He dislikes group work and will refuse to sit near certain pupils. He 'hangs around' in the playground at break times and at the bus shelter after school, always on the fringe of what is going on. Not even girls interest him. Despite their best efforts, the staff have failed to persuade his parents to come to the school on either informal or formal occasions. No-one in his immediate circle shows much interest in Wayne, including Wayne himself, and staff seem powerless to bring about any change.

Abuse

Abuse, on the other hand, may not be as visible as neglect. A distinction is usually made between physical, sexual and emotional abuse (White and Woollett, 1992). While physical abuse may be noticed by teachers, especially in young children, sexual or emotional abuse may never be suspected without a change in behaviour caused by the attendant stress (Lindsay and Peake, 1989). Where there is abuse in the family, the members may turn in on themselves, banding together to keep what is happening secret (Smith, 1992). Those who are abused may not talk about it to anyone, may develop a 'frozen watchfulness' (White and Woollett, 1992) and may even deny strenuously that the abuse is taking place at all. Sexual abuse by fathers is particularly likely to promote emotional distress in the abused. Disclosure of what is happening is very costly as the abused child feels shame and guilt and, in addition, may be held responsible by the other members for any consequent disruption of the family (Holly, 1989). 'Prosecuting abusers and putting children into care may stop the abuse and punish abusers but may in themselves create yet more problems for children' (White and Woollett, 1992, p. 134).

Where the abuse, whatever its nature, is severe, the helplessness and repressed anger which the children feel affects their self-esteem and often leads them into depression (Stern *et al.*, 1995). Both these negative results may prove long-lasting, affecting the victims' ability to establish a satisfying range of interpersonal relationships in adulthood (Harrington and Wood, 1995). Moreover, 'psychiatric disorders aggregate in families' (Kelvin, Goodyer and Altham, 1996) so that, while one member may be the focus of concern at a particular time, other members may well also be involved either then or later, unless they are particularly resilient (Goodyer *et al.*, 1993). Adults in the family also need resilience in order to maintain their balance and feeling of being in control, for without these they may find themselves unable to maintain the family as an entity.

TRAUMATIC EXPERIENCES

Those who suffer traumatic experiences are likely to react, for varying lengths of time, with a paralysing withdrawal from what has happened. They may continue to function in the environment but are isolated from it. The overwhelming stress associated with crises can be felt by children as much as by adults and children too can suffer from post-traumatic stress. The disasters which befall them because of their race or where they live may not only bring them near to death but can also cause deep and lasting despair. Indeed, children are especially vulnerable because they have no more control over war, for example, than they have over natural disasters. Even to survive may be considered negative, not positive, especially if little support is given. Counselling, for example, may be withheld because it is considered unsuitable for children, a belief which is becoming increasingly discredited.

Johnson (1986) separates traumatic events in childhood from those in adolescence. The former he groups into three categories: victimization, loss, and family pathology. At adolescence, secondary traumas may develop from these primary ones, such as drug-taking or substance abuse (Schinke, Botvin and Orlandi, 1991) or attempted suicide, which complicate the situation for both the victim and those who might try to help (Fergusson and Lynskey, 1996). While reaction to Johnson's three categories differs according to the nature of the trauma, those traumatized show certain similarities in how they try to cope.

Victimization

This would include assault, rape and serious accident, experiences of high intensity but usually fairly brief duration, although with prolonged after-effects. The initial impact is followed by a stage of trying to come to terms with what has happened. The victim may try to forget – may even be urged to forget – but finds the event returning again and again, dominating his or her life to the exclusion of everything else. Finally, some sort of resolution of the situation is achieved, not always a satisfactory one.

Loss

The death of a close and loved member of the family must be the greatest loss for any individual but other losses may also be traumatic, say of a friend or even a pet. Illness, separation or the disappearance of a near relative are also likely to cause trauma, especially if sudden and/or prolonged. Children have a concept of death from an early age (Kane, 1979), although their understanding may be neither wide nor deep and will seldom include the possibility of their own death or of one of their contemporaries (Lansdown, 1992). Adults, however, feel that children must be protected from the trauma of death, although this view is of fairly recent origin and not universally held. They avoid discussion or even an open show of emotion, turning their grief in on themselves and perhaps not realizing fully the extent of the children's feelings of loss. Again with the best of intentions, children may be excluded from occasions of mourning and funerals (Kitzinger and Kitzinger, 1989). As a result, children may misunderstand what has happened or misinterpret the adults' behaviour, adding to their bewilderment and anxiety.

Family pathology

Abnormal family patterns include not only disrupted or discordant families (see earlier in this chapter) but also those which are anti-social or unable to cope. Living in such families is highly stressful because adults are inconsistent in their behaviour, often unable to accept responsibility for their children and at times putting demands on them which they have not the maturity to meet. Living in single-parent families may also generate stress as disequilibrium and disorganization have to be worked through following divorce or separation. Boys seem to be affected even more than girls by family break-up. White and Woollett (1992) note that even after two years boys are 'more socially isolated, less co-operative and more obviously unhappy' (p. 106). As has been said before, past experiences play an important part in whether or not any event will be traumatic for those involved in it (Wolff, 1981) and the quality of support offered (see Chapters 7 and 8) may enable the experience to be coped with effectively.

The point has already been made that the other members of the family are also under stress when traumatic events occur. Adults are themselves struggling to cope. Their own feelings may be such that they do not realize how badly the children have been affected (Wallbank, 1992). Stress can overwhelm adults' coping resources, a situation which is affecting teachers more and more often (Dunham, 1992). Children who find themselves under stress at home and attend schools where the stress level in staff is high may need far more help than is available to them.

DISABILITY

While any disability in itself may make it difficult for the disabled individual to join in freely with others, the main barriers which prevent his or her developing positive social relationships are frequently prejudice and discrimination on the part of society. Too often those with a disability, whether physical or mental, are faced with 'exclusion, denial of access and unthinking others' (Beazley and Moore, 1995, p. 100). Where the disability, however severe, is not immediately obvious (as in deafness, for example), the chances of being left out of things increase because others may not make allowances for what seem to them to be strange reactions.

Children themselves, talking about their own physical disabilities and how they had affected their social development, made a number of interesting points (Madge and Fassam, 1982).

- They almost expected to be teased, especially at the secondary stage and especially if they had cerebral palsy.
- They had to put up with considerable name-calling (e.g. peg leg; spastic; shrimp; cloth ears), especially when new to a school.
- While they felt they mixed quite well at school with the other pupils (once the others got to know them), they did not often form real friendships and so seldom met with their classmates out of school unless the activities were specially organized.

The picture which emerges is one of a tendency towards enforced isolation, but whether or not this will have a marked effect on the physically disabled individual's self-esteem or social development depends on many factors, including intelligence, familial support, personality, age and comorbidity (i.e. the number of other disabilities present in addition to the primary one).

The mediating factors listed above have their effect also on those whose physical disability is clearly obvious. Their appearance or their bizarre movements may be disturbing to their peers at first and any inability to join in group games in the playground does not help to promote friendships. Social integration, in the sense of the disabled pupil being accepted as having a contribution to make to any on-going activity, is not easily achieved, although it has been advanced as one of the benefits arising from the integration of pupils with special needs in mainstream education (Hegarty, Pocklington and Lucas, 1981; Booth and Swann, 1987; Dean, 1989).

Boulton (1995) points out that boys who are seldom, if ever, chosen to take part in playground activities have few allies to come to their aid if they are bullied. Disabled children, therefore, may be 'at risk' of becoming easy victims, particularly if their social skills are insufficiently developed. Pupils with learning difficulties, if these are moderate or severe, are similarly vulnerable. Martlew and Hodson (1991), in their study of children of junior school age with mild learning difficulties, found that the older ones reported more teasing/bullying than observers had noticed. While the disabled pupils were not unduly concerned about teasing, bullying did upset them considerably. The worrying point is that the extent of the bullying had not been appreciated by staff (Besag, 1989).

The number of obese children would seem to be increasing today. Body shape is an important facet of how individuals view themselves, peaking in importance at adolescence. Over-fat girls and over-thin boys have the poorest views of themselves in the pre-adolescent years (Pierce and Wardle, 1993), negative perceptions which have been associated with depression (McCabe and Marwit, 1993). Again, a case study may help to show some of the effects of disability on the development of social relationships, even when the disability could not be called severe.

James and his behaviour have already been described in Chapter 3, pp. 40–1. He has been rejected by his peers, who find it difficult to cope with his violent outbursts and minimal social skills. There are so many factors which could be identified to account for his present difficulties that James almost encapsulates the whole of this chapter.

- His temperament has been said by his teachers to be 'fragile and fiery'. Frustration of any kind leads to uncontrolled tantrums followed by remorse. His fury is turned on others, often those younger than himself.
- His family background is an unhappy one. His father left the family home when James was five years of age and his mother died two years later. His sister, who is considerably older than he is, then looked after him. When her fiancé moved in with her, however, there were endless rows with James in which he was sometimes physically abused, and on several occasions he was taken into care by the Social Services.
- James is overweight, with a turn in his right eye for which he should wear glasses. He also suffers from asthma. His physical size protected him to some extent from teasing and taunting at the primary stage, but when he moved into secondary school he became a tempting target. His violent reactions almost inevitably led to his being blamed for the upheavals which erupted around him.
- Both his work in school and his attendance are poor. He shows poor motivation along with a high level of frustration. He has a specially planned programme of work (individual education programme) but he shows little interest in the activities recommended. His learning difficulties and the special help they require serve to emphasize his differences from his classmates.

Any one of these areas could have affected James' social development. In combination they lead to a sense of helplessness on the part of the school. In an attempt to do something to help James, they have tried to tackle his learning difficulties but with little success for the moment. The problems in his social and emotional development seem so dominant that he has little energy to give to cognitive demands. James will be further discussed in Chapters 7 and 9.

Unsuccessful social interactions on the part of disabled individuals cannot be seen as solely the result of negative attitudes on the part of those with whom they come into contact. The concept of synergy again holds good (i.e. the contribution of any individual/group combines with the contribution of another to produce a new and enhanced effect). What the disabled individual brings to the interaction by way of personal characteristics and past experience plays a vital part. Parental strategies in dealing with their disabled child are of particular importance. When the disability is severe, a great deal of adjustment is required at a time when the mother in particular may be least able to cope (Sandow, Stafford and Stafford, 1987). Professionals still do not communicate well when the news of the birth of a disabled child has to be passed on to those most closely concerned (Sandow, 1994). Perhaps there is no satisfactory way of doing this when the disability is severe. Whether the mother withdraws from the child or becomes over-protective, there is an almost inevitable distortion of the early interactions so important for future social development. If the infant has to be hospitalized, this situation may be exacerbated. The surprising thing really is that carers and children remain as positive as they do about interactions with others when faced with the many obstacles which disability puts in their path (Seed, 1988; Wade and Moore, 1993).

THE SCHOOL SITUATION

Educational performance has an important part to play in whether or not pupils feel comfortable in their school community. Failure to progress as the school expects emphasizes any other differences or difficulties they may have and almost inevitably creates a degree of tension within the classroom as pupils, teachers and parents have to adjust to standards of achievement which differ markedly from the norm.

In Chapter 3, mention was made of *Helen* (p. 31) and *Ewan* (p. 33). Neither have friends in school but, apart from that, they really have nothing in common. Helen, while very reserved and self-contained, is an intelligent girl, happily spending time reading. She appears to get considerable satisfaction from her school experiences and continues her school interests at home. Ewan's performance in school, in particular his reading difficulties, were so acute that he could no longer be accommodated within a mainstream class and he is now in a special class. While this move may have reduced the bullying he was receiving at his previous school, it has meant his removal from his neighbourhood school and his presence in a small group of children, all with learning difficulties of one kind or another. He is a small boy, very silent and totally undemanding. He can easily be overlooked in class and may well be 'victimized' again when with other pupils because he is typically 'passive or submissive' (Olweus, 1993).

Educational performance

Pupils may fail to 'mesh in' at school for reasons other than lack of ability to keep up with the demands of the work level of the classroom. They may be very immature and dependent, always in need of attention or reassurance, unable to get on with work on their own. Other pupils (as well as the teacher) find this behaviour irritating because so much time has to be given to coping with it. Any problems in communication, for example speech defects, partial hearing loss or first language other than that of the classroom, inhibit social participation and may lead to children staying silent rather than struggling to make themselves understood. Again, the reactions of the 'slow-to-warm-up' children discussed earlier in this chapter can be misinterpreted by teachers who see them simply as 'slow' and do not give them the space, time and support they require. Factors which have been associated with poor educational performance are too numerous to discuss here, but the concept of learning difficulties is elaborated in, among others, Croll and Moses, 1985; Chazan, Laing and Davies, 1991; Solity, 1992.

A high level of intelligence or outstanding talent in one area is not always an advantage socially (Kellmer Pringle, 1970). As Beveridge (1993) points out, where there is a significant mismatch between learners and the learning challenges confronting them, difficulties may ensue. Unlike *Helen* (see Chapter 3, p. 31), able and talented pupils may simply cease to make an effort to do any more than is required of them to meet the level expected of the class, or may become disliked by others because of the ease with which they dominate in their particular field. Leyden (1985) states that 'the whole question of giftedness is one ... of relationships – of the responses of persons one to another, of the communication or exclusion of individuals or groups' (p. 3).

Because gifted pupils do not react in the conventional and expected way, their behaviour can seem bizarre to others – peers, teachers and even family. They may find difficulty in making friendships with their contemporaries, although the gifted children themselves do not seem to find this a major problem, at least at the junior school stage (Hitchfield, 1973). Their interest in books or computers gives them considerable enjoyment, and when they are with their peers they are often the leaders because they are the ones with the unusual ideas. The latter, of course, are not always welcome in the classroom (or in the home). Again, because highly intelligent pupils grasp new information quickly, they can predict the course of a lesson and link it to their own expertise in a way which can seem deliberately provocative to the teacher and arrogant to their classmates (Docking, 1990a). Gifted and creative children can therefore generate stress in others, especially if they are not extended in their school work (Povey, 1980), and may find themselves becoming isolated in the classroom.

On the whole, however, it is probably the case that gifted and creative individuals feel positive about their ability to achieve. Those who are struggling to understand new material are at risk of negative views of their competence, especially if there are no others in the class who seem to be making even slower progress than they are (Vrugt, 1994). Motivation to master new work may be low. Galloway *et al.* (1995) found that Year 7 pupils in two comprehensive secondary schools, who tested as less able cognitively than their classmates, were significantly more likely than other pupils to show maladaptive motivation. By this is meant that they either adopted self-protective strategies (e.g. saying the tasks were boring; belittling the tasks; avoiding the tasks completely) or they felt themselves helpless to do anything about their poor performance. As the researchers point out, these maladaptive motivational styles are particularly worrying so early in the pupils' secondary career. They are also particularly likely to lead to disruption or frustration of normal teaching routines, identifying the pupils of low ability as different from other pupils and from the teachers' expectations. They may come to exist on the fringes of class activities.

Classroom groups

Group work is not necessarily the answer to motivational problems. Parkinson and Colman (1994) discuss the ways in which individuals appraise various situations, including how they view the presence of others in achievement-related tasks. While the presence of others usually enhances successful completion of a task, failure to achieve 'leads to response inhibition and state anxiety' (Geen, 1994, p. 48). If the task is difficult, learners may suffer from cognitive overload, which is also inhibiting, especially if they believe that their efforts are being evaluated. Motivation may drop in the whole group.

A similar drop may follow an increase in the number of group members, a phenomenon which Geen (1994) calls 'social loafing'. In a fairly large group, some members will 'go along for the ride', doing very little because they believe someone else in the group will do what is required for them. Those in the group who are willing to work realize in turn that they are being made 'suckers' by the others and so reduce their efforts. The effect is, once again, reduced motivation, poor output and, consequently, lack of satisfaction with the group experience among the members. Those held responsible for any negative group outcomes are likely to become excluded. Once isolated, they may not find it easy to restore more rewarding group relationships, especially if their level of ability makes the task difficult for them.

To put a group of children with low motivation together is certainly not the answer, as the most probable result of such a strategy is that nothing gets done at all. It may be that pairing learners together can produce a similar 'social loafing' effect with reduced motivation and negative effect. Even to organize a small 'special' class has considerable implications for the members' ability to interact with other pupils, as such a form of organization considerably reduces opportunities to mix freely. The effect of special class placement on *Ewan* was noted earlier in this chapter. *Eddie* is another pupil who was placed in a special class at the secondary stage and was in consequence even more isolated than he had been at the primary stage. His case will be looked at in greater detail in Chapter 7, pp. 104–4, 118.

NEIGHBOURHOOD/COMMUNITY CONSIDERATIONS

Neighbourhood groups

While children who are brought up in rural settings may be physically isolated from others of the same age as themselves out of school, there are compensations by way of environmental interests, worthwhile occupations and visitors. Those in urban settings are surrounded by potential companions of all ages, but this in itself poses problems for their social development. The many threats inherent in urban living, from traffic density to physical assault or abduction, make the younger children more home-based than used to be the case when safety was accepted and supervision reasonably easy. Where they are allowed to roam freely, there are many temptations for mischief or actual crime. Withdrawn or isolated children are, by definition, seldom involved in group ventures, although solitary anti-social acts are not unknown.

Withdrawal from groups

It is at adolescence, however, that withdrawal or isolation from the group has considerable impact on individual behaviour. This is partly because of the importance of group membership to individual social development (see Chapter 2) and partly because growing maturity moves the focus of the individual's attention to the neighbourhood and the community. Not to be a member of a group, not to have a close friend, not to spend most free time in the company of others, all bring home to the individual what may well be seen as shortcomings. Self-esteem suffers accordingly. What kind of neighbourhood is accessible to young people is also important. Many urban environments have 'high rates of delinquency . . . with poor housing, a declining population, a lack of recreational facilities, high unemployment and so on' (Coleman, 1980, p. 154). Being a member of a group makes the adolescent highly vulnerable to group pressures whether for good or ill. To be excluded from any group makes for deviance and stress.

An example of how the withdrawn individual who is low in self-esteem may react can be seen in drug or alcohol abuse. While young people may be led by their group into experimenting with drugs, smoking or drinking, the effect of drugs in particular is likely to be increased solitariness if addiction occurs (Schinke, Botvin and Orlandi, 1991). Drug and substance abuse can be seen as a way of coping with 'failure (real or anticipated), boredom, social anxiety, unhappiness, rejection, social isolation, low self-esteem or a lack of self-efficacy' (ibid., p. 16). Urban environments make it easy for individuals to move into drug abuse, especially when there are few other attractions. Schinke, Botvin and Orlandi also point out that in America, while alcohol use and cigarette smoking, along with the use of sedatives and tranquillizers, have declined in young people, the use of cocaine and inhalants has increased.

Another negative influence in some areas is racism. While living in the same neighbourhood or working together has brought about understanding and friendship between different racial groups, the media still show sensationalist reports of racial incidents which resonate with deeply held prejudices even within these same well-integrated areas (Troyna and Hatcher, 1992). In today's society, race, class, gender and sexuality still exert potent influences (Gillborn, 1995). To be a member of a minority group can inhibit ease in social relationships for children, young persons and adults and lead to isolation.

Children of refugee families have considerable difficulties in establishing positive relationships in the host community. For the parents to leave their own country is traumatic and if they also lose status, occupation and financial stability, depression may well follow (Lau, 1996). As has been said earlier in this chapter, when the main carer is suffering from depression, the result is often inability to cope with the psychological needs of the other members of the family. Cultural and linguistic differences add to the children's distress because the norms of the school may be at odds with those of the home or of their previous school. In addition, school staff may find it difficult to encourage carers to become involved with their children's education when even the likelihood of their remaining in the country may be in dispute.

One final example can be given of a very different set of circumstances where isolation may also result. Part-time employment is becoming increasingly common in pupils at the secondary and even the primary stage. It is difficult to estimate the prevalence of this as information is patchy and open to frequent change. The effect, apart from possible tiredness during the school day, can be to reduce opportunities for peer group interaction as long spells of out-of-school time are given over to paid employment. Child employment obviously has good and bad implications. For young people to feel a degree of financial self-sufficiency may encourage responsible attitudes in the future. On the other hand, their experience of work may be that it is physically exhausting, badly paid, highly repetitive or exploitative.

Andy was fourteen years old, tall for his age but not very robust. He was one of a large family where making ends meet was a bit of a struggle. His father was in employment but was unskilled with no job security. In the primary school, Andy had begun a newspaper round, which he continued at the secondary stage until he was taken on to stock shelves in the local supermarket. He seemed to be perpetually tired, his school performance deteriorated and he increasingly became a 'loner'. He hung about the edges of the playground, finding quiet corners where he could have an illicit cigarette. He would at times truant but, on the whole, seemed to prefer sitting apathetically through lessons, not doing very much. It is probable that, without his job, Andy would not have been able to acquire any of the symbols of contemporary youth culture and would have felt excluded. On the other hand, his job was beginning to dominate his life. He was brought into contact with a range of people at work, often older than himself, but he had little by way of close, personal relationships. Even at home, there seemed to be little real interest in Andy as a person and more concern about him as an element in the family's attempts at survival.

CONCLUSION

This chapter has looked at a number of factors which may lead to withdrawal or isolation. Some children may be temperamentally disposed to prefer their own company; some may find that their experiences make it difficult for them to feel at ease in social settings; others may find their social uncertainty is reinforced by lack of social success. Withdrawal is not simply the way a child has been brought up. Rather it may reflect poor social skills, unhappy experiences of trying to join in with others, different interests or cultural background, lack of psychological energy to cope with group demands or the attitudes of others who exclude rather than include. Experiences do not just happen to children and young people. They are part of them and their reactions affect present and future interactions. How to bring about changes in the area of social relationships is complicated. But where individuals would be happier to be part of a group rather than always on the fringe of it, there is a responsibility to assess the seriousness of the withdrawal or isolation and try to do something about it.

Chapter 6

Consequences of Withdrawal and Isolation

This chapter will consider the short-term and long-term consequences of withdrawal and isolation in childhood and adolescence. Neither withdrawn behaviour nor a child's isolated situation are necessarily permanent features or even long-lasting. Further, many children who do not enjoy a happy childhood become reasonably well-adjusted adults. However, as will be shown below, withdrawn and isolated children nearly always experience feelings of distress, and may be at risk of continued maladaptive behaviour or future mental disorder.

SHORT-TERM CONSEQUENCES

Some of the short-term consequences of the various patterns of behaviour shown by withdrawn or isolated children have already been discussed in Chapter 3. Shy children, for example, tend to feel embarrassed, uncertain, frightened, and doubtful about their personal merits and capabilities (Crozier and Burnham, 1990). Rejected children experience feelings of loneliness, low self-esteem and social anxiety, and may react to their situation with aggressive and disruptive behaviour (Hymel and Franke, 1985; Hymel *et al.*, 1990; Parkhurst and Asher, 1992). Isolated children, including victims of bullying, may also be unhappy about being outside the group (Perry, Kusel and Perry, 1988; Olweus, 1991). Depressed children and adolescents may show, in addition to withdrawn behaviour, sadness, a feeling that life is not worthwhile, and eating or sleeping disturbances (Goodyer, 1995). A tendency to stand apart from the group is often associated with underachievement in school and general dissatisfaction with school.

If a child has very limited contact with his or her peers, speaking and listening skills may be adversely affected. Shyness and isolation may lead to teasing and bullying, or begin a chain reaction. However, the effects of shyness may be mitigated, particularly amongst younger children, by a child showing willingness to participate in group activities without disrupting them.

The Early Years

It is particularly difficult to know what the effects of withdrawn behaviour will be in the case of young children. As children in the early years divide their time in free play in approximately equal proportions to 'solitary', 'parallel' and 'group' play (Smith and Cowie, 1991), playing on one's own is not necessarily a source of disturbance or distress. However, children show an interest in other children from an early age, and they can understand people's desires and emotions by 3–4 years of age, if not sooner (Harris, 1989). Dunn (1996) asserts that young children may be sensitive to the reactions and opinions of those in their peer group to an extent not fully appreciated until recently. Crozier and Burnham (1990) state that shyness in children aged 3–4 years is linked with wariness, inhibition of behaviour in unfamiliar settings and approach/withdrawal conflict.

In a study in mid-western America, Ladd (1990) considered the potential role that children's classroom peer relations play in their school adjustment during the first two months of kindergarten and the remainder of the school year. Ladd obtained measures of 125 children's peer relations (66 males, 59 females, mean age 5.4 months) on three occasions – at school entrance, after two months and at the end of the school year. Measures of adjustment to school (including perceptions of school, anxiety, avoidance and performance) were obtained during the second and third assessments. The results indicated that children with a larger number of classroom friends developed more favourable perceptions of school by the second month, and those pupils who kept up these relationships liked school better as the year progressed. Making new friends in the classroom was associated with gains in school performance, and early peer rejection predicted less favourable school perceptions, higher levels of school avoidance, and lower performance levels over the school year.

This study suggests that, although young children enjoy a certain amount of solitary activity and friendships are highly fragile in the early years, positive peer relationships are an important factor in children's social, emotional and scholastic development from an early age.

Middle Childhood

By the time children reach the age of 7 or 8 years, they are spending a greatly increased amount of time with their peers in the classroom, playground and neighbourhood. The size of children's groups continues to increase through the mid-school years, although boys may form small, coherent gangs for some of their activities. The segregation of children's groups by sex becomes more marked. Boys tend to emphasize co-operation, companionship and leadership in their social relationships, while girls tend to put more emphasis on intimacy and exclusiveness in their friendships (Smith and Cowie, 1991). Peer relations become increasingly important to children, who grow more susceptible to the influence of other children and more aware of their own status and that of others within the peer group (Strommen, McKinney and Fitzgerald, 1977).

The effects of withdrawal and isolation are now becoming more serious and more obvious. *Laura*, aged 8 (see Chapter 3, p. 40), was rejected as a friend or playmate because of her aggression and inability to abide by the rules followed by her peers. Although she tried to force herself on others, her peers found ways of avoiding her, so that she became increasingly isolated as well as often disruptive and lacking in concentration in class. The isolation suffered by *Robin*, aged 11 (see Chapter 3, pp. 38–9) led to feelings of loneliness, deterioration in his school work, and eventually to an extreme reluctance to going to school, evidenced by feigning illness, crying bitterly and temper tantrums. The shyness shown by *Claire*, aged 11 (see Chapter 3, p. 36), resulted in her being a passive observer both in class and the playground; her isolation encouraged other girls to tease her.

During middle childhood, poor peer relations are often found to be related to general measures of maladaptive behaviour, especially of the internalizing kind (Hartup, 1983), as well as low scholastic achievement (Green *et al.*, 1980). Strauss *et al.* (1986) investigated the association between social withdrawal and internalizing problems in children aged 7+ to 10+ years in the USA. Forty-eight children (from a sample of 640) were identified by teachers as interacting infrequently with other children, and 72 as being outgoing and sociable. When these two groups were compared on a battery of teacher, peer and self-report measures of internalizing difficulties, the low frequency interactors were indeed found to display such adjustment problems. Children who rarely interacted with peers were less well-liked by peers, had poorer self-concepts and were more depressed and anxious than sociable children. These two groups did not differ on measures of externalizing problems. In a study of 396 5th-grade children (10- to 11-year-olds) in Florida, USA, Lazarus (1982) found that 46 per cent considered that being shy led to personal problems, deficient communication, poor self-projection and low self-esteem.

Adolescence

Peer relationships become even more important in adolescence than in previous stages of development, as adolescents turn away from their family base, at least to some extent. In early adolescence large same-sex cliques or gangs become common; then heterosexual relationships are formed; and later various types of crowd become popular (McKinney, Fitzgerald and Strommen, 1977; Smith and Cowie, 1991). It is during adolescence that doubts about the ability to contribute effectively to social encounters and the belief that one will be negatively evaluated by others are particularly likely to lead to inhibited behaviour and social anxieties. Such self-perceptions are likely to shape a social environment that provides few opportunities for rewarding experiences.

The inability of *Susan*, aged 15 (see Chapter 3, pp. 43–4), to keep up with the social demands of her adolescent peer group and her tearful reaction to not belonging led to the hardening of the attitude of both girls and boys towards her and their making hurtful remarks about her. Susan reacted by opting out of school altogether.

The fiery temper and aggressive behaviour shown by *James*, aged 13 (see Chapter 3, pp. 40–1), made him unpopular with the group, who regarded him with fear and contempt and used him as a scapegoat. His aggression towards members of staff led to his temporary exclusion from school.

The isolation and lack of confidence shown by *Joe*, aged 15 (see Chapter 3, p. 42), resulted in him being bullied in secondary school and being generally unhappy with school life.

Loneliness peaks in adolescence and is among the most frequent problems mentioned by the adolescent (Zimbardo and Radl, 1981; Brennan, 1982). Even during pre-adolescence, lonely boys are limited in their formation of relationships with the opposite sex (Rotenberg and Whitney, 1992). Although most adolescents like to be on their own and pursue solitary activities for some part of their time, the intensity of feeling which is characteristic at this stage of development means that extreme shyness, withdrawal and isolation generally have quite severe short-term consequences. These include dissatisfaction with oneself, periods of moodiness and depression, being unhappy in school, deterioration in school work, outbursts of aggression towards others (including members of the close family circle), and physical illness.

LONGER-TERM CONSEQUENCES

It is very difficult to predict with any degree of accuracy the outcome of emotional, social or behavioural problems in childhood and adolescence, particularly in the case of individuals. As already mentioned (p. 2), withdrawal and isolation in childhood are associated mainly with internalizing problems of adjustment. Although research studies on the long-term outcome of emotional and behavioural difficulties in childhood are often flawed, internalizing problems generally show a better prognosis with regard to long-term persistence than do externalizing problems (Rutter and Garmezy, 1983). Nevertheless, a failure to make positive relationships with peers in childhood or adolescence may have adverse consequences in later life (Mellsop, 1972; Cowen *et al.*, 1973; Parker and Asher, 1987).

Researchers have emphasized both the seriousness of behaviour problems presented by children and the complexity of the network of interacting factors which affect the continuity or discontinuity of development in any specific case. For example, Richman, Stevenson and Graham (1982) conclude that behaviour problems even in pre-school children are not usually transient reactions to stress and of little significance in later personality development; once a child's behaviour is established in a maladaptive pattern, it does not readily change. Rodgers (1990), too, asserts that continuity in personality or temperamental characteristics in children carries a risk for disorder in adulthood. For instance, early tendencies towards fearfulness or feelings of sadness are possible precursors of long-term susceptibility to anxiety or depression. However, as Rodgers states, environmental as well as temperamental factors are important in determining outcome; stressful events and situations must occur in adult life in order for childhood neurotic symptoms to be associated with an excess of adult psychiatric problems.

Factors to be taken into consideration

Rutter (1989) highlights the many factors which influence whether and to what extent childhood behaviour and experiences have consequences in later life. These include genetic mechanisms; the shaping of the environment; cognitive and social skills; self-esteem; and habits, cognitive sets and coping styles (see also Robins and Rutter, 1992). In respect of the prediction of the long-term outcome of withdrawal and isolation in children, the following factors need particular consideration:

- the instability of measures of social relationships;
- individual differences in reactions to events and situations;
- combinations of risk factors;
- changes in circumstances;
- significance of withdrawal and isolation at particular stages of development;
- gender;

- membership of ethnic minority groups;
- protective factors;
- intervention.

Many references to these factors have already been made in previous chapters, and so they will be discussed only briefly below in relation to the long-term consequences of withdrawal and isolation in childhood.

The instability of measures of social relationships

The assessment of a child's social adjustment in relation to his or her peers will depend on the particular definition of social status adopted (for example, the sociometric categories used) and the techniques selected to measure social status. In addition, a number of studies have shown that measures of social relationships cannot be regarded as stable over time. For instance, Newcomb and Bukowski (1984), repeating sociometric group assessments over a period of two years with 334 pre-adolescents, found that children in popular, neglected and controversial categories showed low stability; in the case of rejected children, slightly higher short-term stability was evidenced. The findings relating to such limited stability were generally attributed to measurement error and the failure to classify children with different social reputation profiles accurately.

Coie and Dodge (1983) also examined the continuities and changes in children's social status in a five-year longitudinal study. They collected yearly sociometric data on 96 3rd-grade children (8- to 9-year-olds) and 112 5th-graders (10- to 11-years-old) across a five-year period. Social status groups of neglected, rejected, controversial and popular children were identified each year. There was significant continuity of rejected status across all five years for the older cohort, but only for the first three years of the study for the 3rd-grade sample. Peer behavioural descriptions, such as being co-operative or disruptive, increased the prediction of both status categories and social preference scores. Coie and Dodge concluded that the year-to-year stability indices reflected a high degree of stability for both sociometric measures and peer behaviour description variables, that stability tended to decrease with an increasing test–retest interval, but even so, there was a surprising degree of continuity and increasing consensus on who was shy with increasing age. Across the five-year period, 'rejected' children either became 'neglected', moved to 'average' status or stayed 'rejected'; whereas 'neglected' children might move to 'average' or 'popular' status with the passage of time and without intervention. Cillessen *et al.* (1992) also found that a considerable number of children initially rated as 'rejected' in early or middle childhood do not remain in that category.

The long-term prediction of the outcome of poor peer relationships, therefore, rests on an uncertain basis, if reliance is placed solely or mainly on single measures of social relationships in childhood or adolescence. However, Ollendick *et al.* (1991), while acknowledging that the stability of sociometric status should not be exaggerated, assert that the fact should not be ignored that most children rarely make great changes without intervention.

Individual differences in reactions to events and situations

Individuals vary greatly in their reaction to stressful events and difficult situations in which they find themselves (for example at critical points in their life course), when they have to adapt to new roles and relationships (Caspi, Elder and Bern, 1988). As Lindsay and Wedell (1982) state, children can and do compensate for their deficiencies by their resources, and some are able to overcome obstacles in childhood. Some, however, with a relatively trouble-free childhood, may fare badly as adults; and in some cases problems even at an early age become increasingly severe and lead to a disturbed adolescence and adulthood. This wide range of possible responses to troubles in childhood, including those in relation to peers, adds to the difficulties in the way of predicting outcomes in the case of particular individuals, even if those who fall into certain categories of maladaptive behaviour are more likely to be at risk than others.

Combinations of risk factors

Difficulties in childhood and adolescence rarely come singly, and single risk factors seem to have relatively little effect over time (Sanson *et al.*, 1991). Risk factors operate in a cumulative way (Garmezy and Rutter, 1983), and it is a combination of several such factors that tends to be associated with an adverse long-term outcome. For example, withdrawal accompanied by aggression and disruptiveness in children is likely to be a more powerful predictor of mental disorder in adulthood than either form of behaviour exhibited alone (Ledingham and Schwartzman, 1984).

Changes in circumstances

Changes in circumstances may well alter a child's behaviour and social relationships, sometimes radically, for better or for worse. Events within the family likely to have an emotional impact on children include bereavement, divorce, sudden unemployment, separation from a parent or both parents, and moving house. Events related to school that may affect behaviour include having a new teacher, a change of class, or going to a different school. Even in the same class, changes in the composition of the group may result in a child's social status improving or deteriorating. When an isolate or a victim of bullying is befriended, a modification of withdrawn behaviour is likely.

Egeland *et al.* (1990) found that discontinuity of development in children was particularly associated with changes in maternal depressive symptomatology, stressful life-events experienced by the family, and the quality of the home environment. Richman, Stevenson and Graham (1982) also drew attention to disadvantaged home conditions as contributing to the persistence of behaviour problems.

Significance of withdrawal and isolation at particular stages of development

It is not easy to assess the long-term significance of withdrawal and isolation at particular ages, but it would seem that the age at which difficulties in peer relationships are shown has a bearing on the consequences of such difficulties.

Vitaro *et al.* (1992) suggest that children at risk of rejection can be identified during nursery and kindergarten years. Egeland *et al.* (1990) found that the majority of a sample of pre-school children presenting behaviour problems, including withdrawal, continued to have problems of this kind in the first three years of elementary school. Malik and Furman (1993), too, draw attention to studies which have shown solitary passive play in the pre-school years to be associated with subsequent internalizing difficulties, though findings have not been altogether consistent.

Younger, Schwartzman and Ledingham (1985) assert that social withdrawal becomes increasingly maladaptive with age, finding that items relating to withdrawal cluster poorly at 1st grade, but become a more cohesive category of behaviours as the children grow older. A number of other researchers, too, consider that the strongest evidence of the long-term adverse effects of being poorly accepted comes from follow-up studies of rejection at adolescence (Parker and Asher, 1987; Parkhurst and Asher, 1992; Cillessen *et al.*, 1992).

Hymel *et al.* (1990) found that internalizing problems in middle childhood (around the age of 10 years) were significantly related to earlier social difficulties about three years previously, including poor peer acceptance, social isolation and perceptions of social incompetence. Cowen *et al.* (1973), in a eleven-year follow up of a large number of 8-year-olds, reported that those needing psychiatric help during this period were much more likely than others to have had negative peer ratings at 8 years. In fact, the peer ratings were the best of all the earlier measures at predicting future appearance in the mental health registers.

In the Waterloo Longitudinal Project in Canada, Rubin (1993) found that solitary-passive activity in the kindergarten predicted problems such as low self-esteem, loneliness and depression up to Grade 5 (age 10+). However, four years later the children who had been withdrawn at an early age did not show internalizing problems. Rather, they reported that social interaction was unimportant to them and emphasized academic achievement. However, solitary-passive activity in Grade 2 (age 7+ years) or later was rather strongly associated with internalized problems up to Grade 9 (see also Rubin, Hymel and Mills, 1989).

Gender

By the age of seven, a clear-cut difference is found in the overall prevalence of emotional and behaviour problems between boys and girls (McGee, Silva and Williams, 1984; Stevenson, Richman and Graham, 1985; Achenbach *et al.*, 1987b). Far more boys than girls are reported in numerous studies as showing externalizing problems, whereas in the case of internalizing difficulties, little difference is found in prevalence between the sexes; or else more girls than boys are referred for such problems, particularly in adolescence. Richman, Stevenson and Graham (1982) concluded that gender (being male rather than female) was an important contributing factor in the continuity of behaviour problems from early childhood. Mellsop (1972), on the basis of a twenty-year follow-up of children referred to a psychiatric unit in Australia, found that delinquent girls and girls with behaviour problems were particularly at risk of psychiatric illness as adults.

Dunn and McGuire (1992) emphasize the need to take gender into account in considering peer status as a predictor of future emotional, social and behavioural difficulties. Kupersmidt, Coie and Dodge (1990) also assert that different patterns of variables are involved in the prediction of behaviour problems in boys and girls; the form of social behaviour that accompanies peer rejection in childhood may be quite different for males and females. In general, withdrawal seems to be linked to risk for schizophrenia among females who are lonely, isolated and socially inept (see also John, Mednick and Schulsinger, 1982).

Simpson and Stevenson (1985), too, produce evidence to show that boys and girls should be considered separately in the search for associations between temperamental characteristics and family interaction. For example, in the early years members of the family tend to respond differentially to shyness in girls or boys. At 42 and 50 months, parents are likely to react negatively to shyness in boys, but positively to shyness in girls. Caspi, Elder and Bern (1988) found that the long-term outcome of shyness in late childhood (ages 10–12 years) was somewhat different for boys and girls (see below, pp. 98–9, for a further discussion of this study).

Although a number of studies, as pointed out above, have stressed the importance of taking gender into account as a variable affecting the outcome of poor peer relationships in childhood, research evidence on this issue is still limited. Samples of girls have only infrequently been included in studies of rejection by peers (Malik and Furman, 1993), and gender differences in behaviour during childhood and later are beset with problems of measurement and interpretation (Whitehead, 1979; Hay, 1994).

Membership of ethnic minority groups

Children of different ethnic groups often mix well in school and the community, and have friends from other minority groups. However, children from ethnic minorities are not always fully accepted in classroom, playground or neighbourhood settings. They are particularly vulnerable to racist taunts; Moran *et al.* (1993), for example, found that Asian pupils suffered to a considerable extent from name-calling with reference to their colour. Where there is a minority of 'black' children, they tend to be isolated (Gordon, 1992). Negative attitudes towards children from other races are present in early childhood, and are exacerbated by the tendency for children of particular ethnic groups to interact with one another rather than with those from other groups (Hartup, 1983; Stephan, 1985).

It is plausible to suggest that members of ethnic minority groups who are withdrawn, rejected or isolated in childhood will find it particularly difficult to change their behaviour and situation later on, as they may meet with prejudice and discrimination in adolescence and adulthood. However, they may have normal and positive social relationships within their own ethnic groups.

Protective factors

Precisely what factors act as moderators, protecting children from highly adverse effects of events or situations which they may experience, is not yet known. Garmezy (1985) lists as potential protective factors: (1) positive personality dispositions; (2) a supportive family milieu; and (3) an external support system, such as a caring school environment, that encourages a child's coping efforts. Problem-solving skills and children's own beliefs about their control over situations also act as protective factors (Berden, Althans and Verhulst, 1990; Rossman and Rosenberg, 1992). Goodyer, Wright and Altham (1990) put special emphasis on close, affectionate relationships with parents, in whom the child can confide, as decreasing the risk of conduct disorder even in the presence of marital disharmony. Teachers sensitive to the emotional and social needs of their pupils are also likely to contribute to protecting them from the worst effects of difficult situations within the classroom or playground group.

Rutter (1983) points out that intelligence and good progress at school may serve as moderating factors in childhood disturbance. He suggests that there is a slight but consistent tendency for children of above average intelligence to have rather low rates of psychiatric disorder and sociobehavioural deviance generally. Intellectually able children may have better self-esteem, greater problem-solving skills, or be constitutionally more resilient. On the other hand, intelligent children who are isolated or rejected may view their situation with particular sensitivity and suffer all the more.

Intervention

Clearly, if intervention strategies are applied successfully in the case of childhood difficulties in social relationships, this should lessen the risk of continuity of such difficulties into adult life. In the case of shy children who want to participate in social activities, even very simple interventions may be of considerable help. These include sympathy and encouragement from parents and teachers, as well as support from peers who are mature and sensitive enough to be able to help a shy and inhibited child. Many forms of intervention may be tried which can change behaviour and attitudes radically, though intervention does not work in every case. Intervention strategies are discussed elsewhere in this book, especially in Chapters 7, 8 and 9.

LONG-TERM CONSEQUENCES OF SPECIFIC KINDS OF WITHDRAWAL

Shyness

Rutter (1989) points out that shyness does not seem to carry the same long-term risks as rejection allied to aggression. However, shyness evident at an early stage of development tends to show a causal chain. Shy children may become trapped in a feedback loop involving withdrawal from peers, rejection by peers and internalizing problems (Rubin, LeMare and Lollis, 1990; Rubin, 1993). Increasing non-acceptance by peers as a result of shyness is likely to lead to increased withdrawal and inhibition.

Caspi, Elder and Bern (1988) used data from the Berkeley Guidance Study (Macfarlane, Allen and Honzik, 1954) to identify individuals who were shy and reserved in later childhood (aged 10–12 years). They traced the continuities and consequences of shyness and inhibition across the subsequent 30 years of their lives. Shy boys were more likely than their peers to delay entry into marriage, parenthood and stable careers; to obtain less occupational stability; and to experience marital instability. Shy girls were more likely than their peers to follow a conventional pattern of marriage, childbearing and homemaking, often with no work history at all. Women characterized by shyness and reserve in late childhood manifested no distinctive problems through mid-life.

In the study by Caspi and colleagues, childhood shyness did not produce pathological or extreme outcomes, but it did have significant consequences for later adult life. These consequences resulted from their progressive accumulation (cumulative continuity) and from their tendency to evoke maintaining responses from others during reciprocal social interaction (interactional continuity).

Neglect

As previously mentioned (p. 37), 'neglected' sociometric status has rather poor stability, and children neglected by their peers at particular times may well improve their relationships with other children. Coie and Dodge (1983) found that over a five- year period from the age of 8+ years, 'neglected' children might move up to 'average' or 'popular' status even without intervention. They report that children neglected in elementary school almost never became 'rejected' or 'controversial'. However, a sizeable number of children 'rejected' at elementary school became 'neglected' later in junior high school; this suggests that 'neglected' status has a different meaning at the two stages.

Most 'neglected' children do not show seriously maladaptive behaviour to the extent that 'rejected' children do, and are probably not greatly at risk of future long-term difficulties. However, studies have not always made a clear distinction between peer rejection and neglect (Parkhurst and Asher, 1992), and those children who are seriously neglected or ignored by their peers may well continue to have problems (Malik and Furman, 1993; see also Ollendick *et al.*, 1991). Where isolation and neglected social status are associated with continued withdrawal in childhood, neglected children are likely to see themselves as lacking in social, cognitive and physical competence, as well as in general self-worth in regard to the group. Such perceptions may well have adverse consequences in relation to social adjustment and school progress (Rubin, LeMare and Lollis, 1990).

Rejection

Rejection is a more stable category than other sociometric classifications, and many rejected children quickly become disliked again even when put into new groups of children (Coie and Dodge, 1983; Newcomb and Bukowski, 1984). Children's experience of rejection by classmates may pervade and disrupt many areas of their life. Rejected children in primary school, particularly when they are aggressive, are more likely than others to achieve poorly at secondary school, play truant, become delinquent and experience mental health problems in adulthood (Parker and Asher, 1987; Kupersmidt and Coie, 1990; Hymel *et al.*, 1990; Frederickson, 1991). Many rejected children have enduring personal characteristics that lead to difficulties in their peer relations, loneliness and feelings of depression (Asher, 1990).

Many adolescents and adults with disorders tend to have a history of non-acceptance by peers, but by no means all children who are rejected by other children have later problems. Prediction is better for school drop-out problems and criminality than for adult psychopathology (Dunn and McGuire, 1992).

Anxiety and fearfulness

Internalizing emotional and behavioural problems, in which anxiety and fearfulness play a considerable part, tend to have a relatively favourable prognosis as compared with externalizing problems or psychotic disorders (Robins, 1972; Esser, Schmidt and Woerner, 1990). Fears decline with age, especially in boys, and even phobias may respond well to treatment. For example, although some children and adolescents with problems of a fear of school are at risk for psychiatric disorder in later life, most school refusers become normal adults (Hersov, 1985).

However, individual fearfulness tends to be stable over time and is partly under genetic control (Marks, 1987). Some fears may persist from childhood to adulthood, and temperamental tendencies towards fearfulness shown in childhood are possible precursors of later emotional susceptibility to anxiety (Rodgers, 1990). Kagan and Moss (1982) found that extreme inhibition in face of the unfamiliar in the first three years of life was a strong predictor of withdrawn behaviour in later childhood, adolescence and adulthood. Children who were extremely inhibited until age three were likely to withdraw from social interaction during the subsequent three years and be socially timid at ages 6–10 years. Inhibited boys tended to avoid typically male activities as adolescents and masculine vocations as adults.

Depression

Although not all depression in adulthood has its origins in childhood, and not all depression in childhood or adolescence leads to depression in adult life, there is an association between episodes of depression in children and adolescents and major depression later on. Carlson (1984) has suggested a link between depressive disorders in the pre-pubertal age range and depression in adolescence, and Kandel (1986) has found a relationship between depression in adolescence and similar symptomatology in later life (see also Garber *et al.*, 1988; Keller *et al.*, 1988; Zeitlin, 1990; Harrington *et al.*, 1994 and Hammen, 1995).

Merikangas and Angst (1995), in a review of the relevant literature, state that the results of longitudinal studies of clinical samples of depressed adolescents suggest that these young people show a marked recurrence of affective symptoms and syndromes over time. In general, continued depression is most likely among those with an early onset of depression, and depression occurring with substance abuse, anxiety disorders or personality disorders. The poor social functioning of adults with a history of adolescent depression may be associated with its interference with the development of educational, social or occupational skills.

As Cantwell (1990) points out, depression takes a variety of forms in children as well as in adults, and different subtypes in childhood may have different outcomes in adulthood. The interpretation of any links found between depression in childhood and later is complicated by the fact that children with depressive disorders often have other psychiatric disorders, such as anxiety states and disruptive behaviour. It would seem that children who are diagnosed as having a major depressive disorder have a worse outcome than those diagnosed as having an adjustment disorder with depressed mood (Kovacs *et al.*, 1984a, b).

There is a high degree of recovery in a number of cases of depression in middle and late childhood, but the outcome depends on the type of depression (Kovacs and Gatsonis, 1989). In general, according to Kazdin (1990), the findings relating to children and adolescents are similar to those relating to adults, where good recovery rates are reported for episodes of depression but there is a high risk of relapse.

Autism

As autistic children grow older, some improvement is often reported in respect of developing attachments to familiar adults and showing affection towards their parents. The extreme aloofness of many young autistic children may subside (Frith, 1989). A small number become independent enough as adults to find some form of paid employment; and some make good progress, even if still needing a sheltered occupation (Wing, 1980).

However, despite possible changes in behaviour, autism is likely to remain throughout life, and serious social difficulties tend to persist (Lord, 1984; Howlin, 1986). In particular, autistic individuals continue to show a lack of social responsiveness in their interactions with peers, avoiding contact with them and preferring to spend time in solitary routines. Good intelligence is likely to help autistic people to compensate for their handicaps, but many show cognitive deficits severe enough for them to remain classified as retarded throughout their lives (Ritvo *et al.*, 1976).

Schizophrenia

Schizophrenia in childhood or adolescence generally has a gloomy prognosis in terms of the recurrence of psychotic symptoms in adulthood, although recovery is possible (Zeitlin, 1990; Asarnow, 1994). Persistently disturbed interpersonal relationships, in particular, point to a poor outcome (Strauss and Carpenter, 1972).

Eggers (1978), carrying out a twenty-year follow-up of 57 children with schizophrenia before the age of 14 years, found that 11 recovered completely, and altogether about one-half of the sample had improved in mental health. Eggers concluded that the worst prognosis was associated with an onset of schizophrenia before the age of 10 years and in children with previously abnormal personality characteristics (see also Steinberg, 1985).

Steinberg (1985) states that, in cases of schizophrenia arising in adolescence, there is either an early substantial recovery or continuing incapacity frequently resulting in prolonged hospital care. Gillberg, Hellgren and Gillberg (1993) followed up 55 cases, at age 30, of individuals diagnosed in adolescence as suffering from a psychotic condition; they concluded that the outlook for such young people was poor with respect to later psychosocial adjustment. Cawthron *et al.* (1994), too, carrying out a retrospective follow-up of 58 psychotic adolescents between 12 and 17 years, reported that the outcome of schizophrenia in adolescence was poor.

Selective mutism

Not a great deal is known about the long-term consequences of selective mutism in childhood. As Herbert (1991) states, the lack of follow-up data probably reflects difficulties in keeping track of clients over a long period, the initially low incidence of the condition, and the sporadic way in which most therapists come across it. Rutter and Garmezy (1983) suggest that the long-term prognosis is quite good, especially for younger children where this condition begins soon after school entry. Herbert, too, while acknowledging that the use of behavioural techniques does not always provide a quick solution to the problem, considers that children given individual behavioural programmes are likely to respond better than those receiving less focused treatment.

However, Kolvin and Fundudis (1981) report that after a follow-up period lasting ten years, only half of their 24 cases improved. When marked improvement occurred, it did so before the age of ten, suggesting that those who fail to progress by this age may be suffering from a more intractable form of selective mutism. The sample was too small to identify which children were likely to improve, but rather more of those children who did not respond to treatment had parents with personality problems than those who did.

CONCLUSION

This chapter has shown that, although withdrawal and isolation may not always be long-lasting in childhood and adolescence, poor peer relationships are likely to lead to distress and emotional upset, even in the short-term. It is difficult to predict with accuracy what the long-term consequences of withdrawn behaviour may be, since status in the group is subject to change over time, and so many other variables are involved. Shyness in childhood may not have serious implications for mental health in adult life, but rejection, particularly when accompanied by aggression, is often a precursor of later delinquency and poor psychosocial adjustment. In the case of depression, autism and schizophrenia occurring in childhood or adolescence, the prognosis is gloomy, although partial or complete recovery is possible.

It is important to be cautious in the interpretation of any associations found between withdrawal in childhood and later problems of adjustment. Parker and Asher (1987) emphasize that causes and consequences influence one another in a transactional process. The failure to experience inclusion in the group may deprive children of necessary support in their development and contribute to later difficulties. However, it is also feasible that initial poor adjustment may lead to deviant behaviour, which results in low peer acceptance and maladaptive outcome.

Rubin, LeMare and Lollis (1990) trace two developmental pathways leading to long-lasting withdrawal and isolation. One pathway has its beginnings in unsatisfactory parent–child relationships in the early years, which result in inappropriate, negative and perhaps aggressive interchanges with peers. Peer rejection follows, exacerbating tendencies towards excessive engagement in solitary activities. The other pathway relates to children with a temperamental disposition from infancy to show limited responses to social stimulation. As such children grow older, they acquire negative reputations in the peer group and they may also meet with hostile parental reactions if they are difficult to bring up and relate to. Faced with negative or even hostile attitudes on the part of both peers and parents, these children become increasingly withdrawn, anxious and possibly also depressed.

Chapter 7

How Schools and Teachers Can Help

The concerns which withdrawn and isolated pupils raise in their teachers are very varied and there is, therefore, no one way to deal with them. Help is needed, however, if present and future social difficulties are to be alleviated, as previous chapters have shown. An example might serve as an introduction to this chapter, which will then go on to look at what can be done by way of:

- 'whole-school' approaches;
- school management;
- working through the curriculum.

Eddie, in his first year at secondary school, is small and almost totally uncommunicative. He seems to have considerable language problems, allied to learning difficulties. These learning problems were the focus of the statement of his special educational needs which was drawn up in his primary school, and which has now led to Eddie's placement in a small special class for most of his secondary school day. His lack of progress in the primary school convinced the staff there that he should spend an extra year with them, the result being that Eddie is now a year below his previous classmates, with few immediate contacts in his new school. His elder sibling, who offered him some protection for most of the primary stage, moved on to a different secondary school.

At breaktimes Eddie wanders around the playground attempting to avoid large groups of pupils. He has been teased by other pupils but this was dealt with by the Head of Year and by Eddie's mother, who decided that he should come home for lunch, thus avoiding any unwelcome attention. He makes little contact with the other seven pupils in his class and will not even ask for help from his teacher. Without constant supervision, he does virtually no work at all.

What has his school experience so far done for Eddie? Staff believe they have stopped any teasing or bullying; a statement of his special needs has been drawn up and to some extent implemented, although his academic performance and his communicative skills remain poor. The delayed transfer to the secondary stage and his placement there in a special class have not helped to reduce his isolation from his peers. If anything, this is now more pronounced, as the opportunities to establish relationships are somewhat limited, what with the small size of his class and his lunchtime arrangements. Everything has been done in Eddie's best interests but his problems remain. Teachers are anxious to improve his school experiences but are aware that they are failing to do so.

'WHOLE-SCHOOL' APPROACHES

The ethos of the school

In today's educational climate, where competition between schools is being encouraged and security is an ever-present concern, it is difficult to maintain a relaxed, friendly atmosphere where there is room for individual variations. Stress is high among many staff; pupils do not always see the relevance to their own lives and prospects of what they are expected to do.

Pollard and Tann (1987) argue for 'incorporative classrooms' at the primary stage. By this they mean classrooms which are 'consciously designed to enable each child to act as a full participant in class activities and also to feel him or herself to be a valued member of the class' (p. 98). To achieve these aims, co-operation needs to be stressed rather than competition, with more emphasis on effort than on achievement and a respect for all class members whatever their level of success. Teachers, at all stages, need be 'reflective' (Clegg and Billington, 1994), balancing responsibility for each pupil as an individual learner with society's expectations for education. This is no easy task. It is true, however, that if such an atmosphere could be achieved in schools and classrooms, withdrawn and isolated children would be helped. They find evaluation threatening, especially to their self-esteem, and seem unable to acquire status in any way. They participate little in class activities and need encouragement to make any effort at all.

Where the atmosphere in the school is one of co-operation and respect for every member of it, pupils, parents and school staff feel there is a common purpose. While stress is probably inevitable in teaching (Cole and Walker, 1989; Johnson, 1989), teachers find the pressures bearable in a supportive working environment, and pupils see that their views, despite their immaturity (Peters, 1973), contribute to the working of the school as a whole. There is easy communication with parents and they feel welcome in the school (Jowett and Baginsky, 1991).

Such a school is an ideal one. However, when the ethos of the school approximates to one in which the main elements are co-operation, respect, support and welcome, discrimination will be avoided, including racism and sexism. Alienation from school (Docking, 1990a) will also be reduced. As Peters (1973) points out, teachers have to try to be in authority and to be an authority, without being authoritarian. Further discussion of the source and implications of the school ethos (as well as of how it might be changed) can be found in the references given in this section and in Garforth, 1985; Walsh, 1991; Brubacher, Case and Reagan, 1994; Edwards, 1995.

'Whole-school' policies

Disruptive pupils make sure they are never overlooked for long. For withdrawn and isolated children, the situation is somewhat different. Policies on behaviour and discipline, as well as school rules (Coulby and Coulby, 1990), should include reference to the particular problems of pupils whose inadequate social skills leave them vulnerable to isolation or victimization. These policies, like the others which are required in the present educational climate, have to be the result of work by all the staff concerned, agreed by all of them and implemented by all. In the case of school rules, pupils (and parents) also have to be closely involved. Pious expressions of care and concern for those who are lonely or miserable in school, or even afraid to attend, will not be effective. Teachers must recognize the problems faced by withdrawn and isolated pupils and be aware of the guidelines in their 'whole-school' policies (i.e. agreed by everyone) for trying to alleviate these problems.

Dealing with bullying is a good example of the value of a whole-school exercise, calling for an agreed policy known to all concerned. The naming of a 'key' person who is easily contacted ensures the implementation of the policy (Roberts, 1994a). Details of the contents of an anti-bullying policy can be found in Tattum (1993), Sharp and Smith (1994) and DFE (1994a), and a discussion of the difficulties which may arise in drawing up such a policy, and whole-school policies in general, in Hargreaves and Hopkins (1991). Where implementation of policies involve changes in staff thinking or school organization, it may take time and effort to alter previous procedures (or lack of them). Fullan (1991) and Hargreaves and Hopkins (1991) discuss how change can be accomplished and 'institutionalized', that is, become part of the culture of the whole school and its pupils. Anti-racism policies and their particular difficulties are looked at in Bagley (1992).

While the construction of whole-school policies is time-consuming, because all staff members need to be involved and in agreement, there are advantages:

● guidelines for action have been clearly set out;
● newcomers to the school, adults or pupils, can quickly understand accepted procedures;
● 'supply' teachers can fit in easily;
● school governors, who are, after all, ultimately responsible for trying to ensure that pupils' special educational needs are met, are also in agreement with the approved procedure.

In a number of the case studies which have been presented so far (e.g. *Peter* in Chapter 5, p.76), the comment has been made that staff were well aware of the children's difficulties, with regard to their social relationships, but were unsure about what to do to help. The existence of a policy which has resulted from discussion by the whole staff and which covers all types of behaviour, not just 'acting out' behaviour, must be helpful to all concerned.

Counselling

The emphasis here is not on professional counselling in schools (see Chapter 9 for a discussion of this), although this can do much to support withdrawn and isolated pupils and help them towards establishing effective interpersonal relationships (Cowie and Pecherek, 1994). The suggestion is rather that all staff have a part to play in counselling, especially class teachers at the primary stage. Enhancing pupils' views of themselves as members of the primary school community (Gurney, 1990) can only be helpful to them when they transfer to the larger, more impersonal conditions of secondary school.

The way in which the ethos of the school affects all aspects of the lives of those who are its members has already been looked at briefly in this chapter. Concern for the individual is, of course, vital within the classroom. It is important that teachers should:

● be aware of those in their class who are unhappy or ill at ease in interpersonal relationships;
● find time to talk to these pupils in a non-threatening, relaxed manner;
● avoid adding to the stress which many of these withdrawn and isolated pupils feel in a setting where individual performance is often commented on or working effectively with others is expected;
● use praise, attention and reward sensitively to increase these pupils' self-esteem, without singling them out unduly;
● work along with parents to try to develop social skills where these are inadequate.

Lang (1990) stresses that what is required is planning and review. Leaving support of the individual pupil to chance is not likely to be successful, because it is only too easy to overlook withdrawn and isolated pupils when coping with the whole class. They need to be in the teacher's mind when lesson strategies are being considered, so that they find it fairly easy to make their contribution because of the tasks set or the way groups are arranged. In turn, the success or otherwise of the strategies has to be reviewed and adapted if necessary. In particular, the reaction of withdrawn and isolated children to noise, lively discussion and movement between activities should be watched to see how these affect response and performance.

Teachers who are in daily contact with pupils are well placed to notice changes in reaction which may indicate stress or trauma and, at the immediate level (Hamblin, 1993), they have a responsibility to do something about the situation (Galloway, 1990). At the same time, because teachers are not usually trained to be counsellors, they must realize their limitations and know when more intensive support than they can give is needed. Whole-school policies should give clear indications of how pupils who may be under considerable strain outside school can be counselled, so that there is recognition of the difficulties they are facing and sympathetic, constructive concern.

Individual counselling sessions are more likely to be available at the secondary level, but a separation of academic and pastoral-counselling activities is not always the best approach (Bulman and Jenkins, 1988). It may be more effective to plan curriculum content in such a way that opportunities arise within the selected topics for consideration of personal concerns. General discussion can help specific individual problems and suggest potential action which the pupil under stress might not have considered, including asking for help outside the normal class setting. Such help should be available at both the primary and secondary stages, whether from different levels of school management or from other professionals. Personal and social education within the normal curriculum will be discussed later in this chapter.

Teachers themselves are under considerable stress (Dunham, 1992). Their role is often ambiguous and open to conflicting pressures, a situation which should help them to appreciate pupil stress. How to alleviate teacher stress is covered in Dunham (1992) and Gray and Freeman (1988), among others. As in the case of pupils under stress, teachers need to feel they have support from others, are at least holding their own in difficult circumstances, and have access to further help or additional self-help skills (such as relaxation or meditation) as required. Withdrawn and isolated pupils may not be seen by teachers as sources of stress. It is all the more important that positive, co-operative strategies exist in schools to help these pupils. Otherwise, they may continue to fall below their teachers' attention level or be left without help because of pressures of time, curriculum content or more vociferous 'acting out' behaviour.

SCHOOL MANAGEMENT

The way in which a school is managed lies at the heart of its effectiveness, academically and socially. To achieve quality of schooling, there must be continuous, dynamic movement, resulting from collaborative evaluation of present policies and aimed at achieving clear and agreed educational aims (Holly, 1994). Only top and middle management can provide the underlying stability which can enable change to be creative and constructive as opposed to chaotic or ephemeral. This section will look at some of the ways in which effective management might be achieved with regard to the school as a whole, what goes on within the classroom, and relationships outside the classroom.

Democratic consultation

If a school is managed in an authoritarian way, with status strictly dependent on the established hierarchy, then co-operation and collaboration with, and concern for, those who appear to make only a minimal contribution to its life do not feature very highly. Research studies (e.g. Brown and McIntyre, 1993 and Cooper and McIntyre, 1996) have shown the effects of different organizational and educational strategies on pupil learning and have stressed the extent to which successful management of learning depends on how far teachers feel they are appreciated, supported and facilitated in their classroom work. Teachers reflect in their classroom behaviour the strategies which they themselves experience. And it is tempting to extend this finding by saying that the way in which pupils interact with each other also models senior management behaviour.

'Restructuring' schools (see Hargreaves, 1994) ought, in theory, to help withdrawn and isolated pupils. Traditional patterns of schooling have tended to lead to their being overlooked, inasmuch as they make few demands on teachers. Hargreaves points out that restructuring includes attempts to 're-define relationships between teachers, students, principals and parents in fundamental ways' (p. 243), involving positive classroom environments and innovative curricula. Schools are seen as becoming more responsive to all who are part of the school community. Some of the ways in which this responsiveness might be achieved have already been touched upon in this chapter.

To give pupils a more active and participating role in their learning (Kyriacou, 1986) entails ensuring that they have the social skills, as well as the educational competence, to make such a contribution (see later in this chapter).

Participation, whoever is concerned (pupils, members of staff, parents), is very easily inhibited. Sotto (1994) lists seven constraints on participation, including the conflict in the teacher's role between the desire to impart information as quickly as possible and the hope of involvement from others concerned. He says that, in spite of themselves, teachers are 'like a coach who never passes the ball' (p. 151). If the participant feels that any response made will be evaluated, involvement is even harder to achieve. Working with parents of withdrawn and isolated children is a good example of the problems involved in participation. They may be unwilling to recognize that there is any need for action at all; they may not welcome moves to increase their child's relationships with his or her peers; they may be too overwhelmed by their own difficulties to try to participate. As senior management has often found out to its cost, democratic consultation takes time and patience if it is to become sufficiently well established as a strategy that will effectively involve those concerned.

A great deal has been written recently about all the points raised in this section. How to avoid the dangers inherent in management change is dealt with in, for example, Paisey (1981), Shipman (1990), Bottery (1992), Caldwell and Spinks (1992) and Preedy (1993). Sotto (1994) also discusses how the constraints that he enumerates can be overcome. Cangelosi (1988) looks at how pupil co-operation can be increased and Docking (1990b) advises on parent co-operation at the primary stage. The secondary school is examined in Harber and Meighan (1989). They quote E. M. Forster as saying: 'So two cheers for Democracy: one because it admits variety and two because it permits criticism. Two cheers are quite enough: there is no occasion to give three' (p. x).

Classroom considerations

The basic organization of the classroom, with regard to seating arrangements, resource areas and teacher's station, reveals a great deal about the nature of the relationships between teacher and pupils as well as between pupil and pupil (Waterhouse, 1990). If teachers want to help withdrawn and isolated pupils, they could begin by considering what messages are conveyed by their classroom setting, the way in which educational tasks are allocated, the teaching strategies they adopt and the way in which they evaluate the success of their lessons. Where the forms or organization and interaction adopted by school staff are deliberately intended to benefit pupils' social and personal development, as well as their academic development, schools achieve effectiveness and promote their pupils' feelings of self-worth (Cooper, Smith and Upton, 1994).

What does this mean in practice? Teachers really have to work their way to their own solutions in the light of the kind of persons they are and the pupils in their current class. But the following questions may help to point the way forward.

- How far do teachers themselves exemplify the kind of interpersonal behaviour they feel might help withdrawn children? Body posture, expression, eye contact and gesture communicate to class members how teachers see their pupils as learners and as individuals (Bull and Solity, 1987).
- How is entry to the classroom organized and seating arranged or rearranged? When other pupils push and shove withdrawn pupils to the back of the queue, protest about their placement in a group, make it clear that such withdrawn children are only chosen as a last resort and fail to listen to their contributions, nothing is done to reduce feelings of isolation and failure.
- How does the teacher deal with derision or laughter aimed at particular pupils (Woods, 1990)?
- What tasks are allocated to withdrawn pupils and how realistic is it to expect them to succeed in what they have to do? To set learning challenges which are too low is as bad as setting those which are far too high (as the example of *Wayne* in Chapter 5 showed). Whatever teaching approach is used – whole class, group, pairs or individual – withdrawn children have to be adequately challenged if their completion of the task is to lead to a feeling of satisfaction. It is seldom possible to strike this level of difficulty on the spur of the moment. It requires careful consideration, knowledge of the pupil and planning, often imaginative planning. Perhaps because of these requirements, withdrawn and isolated pupils are at a particular disadvantage at the secondary stage, where they are faced with a series of teachers, pressures of time are constant and planning can be knocked awry by any disruption.

Withdrawn and isolated children pose problems whatever form of classroom organization is adopted. They tend to be overlooked when the class is taught as a whole, yet grouping or pairing may not be the answer. Groups often do not achieve the combined contribution from their members that teachers hope for and may, in fact, be just a collection of individuals working as best they can on their own (Galton, Simon and Croll, 1980; Tann, 1981; Bennett *et al.*, 1984). Where the group does cohere, there can be considerable social and/or cognitive benefits, making grouping a useful strategy for teachers to consider among others (Bennett and Dunne, 1992). Practical advice on setting up and managing groups and their activities can be found in Dunne and Bennett (1990).

Pairing of pupils can also be effective. This certainly seemed to be the case for **Christopher**. At 8 years of age, Christopher was a lonely, over-anxious, tearful boy, eager to help adults but virtually friendless in school. He had become friends with another isolated boy, who was overweight and unpopular, but this child had a prolonged absence from school because of a congenital heart problem. Christopher's teacher realized that placing him in a group was not going to be successful as he had a dread of speaking in front of others and found oral lessons, such as Welsh or Drama, almost unbearable. She decided to increase the use of paired working arrangements in the class and carefully selected the pairs, choosing for Christopher's partner a boy, Toby, who was rather quiet but well-organized and able to mix with the others in the class. Toby gave Christopher the support he needed without dominating him and, while neither boy was academically very gifted, they worked conscientiously and Christopher achieved a level of performance and success above his usual. Pollard and Tann (1987) point out that, once pairs have been established in this way, they can at times join another pair to discuss findings. Gradually groups can be built up in a 'pyramid' fashion.

'Peer tutoring', another form of co-operative learning, takes many forms but basically involves a 'tutor' who has greater skill or knowledge helping one who has less. As Topping (1988) points out, 'the quality of the teaching . . . may not quite match that of professional teachers but [it is] suffused with the rosy glow of companionship' (p. 4). It is not only the tutee who gains from this kind of pairing but also the tutor, whose self-esteem is enhanced by the responsibility placed upon him or her. Older pupils can help younger ones and parents can also be involved when the idea of tutoring is extended beyond the classroom (Topping, 1995).

Classroom management has, therefore, a great deal to contribute to how withdrawn and isolated pupils can be encouraged to see themselves as achievers in a social setting. The plight of *Eddie* was described at the beginning of this chapter. Perhaps more effort should have been made to begin to develop contacts at a social level rather than concentrating solely on his meagre academic skills, an emphasis which, almost inevitably, made him feel worse about himself. He also had his problems in the playground and some attention must be given to this important aspect.

Breaktimes

Ross and Ryan (1994) comment that the playground is a social system 'which is based on unspoken rules, values and codes, all too often rooted in an ethic of power and powerlessness' (p. 173). For withdrawn and isolated pupils, time at school spent outside the classroom is a particular trial. They have no power and no friends who might help to protect them. They are vulnerable to harassment, if not outright bullying.

Yet breaktime experiences are valuable for many pupils, allowing them to practise their developing social skills and cement tentative relationships. Joining in playground activities can help active learning in the classroom and offer opportunities to show different abilities and skills which are not classroom-related (Blatchford and Sharp, 1994). Can these benefits be extended to those who, because of their inadequate social skills, inhibition, race or sex find themselves excluded rather than included?

- Again, decisions have to be taken by all concerned – school staff, supervisors, parents and pupils. Without such collaboration, any decisions taken are unlikely to be fully implemented.
- The playground environment itself needs to be considered, so that the best use is made of the space available and suitable areas are set aside for quiet activities as well as organized games or running and chasing.
- The environment needs to have within it enhanced opportunities for various activities. It is not just young children who require play equipment.
- Staff and supervisors should be aware of those pupils who never participate fully in any activity and pass on their concerns to the appropriate person (e.g. class teacher or head of year).

Practical advice on how to improve the playground experiences of all pupils can be found in Ross and Ryan (1990) and Blatchford and Sharp (1994).

Looking for ways of improving the school grounds is not the whole story. Training may be required for supervisors or voluntary helpers (Fell, 1994; Sharp, 1994) and regular monitoring of any changes is essential. Secondary schools in particular need to be alert to the possibilities for intimidation and discrimination which many school playgrounds present and not just react to crises when they occur (as happened in the case of *Eddie*). Teasing has to be distinguished from bullying, and rough-and-tumble play from fighting (Mooney, Creeser and Blatchford, 1991; Boulton, 1996). The impact of social skills training (see next section) can be lost if relationships which begin to emerge tentatively in the classroom are wiped out by playground experiences.

WORKING THROUGH THE CURRICULUM

There is a great deal of interest today in what makes a 'good' school. Some may place emphasis on comparing achievements at different levels (or even across different countries) but others have shown that if the school is not a success as a social institution, the cohesion and drive needed to reach high standards in academic work may not exist or may be present only in certain groups of pupils (see, for example, Rutter *et al.*, 1979). Fontana (1994) notes that the curriculum has a considerable part to play in whether pupils feel part of the school or alienated from it. If the curriculum is to be positive and purposive, it needs not only to be relevant but also to engage pupils through the opportunities it offers for social and emotional, as well as cognitive, development.

Social skills training (SST)

Programmes in this area have tended to concentrate either on developing prosocial behaviour (e.g. play; friendship; conversation; helping others) or cognitive processes, such as problem-solving, role-playing, or taking on the perspective of others. Sometimes both aims are pursued. A number of these programmes exist and offer useful guidelines for teachers (e.g. Spivack, Platt and Shure, 1976; Oden, 1980; Spence, 1980; Ellis and Whittington, 1981; Wiltshire Education Department Psychological and Advisory Services, 1989). More will be said about SST in Chapter 9.

It should be noted, however, that SST approaches have often been aimed at disruptive pupils and have attempted to establish a fairly wide range of behaviours at a variety of ages (Herbert, 1986). Perhaps because of these factors, evidence for the long-term success of most SST programmes is sparse. It would seem, however, that opportunities to practise useful interpersonal skills in a supportive environment should be beneficial, especially for younger children. Teachers of pre-school children are particularly aware of the importance of social skills training as children enter formal schooling. For older pupils, the encouragement of personal and social skills, either alongside or within the National Curriculum, may be the way forward. As with all skills, however, practise is essential.

Personal and social education (PSE)

To consider personal and social education separately from social skills training emphasizes that the two concepts do have distinct differences, although it is true that the skills which are the focus of SST have to be displayed if personal and social development is to be considered adequate. PSE, however, is a wider concept than SST and encompasses a major educational aim, namely the socialization of young people. Some might argue that this is the school's major aim, being more important than the acquisition of knowledge. It may be more accurate to say that both these educational aims are essential and each contributes to the other. Indeed, so much can be included in personal and social education that it is in danger of becoming merely a 'pot-pourri' (Pring, 1984) of vague hopes and poorly defined skills.

If such a danger is to be averted, careful consideration needs to be given by the staff to the content of a PSE programme and its status in the curriculum as a whole. Fontana (1994) defines a relevant curriculum as one that teaches 'information and skills which help [children] understand themselves and others, and which not only help prepare them for a vocation but also enrich their leisure time' (p. 48). The cognitive and social overtones are evident in this definition. It is also clear that PSE ought by definition to be relevant to all pupils and, instead of being an extra which is tagged on and even seen by pupils as unimportant, should provide an over-arching framework for what happens in school. What is not required is 'lack of coordination, absence of support from unconvinced heads and sometimes mediocre practice resulting from teachers working in isolation' (Hargreaves *et al.*, 1988, p. 6).

At the primary stage, PSE programmes may be easier to devise than at the secondary stage, especially when withdrawn and isolated children are considered. These children may well:

- not know how to approach others efficiently, join in with others effectively or make an acceptable contribution to the group effort;
- never have had a friend and so never have learned the benefits and vicissitudes of friendship (Roffey, Tarrant and Majors, 1994);
- not have the body language or linguistic abilities to enable them to interact with their peer group in a working relationship.

Leech and Wooster (1986) suggest that activities designed to build up friendships are appropriate for primary school pupils. There are three stages in their programme: encouraging discussion of what class members have in common in order to learn more about each other; exploring rules and values and what effect these have on individuals; and beginning to understand the point of view of others, children and adults, so that co-operative work and play become possible. This programme could seem threatening to pupils with low self-esteem. It is important, therefore, that:

- the atmosphere in the classroom is relaxed and non-competitive;
- pupils' privacy is respected – children should be able to 'pass' or contribute when they wish;
- models of behaviour, withdrawn and more forthcoming, are presented in story or picture form, encouraging imaginative discussion; by listening to what others say and do, withdrawn children may come to realize the range of potential reactions open to them which they had never previously considered; the use of film, TV and tapes can also provide models of behaviour, as can the use of drama, mime and puppetry;
- materials and activities are selected sensitively and their implications carefully worked out beforehand.

The National Curriculum provides guidelines for this kind of work in the early school years, moving from consideration of 'Myself' at home and school to wider issues. Coming to see oneself as an individual and empathizing with others should help the social development of withdrawn and isolated children, as should cognitively-oriented activities such as problem-solving or thinking up different endings to stories. It may be that they will also benefit from the effect of the PSE programme on the other class members if it encourages increased care and concern for others.

At the secondary stage, there are considerable problems in establishing effective personal and social education programmes and withdrawn or isolated pupils are particularly vulnerable. Pressures on an individual's self-esteem increase at adolescence. Normal development leads to concern over personal appearance and performance and to sensitivity to reactions from others and acceptance by them (see Chapter 2). *Robin*, who was discussed in Chapter 3, is an example of how isolated pupils interpret (or misinterpret) the behaviour of fellow school members and how the social pressures they feel affect their attitude to school.

Ryder and Campbell (1988) present four models of PSE, which they extend to include Health Education.

- *Pastoral/individual* Programmes of this type aim to promote individual self-awareness and self-esteem. Pupils work in groups and constructive feedback from group members or other groups is encouraged. (The problems faced by withdrawn pupils in this type of approach, as well as the advantages, have already been discussed.)
- *Educational/rational* These programmes have mainly a cognitive, problem-solving emphasis and encourage pupils to examine their beliefs and behaviour closely to improve their within- and out-of-school performance.
- *Radical/political* Social situations are the focus here and how they can be changed through collective action. Shared responsibility is stressed.
- *Medical/traditional* Emphasis is on the imparting of information with the intention of establishing 'pre-determined, approved behaviour' (p. 66).

Ryder and Campbell go on to suggest that aspects from all these models may need to be included if PSE (they would add in H for Health) is to be effective, most emphasis being given to the first three of the models.

A further problem with regard to PSE is how it should be timetabled. It may be theoretically easy to argue that all subjects contribute to PSE. In practice, it becomes clear that personal development and academic objectives do not always blend together within the constraints of a subject-oriented curriculum. McNiff (1985) discusses the effects of seeing PSE (at the secondary stage) either as part of the whole curriculum, or as operated through form tutors, or as part of religious education, health and sex education, integrated studies or careers education. Clearly different forms of organization lead to different outcomes. For withdrawn and isolated pupils, the vital consideration would seem to be the extent to which they can become involved in a carefully planned programme which the rest of the class members are prepared to accept. The absence of academic pressures may to some extent compensate for the difficulties withdrawn pupils have with informal approaches which focus on the very areas where they feel most inadequate.

Other curricular areas

If personal and social education is to assume a position of importance in any school, however, consideration of the issues involved cannot really be confined to one specific area of the curriculum, whatever that area is called. Withdrawn and isolated children do need to be considered in every lesson so that their particular needs affect its content and organization. It may be that, if they lack specific social skills, direct experience of prosocial behaviours can be offered in certain timetable slots. But opportunities to continue to think about such new skills, see the effect of changes in behaviour on how others react, or practise interacting with peers and adults, should occur throughout the school day.

This does not mean that any one form of classroom organization has to be implemented. Small group work or pairing may be more appropriate in some subjects than others. For example, practical subjects, like Science or PE, lend themselves to working in small groups. But so do English, RE, History and Geography at times, and they also offer opportunities for the whole class to discuss events in the light of how people behaved or might behave. Discussion also plays a very important part in Art, Music and Drama. Even if withdrawn pupils do not contribute much, they are made aware of a variety of possible actions and their consequences. Teachers often hope that prosocial attitudes and behaviour will be 'caught' and may not need to be 'taught'. While this may be so for pupils whose social and emotional development is progressing adequately, for those who cannot or will not join in, deliberate indication of alternative behaviour may be essential. Teachers clearly need to consider the implications for their own classrooms of personal and social education in its widest sense. A useful framework is provided by Galloway (1989) for the primary sector and Mitchell (1991) for the secondary.

Consideration of the needs of withdrawn and isolated pupils can be linked to consideration of other groups who may also need support. For example, how does the content of the History or Geography lesson represent other nations and their peoples? Is there equality of opportunity for girls and boys in Mathematics and Science? Care has to be taken to ensure that the materials used in any lesson 'do not contain gross stereotypes, glaring omissions and serious distortions' (Burgess-Macey, 1992, p. 270). Indeed, teachers are at risk of stereotyping withdrawn and isolated individuals and developing attitudes towards them or expectations of them which reinforce that stereotype rather than trying to find an approach which would enable them to be more educationally and socially successful.

Eddie, who was described at the beginning of this chapter, does not fit easily into the proposals for positive action made in this section. Because of his communication and learning difficulties, he was not able to take an active part in any form of discussion at the secondary stage. Had his lack of social skills been tackled early in his school career, his difficulties might not have been so marked. His poor speech development must have been noted from pre-school onwards but, for whatever reason, this had been largely left to remedy itself. While it may be the case that children who are reluctant to speak or who produce poor speech are helped when they go to school and have to communicate with others, it may also happen that they are overwhelmed by the school's communicative demands, especially if they find it very difficult to keep up with what the other children are learning. With the benefit of hindsight, it could be said that probably a statement of Eddie's special educational needs should have been drawn up even before he entered school so that teachers, therapists and his parents knew what might best be done to help him. What was eventually done was too late, and the fact that his primary school retained him for an extra year would seem to indicate that his teachers realized this. When social and emotional development is the cause for concern, being proactive is better than being reactive – in other words, it is best to consider how the situation can be helped sooner rather than later.

PSE across the curriculum

It is current practice in schools to see personal and social education as a major cross-curricular dimension (along with equal opportunities and multicultural education). A good argument could, as has already been said, be put forward for it to be the major dimension, incorporating the other two. Watkins (1995) argues that all pupils are entitled to personal–social experiences which enable them to maximize their academic achievement, both at and after school, and lead a satisfying life when adult.

No-one could disagree with these aspirations. The problems lie in how they are to be achieved. Watkins presents a list of objectives through which this might be accomplished, as does Hamblin (1986), who distinguishes a pastoral programme from a pastoral curriculum. By that he indicates the difference between what is done in one specific part of the curriculum and what is to be seen as an overarching concern of all school experience.

Withdrawn and isolated pupils have, as has already been emphasized, particular problems in this view of PSE as involving the whole curriculum. Basically, what they have to acquire is:

- the ability to interact with others to a degree and with a competence that satisfies their needs, both educational and social;
- the ability to 'decentralize' (Roffey, Tarrant and Majors, 1994), that is, to be able to see things from other points of view.

While they may never become as skilled in these areas as some other pupils, they can benefit from opportunities to develop interpersonal skills when these have become an accepted part of the school's ethos and total approach. There are dangers.

- Withdrawn pupils can be overlooked in this curriculum too, especially if they have specific problems such as learning difficulties, partial hearing, a mother tongue which is other than English, physical disabilities or poor language development.
- PSE aspects can themselves become overlooked. While everyone, teachers, pupils and parents, may agree on their importance, pressures of time and subject-based demands may reduce the visibility of long-term aims of education as against short-term subject objectives. The specific problems of some disruptive pupils then exacerbate the situation.
- Teachers may feel that the aims of PSE, while admirable, are too distant or too ideal ever to be achievable. There is a temptation to pay lip-service to them while concentrating on something else. To go back to *Eddie* (or indeed to many of the other children described in this volume), his isolation in school had so many facets that his teachers may simply not have known where to begin. To improve his reading skills may have seemed a practical area to tackle but, in fact, without considerable attention being given to his social and emotional development, his inability to cope with school was likely to persist.

The best ways to avoid such dangers may be to be aware of them and constantly vigilant. It is unlikely that the social competencies which withdrawn and isolated individuals need for adequate personal development can be acquired successfully out of school, without well-planned, in-school learning opportunities.

CONCLUSION

Unless the whole school is involved in decision-making and planning, as well as in evaluating the development of any decisions and plans, change is unlikely. At the moment, few schools appear to be as concerned about withdrawn and isolated pupils as they are about disruptive and aggressive pupils. To remedy this situation, all aspects of life in schools need to be considered, from the whole ethos of the school to the daily management of each classroom. Withdrawn and isolated pupils do not draw attention to themselves. Indeed, they may deliberately expend energy in making themselves as invisible as possible to teachers and fellow pupils alike.

It is on class teachers that the success of any strategy to improve pupils' interpersonal relationships depends. They are able to see what is happening and gauge the effects of inadequate adjustment. By incorporating opportunities to develop social skills in their presentation of the curriculum, they can offer specific help to pupils in difficulties. General support can come from the existence of a whole-school policy, which is known and accepted by all staff, pupils and parents. This policy, through school rules, strategies for action when problems arise, and clear identification of concerned members of staff, should alleviate distress felt in or out of the classroom. It is not so much a question of finding room in the National Curriculum for teaching personal–social skills, but rather of seeing the whole curriculum as offering opportunities to increase pupils' self-esteem and social development. 'The fundamental question is how we educate, not what we educate about or where we do it' (Whitaker, 1995).

It has been difficult to be specific in this chapter. There is little agreement in the literature as to what being socially competent involves either at school or after school (see, for example, Durkin, 1995). Cultural values determine what is seen as competence in any country at any particular time. Adaptation is crucial to enable individuals to function in our present society. This point of view inevitably leaves schools with few specific, generally agreed aims for personal–social programmes.

Without help, withdrawn and isolated children and young people are unlikely to be able to make the most of their abilities, including their cognitive abilities. What schools have to do is to work out how best they can encourage co-operative, productive interpersonal relationships in the particular circumstances in which they find themselves. There are so many differences between schools and individual pupils that only rather generalized guidelines can be given.

This chapter has attempted to provide some of the background for discussions on a number of aspects of school and class management which might help withdrawn and isolated pupils, on the curricular implications of programmes aimed at personal and social development and on the particular problems which some pupils face in and out of the classroom. It is important that staff have the opportunity to take part in such discussions and formulate policies which take withdrawn and isolated pupils into consideration. The next chapter will look at what might be done to help by others concerned, especially parents and peers.

Chapter 8

The Role of Parents and Peers in Helping Withdrawn Children

THE ROLE OF PARENTS

The effects of parental attitudes and child-rearing practices on the social development of children have been discussed elsewhere in this book. The importance of parental co-operation with the school and support services is also emphasized in several chapters.

Chapter 5, in particular, showed that all aspects of a child's development are affected from the earliest days by the ways in which their parents behave towards them, and it stressed the need for children to experience affection and flexible yet consistent discipline from their carers. The chapter drew attention to certain tendencies, e.g.,

- children whose main carers are lacking in warmth tend to be withdrawn and dispirited, with few friends;
- children who are neglected and/or abused at home are at risk of becoming passive and withdrawn;
- family discord often leads to children being unhappy and possibly unable to make or sustain relationships with peers.

However, the chapter stressed that it is difficult to generalize about the effects of particular child-rearing styles. The parent–child relationship cannot be considered in isolation from other influences on the family; and parenting is a two-way process, with children themselves making a significant contribution to the way in which relationships at home develop.

Malik and Furman (1993) advise that the clinician dealing with peer relation problems should ascertain whether there are also family difficulties which require attention, although it is not certain that the treatment of family problems will eliminate any problems of peer relationships which have developed. Family therapy is discussed in Chapter 9 (pp. 151–2).

Close relationships between parents and school will help to ensure that a child's problems over peer relationships will be identified and dealt with at an early stage. In recent years, home–school collaboration has improved to a considerable extent. Such co-operation is achieved through a variety of means, including informal contact; regular meetings between teachers and parents to discuss individual children; parent–teacher associations; home visits by teachers; and partnership projects seeking to encourage and support parents in teaching academic and social skills to their children. Parents are becoming increasingly involved in the development of the curriculum, school policies, records of progress and provision for children with special needs (Chazan, 1992; Gascoigne, 1995; Bastiani and Wolfendale, 1996). However, involvement in school decision-making processes is still often limited to a small number of parents, and parents with considerable problems of their own are the least likely to seek contact with schools (Hughes, Wikely and Nash, 1994; Malek, 1996).

This chapter will discuss parental supervision and management of peer interaction, with particular reference to the role of parents in helping or hindering the development of social competence and ability to resolve conflicts in their children, within and outside the home.

Parental supervision and management of peer interaction

There is much variability in parents' perceptions of their role in supervising and managing their children's interaction with their peers (Dunn and McGuire, 1992). Some parents prefer to grant their children considerable independence in developing their peer relationships; others consider it their province to keep a close watch on how their children behave towards other children. Such parents may attempt to control both the frequency and type of social interactions in which their children engage, in the hope that the children will learn to behave correctly (Rubin and Sloman, 1984). They will intervene frequently in any social activities involving their children that they have the opportunity to observe. They are likely to reward what they consider to be socially appropriate actions.

Finnie and Russell (1988) stress that the importance and characteristics of the parents' role in relation to children's social activities may change markedly as the children grow older. However, they acknowledge that even in mid-childhood and adolescence parents have a part to play in guiding and assisting their children in their peer relationships, though mostly in more indirect ways such as discussion and consultation.

Much will depend on the reactions of children themselves to parental intervention in their social life. As Lollis, Ross and Tate (1991) caution, researchers need to be aware of the influence of children on their parents as well as the influence of parents on their children. Some children will resent any parental interference in their interaction with friends and other peers. This may occur at the primary school stage, but will be particularly the case during adolescence. Many adolescents go through a phase of reacting adversely to parental dictates or even advice on any issue, but especially in regard to their social relationships at school or in the neighbourhood. During the teenage years, it will be very difficult for parents to exercise their authority when, for example, they do not wish their children to associate with peers who have delinquent tendencies or are taking drugs. Parents need, therefore, to handle discussions with their children about peer interaction with great tact and sensitivity.

Parental supervision and social competence

Parke and Bhavnagri (1988) point out that parental management can produce both negative and positive consequences for children's competence in forming and maintaining relationships with peers. Positive outcomes include the ability of children to take turns, co-operate well in play with others, and show persistence in collaborative activities. On the negative side, parents who continue to manage their children's relationships actively when this is no longer necessary may be curtailing or retarding social and emotional growth by denying children the opportunity to learn, practise and implement their emerging social skills independently.

As Putallaz and Heflin (1990) assert, a friendly, warm yet instructive home environment is likely to be one in which children engage in and discuss social behaviour. If children are brought up in a family setting where visitors, including the children's friends, are given a welcome and social gatherings are encouraged, they will be helped to develop positive social attitudes. If, however, the parents are inward-looking and reclusive, discouraging their children from bringing their friends into the home, the children may well model their own social behaviour on their parents' negative attitudes to others.

In the case of young children, there is evidence that they show higher levels of social competence when parents supervise their activities with others (Dunn and McGuire, 1992). For example, MacDonald and Parke (1984) studied the relationship between father–child and mother–child play and children's competence with pre-school peers (aged 3–4 years). They found that the stylistic differences of both parents were related to popularity ratings in school and the quality of peer interaction, though in different ways for boys and girls. The popular boys had parents who actively participated in the play sessions and aroused emotional reactions such as laughter, mothers who were verbally stimulating, and fathers who were physically playful but not directive. The popular girls had physically playful and emotion-arousing but non-directive fathers, and mothers who were directive.

Ladd and Golter (1988) carried out a study of the relationship between parents' efforts to initiate and monitor children's peer contacts and the qualities of young children's peer relations in and outside school. 'Monitoring' included both direct (being involved in children's activities) and indirect (not involved, but aware of what was going on) methods of supervision. The parents of 58 children, aged between 49 and 68 months, completed diaries of their practices with regard to initiating and monitoring their children's contacts with peers. On this basis, they were classified as high or low initiators, direct or indirect monitors. In school, the children were observed in class, assessed by their teachers and rated sociometrically by their peers. Ladd and Golter concluded that parents who initiated a high proportion of peer contacts tended to have children who had a larger number of different play partners and more consistent companions in non-school settings. For boys but not for girls, higher levels of parental initiation were also associated with greater acceptance by peers and lower levels of peer rejection in school. Neither direct nor indirect forms of parental monitoring were related to children's peer relations in non-school settings, but directive styles were predictive of children's poor social adjustment in school.

The evidence about the effects of parental management of their children's social relationships is less clear in the case of older children. Steinberg (1986) found that adolescents whose parents monitored their activities after school and were not reluctant to exercise their authority were less likely to be susceptible to undesirable peer pressure to engage in anti-social activities. However, Ladd, Muth and Hart (1991) report that parental supervision of older children is related to lower levels of competence in interacting with peers. They suggest that such parental management may be both a cause of and a response to children's behaviour: children with higher levels of social competence may be granted more independence from their parents. Putallaz (1987) also recognizes that children's behaviour may produce particular responses in their mothers: difficult, squabbling children may arouse disagreeable responses from their mothers, while pleasant, compliant children may facilitate positive maternal behaviour.

On the basis of their own and others' research, Russell and Finnie (1990) consider that the links between the social skills of children and those of their parents could be due to modelling or genetic factors. They point out that it has to be recognized that many home variables are likely to be associated with children's competence in their relationships with peers, and that the links between parent and child behaviour are unlikely to be directly between specific experiences and specific peer skills.

Parental supervision and management of their children's peer interactions will be considered further below, with reference to two main aspects:

- the connection between parental supervision of peer interactions and low sociometric status;
- how the responses of parents in conflicts between children may affect social development.

Parental supervision and low sociometric status

It is desirable that the problems of children who are failing to make satisfactory peer relationships should be identified and dealt with at an early stage, but Rubin, LeMare and Lollis (1990) warn that, as far as parents are concerned, early identification has its hazards. They argue that, during the pre-school and early primary school years, teachers may alert parents to problems of withdrawal and anxiety experienced by pupils. Such knowledge may lead parents, especially those already inclined to non-affectionate, insensitive or hostile attitudes towards their children, to take maladaptive courses of action. They may be motivated to teach autocratically academic or social skills deficient in their child's repertoire, or else to distance themselves psychologically or physically from the child. The combination of what takes place in the family circle and the teachers' perceptions may reinforce the child's feelings of anxiety and insecurity.

A number of studies, mostly involving young children, have suggested that parental attitudes and practices are related to children's status in the peer group. For example, Finnie and Russell (1988) have studied differences in the help and supervision given by the mothers of popular, rejected and neglected children. They compared mothers of pre-school children of high social status (HSS) (mean age 4.8 years) with those with children of low social status (LSS). In one study that they carried out, mothers of HSS and LSS children differed in their supervisory behaviour when asked to help their children to join in the play of an unknown pair (dyad) of the same sex. The mothers of the HSS children encouraged them to integrate into the play of the others without modifying the essential nature of the activity as established by the dyad. The mothers of the LSS children were less skilful: they avoided the task, or attempted to use their authority in a hostile way to gain entry for their child, or else disrupted the ongoing play by asking questions. In a second study, mothers of HSS children showed more knowledge about effective social behaviour, particularly in respect of their own supervisory role, than mothers of LSS children.

Roopnarine and Adams (1987) studied the interactional teaching patterns of mothers and fathers with children who were popular, moderately popular or unpopular at school. They used a structured animal puzzle of nineteen pieces to examine how parents monitor their children (aged 46 to 60 months). The parents of popular children used more explanations than the parents of moderately popular or unpopular children, with the mothers intervening more than the fathers with explanations, suggestions and questions. The investigators concluded that social interaction between parent and child may be associated with the quality of peer interaction in pre-school settings: popular children are exposed to interaction patterns with their parents that are conducive to encouraging prosocial characteristics in children.

Kolvin *et al.* (1977), in a study of the correlates of deviance in somewhat older children (aged 8 years), found that a significantly higher percentage of parents of children rejected in school used physical punishment and deprivation of privileges than in a control group. In the case of isolated children, no differences in management were evident between the mothers of these children and a control sample. However, the mothers of both rejected and isolated children were significantly less sociable than the controls. Whereas the group of rejectees contained vulnerable children coming from vulnerable families with substantial problems, the isolated children did not tend to come from families with many pathological features, but rather seemed to reflect their mothers' own social isolation.

Responses of parents in conflicts between children

Skill in resolving conflicts is an important component in the maintenance of virtually all interpersonal relationships (Bryant, 1992), and so the way in which parents help their children to acquire such skill is likely to affect their social development. As Cowie and Sharp (1996) observe, conflicts are typically resolved by children and adolescents themselves, and through this process they learn important things about themselves, their peers and social relationships. Conflicts can have damaging effects on groups as well as on individuals, but by the teenage years most young people learn to manage conflicts in such a way as to minimize their disruptive effects.

Most children are involved, to a greater or lesser extent, in conflicts at home – with their parents, siblings and other children who come into the home. Dunn (1984) states that parents take very different views about how far they should intervene in children's quarrels at home, or how far the children should be left to sort out conflicts for themselves. Some parents stress that, as the children are going to have to cope with fights and aggression outside the home, they need to learn at home to be independent. Other parents feel that they should step in and act as arbitrators and try to get each child to understand the other's point of view, especially if physical violence is involved.

Ross *et al.* (1991) studied mothers' interventions in conflicts over ownership and possession of objects in pairs of children aged 20 to 30 months, playing with same-aged, same-sex peers for eighteen 40-minute sessions. The mothers of both children were present and free to respond to their children, but were asked not to direct the children's play. The mothers frequently intervened and overwhelmingly favoured the other child rather than their own. They did not act consistently, and thus did not provide the children with a coherent basis for understanding the principles of entitlement. Rather, the mothers' interventions were aimed at restoring harmony between the children by urging their own children to yield to their peers.

Children can learn much from the way in which conflicts are handled in the family circle, but, whatever the attitudes and intentions of parents may be, parents are likely to make use of their authority to resolve conflicts at home. Therefore the principles of conflict resolution within the family may not readily transfer to the peer group outside the home, where there is often no adult present, and where conflicts tend to be resolved reciprocally rather that unilaterally, if at all (Youniss, 1980). Indeed, from a young age children seem increasingly able to settle their disputes without adult intervention (Smetana, 1989), especially if the disputes are between friends (Hartup *et al.*, 1988). The way in which children deal with conflicts with peers may well affect their status within the group and, if they usually emerge from conflicts without success, may lead to withdrawal from social activities.

Bryant (1992), in a study of children aged 10–12, found that children who were socially preferred were identified by peers as more likely than others to use a calm approach to resolve conflicts and less likely to use anger-retaliation or avoidance approaches. Rejected children and those of 'controversial' sociometric status were seen by their peers as using anger-retaliation strategies more than did popular, neglected and average children; popular children were viewed as using a calm approach more than rejected, neglected and average children; and rejected children used a withdrawal-avoidance strategy more than popular, neglected and average children.

THE ROLE OF PEERS

As the problems of withdrawn and isolated children are related mainly to functioning in a group setting, it makes sense to think of intervention being particularly appropriate when groups are involved. The individual needs of the child will need to be borne in mind at all times, and even when group strategies form the main approach to helping the child, it is desirable that advice, counselling or therapy should also be available on a one-to-one basis.

The use of groups in intervention is discussed in several other parts of this book. In Chapter 7, consideration is given to peer tutoring and group work in various aspects of the curriculum, including personal and social education. In Chapter 9, attention is given to group approaches used by counsellors and psychotherapists, as well as in social skills training. Here, the following aspects of intervention involving other children will be discussed:

- children's responses to peers in distress;
- pairing;
- peer counselling.

Children's responses to peers in distress

Studies have suggested that children can be encouraged to help others to a greater extent than they usually do. This can be done through showing altruistic and helpful models of behaviour, as well as by reinforcement of supportive actions and direct instruction (Bryan, 1975). Denham (1986) asserts that young children's ability to respond to emotional displays has been underrated: children from an early age can infer others' emotional needs and act in a helpful way. Even 18- to 24-months-old children are able to comfort distressed companions and members of the family in a variety of ways and to change strategies when their attempts are unsuccessful.

Caplan and Hay (1989) observed the spontaneous responses of a sample of 3- to 5-year-olds (mean age 4.1 years) to the distress of their peers in the classroom. Distress included injury, crying, appeals for help or comfort, and standing off in a remote area of the room. The children clearly noticed the distress of peers. However, active forms of responding to others in trouble were not frequent, although most of the children helped, shared with, touched or gave verbal comfort to a distressed peer on at least one occasion. Caplan and Hay concluded that initially all the children could respond in an active, prosocial way, but rarely did so. The children held definite beliefs about how to aid a distressed companion, but did not believe that they were supposed to help when competent adult caregivers were present. Indeed, the adult caregivers tended to respond promptly to their charges' distress but did little to encourage the children's own prosocial responses to peer distress, at least in real situations, so that the children rarely put their knowledge into practice.

On the basis of a study of children aged 4–12 years, Chapman *et al.* (1987) suggest that children are helpful to others in distress not only as a result of the emotional arousal caused by seeing such distress but because of the sense of responsibility that they feel towards the person in need. However, Sharp (1996), discussing children's responses to bullying behaviour affecting others, notes that helping approaches are often inhibited by the presence of age-mates, especially after the age of about nine. Peers, in fact, often encourage and collude with bullying by ignoring it. Even so, children can be taught, perhaps through role play, how to respond effectively when they witness a peer being bullied.

In recent years, a number of projects have been reported which aim to increase the awareness of others' distress and isolation and encourage peers to support those in their group who need help. For example, the Circle Approach developed by Mosley (1993) brings in the whole class as well as the teacher, and plans a wide range of activities to achieve certain behavioural targets for a child. Children are encouraged to think more about the effect of their own behaviour on others and to share in the responsibility for creating a better learning and caring atmosphere (see also Latane and Darley, 1970; Latane and Nida, 1981; and McCaffery and Lyons, 1993).

Pairing

Pairing a withdrawn or isolated child with a mature member of the group or another child can be a relatively simple yet often effective form of intervention. Pairing may be used in planned play activities, befriending or therapy. An example of how an isolated child can be helped by being paired with another child, chosen by the teacher, for co-operative activities in class is given in Chapter 7 (pp.111–12).

It is usually practicable to pair a child only with a peer in the same class, but in the case of pre-school children, a younger child may be involved. In a study, for example, by Furman, Rahe and Hartup (1979), 24 socially withdrawn pre-school children (mean age 52.8 months) were assigned to three conditions: (a) socialization with a younger child during ten play sessions; (b) socialization with an age-mate during a similar series of sessions; and (c) no special intervention. The socialization sessions, particularly those with a younger partner, were found to increase the sociability of the withdrawn children in their classrooms. The withdrawn pupils engaged in co-operative play and some form of prosocial behaviour (such as helping, giving or sharing) to a significantly greater extent after the play sessions than before. Furman and colleagues suggest that younger partners provide the isolate with more opportunities to display initiative and direct play successfully than do age-mates, who may be very active and direct most of the play.

Asking one child in the class or other group to befriend an isolated or withdrawn pupil may serve to afford the child who has no friends considerable comfort and support. Children are usually very willing to volunteer their services in this way and able to carry out the task effectively.

Pairs have been used in therapy by Selman and Hickey Schultz (1990). The pair meet with the therapist, usually weekly for a year or longer. Malik and Furman (1993) find this approach of interest, and consider that peer interaction may facilitate therapeutic intervention. However, this form of therapy has yet to be fully evaluated.

Peer counselling

Counselling of children with social and emotional problems as a form of specialized help given by adults with appropriate training is discussed in Chapter 9 (pp.134–7). Recently some schools have introduced a peer counselling service, through which senior pupils take on some of the responsibility for counselling children who require support of this kind.

The task of peer counsellors is usually seen as helping pupils to help themselves, and not as telling them what to do; those acting as counsellors need to be sympathetic, non-judgemental listeners, encouraging 'clients' to express their feelings and opinions and showing them that their views are valued (James *et al.*, 1991). However, non-directive counselling often proves difficult to sustain, and counsellors tend to come under pressure to advise about courses of action which might solve a problem.

Peer counsellors are given some training, usually of short duration, in relevant skills, including listening, reflecting back feelings, paraphrasing what the 'client' has said, showing empathy and developing a vocabulary of feelings (Cowie and Sharp, 1995).

Opinions are sharply divided about the desirability and value of peer counselling (Cowie and Sharp, 1995). The critics of peer counselling, who include many professional counsellors, stress its disadvantages and even dangers, considering that adolescents are not mature enough to understand the complex emotions and problems they have to deal with; that they lack adequate experience and training; and that problems relating to maintaining confidentiality and taking responsibility are more difficult to overcome than in the case of counselling by professional adults. The supporters of peer counselling assert that adolescents are frequently willing to discuss personal issues with peers when they will not do so with an adult; that peers have ample time to listen; and that adolescent counsellors possess the language and shared culture which enable them to empathize with someone of the same age group and which make communication easy (Duck, 1991).

Hamblin (1986) advocates that adolescents should not only be involved in the pastoral programme in schools, but should also take major responsibility for counselling one another. However, Hamblin acknowledges that some form of monitoring, through reporting back of progress, is necessary, and that there is no guarantee that peer counselling will always work: there could be times when it is harmful. James *et al.* (1991) assert that, as adolescents are more likely to take notice of the opinions and comments of their contemporaries than those of adults, peer counselling can be a very useful supplement to existing helping strategies. This is illustrated by a study carried out by Murfitt and Thomas (1983) to investigate the progress achieved in the self-concept and reading attainments of secondary school slow-learning pupils through peer counselling in addition to classroom-based general education. They used a group of sixth-form counsellors aged 16+ years. The role of the counsellor was non-directive, non-critical and client-centred, along Rogerian lines. Positive results relating to both reading and self-concept were recorded and Murfitt and Thomas concluded that the use of sixth formers as peer counsellors was a worthwhile form of help for the clients, and that the counsellors themselves obtained much satisfaction from their involvement.

Cowie and Sharp (1995), reviewing the principles and practice of peer counselling in schools, are able to state with some confidence that peers have a part to play in alleviating personal and social problems, including relationship difficulties and friendship problems. Sharp (1996) asserts that pupils are very capable of providing a caring environment for peers where their concerns are listened to and they can explore possible solutions. However, Sharp recognizes that peer counselling can be a failure, and emphasizes the need (1) to regard peer counselling as supplementing rather than replacing counselling by adults; (2) to provide training and supervision of good quality; (3) to ensure that confidentiality is maintained as far as possible; and (4) for the school to take action when a peer-counselling service is experiencing serious difficulties.

CONCLUSION

This chapter has shown that there are many ways in which parents and peers can help withdrawn and isolated children and adolescents. Parental management styles can have positive consequences for children's competence in forming and maintaining relationships with others. In particular, parents can help their children's social development by providing, from the early years, a warm, secure and affectionate home base and offering a model of positive attitudes and behaviour towards others. They need to grant their children increasing independence in their relationships with their peers as they grow older, supervising and intervening in peer interaction with sensitivity and insight. Parents should also exercise considerable care if their child is said to be withdrawn or isolated at school, and guard against autocratic action in such cases which might make matters worse. They should be prepared to work closely with the school and support agencies if difficulties over peer relationships are experienced by their children.

Only recently has the considerable contribution which peers can make to alleviating relationship difficulties been recognized. An increasing number of projects have been set up, mainly in schools, to encourage pupils to be more aware of distress in their peers and teach children appropriate ways of giving help to those in need. Peers have also been involved in planned attempts to provide lonely children with friends and offer a counselling service. Befriending schemes seem to be a relatively uncomplicated but usually effective way of reducing loneliness and isolation, but peer counselling, while having some advantages, has its dangers, mainly arising from the inexperience of adolescents who often find themselves caught up in quite complex problems. If a peer counselling service is established, adequate safeguards need to be provided by the adults overseeing it.

Chapter 9

Specialized Help

In the previous two chapters, discussion centred on how school organization, school staff, parents and peers can help withdrawn and isolated children and adolescents. This chapter will look at various forms of specialized help which can be offered, both inside and outside the classroom. Four different strategies will be considered:

- counselling;
- behaviour modification;
- strategies designed to improve social competence;
- psychotherapy.

Some of these have already been discussed briefly, but more attention will now be given to their underlying principles and the detail of their procedures, which overlap to a certain extent. From the beginning, however, it is important to stress the need for co-ordination between all concerned with withdrawn and isolated pupils if help is to prove effective.

CO-OPERATION BETWEEN SCHOOLS, PARENTS AND HELPING AGENCIES

While other professionals, such as psychologists, psychiatrists, social workers or therapists, may be responsible for the planning, execution and monitoring of specialized programmes, teachers, parents and peers are also involved in their successful implementation. Teachers in particular have to be aware of the implications of any particular strategy adopted for their own approaches to withdrawn pupils. Inconsistency in adult approaches to children and young people clearly acts against the establishing of behavioural change. Peers, too, can very easily cancel out advances in social development if they fail to respond positively to attempts at initiating changes in relationships.

There has to be collaboration between all who come into contact with those receiving specialized help. Without information, co-operation is virtually impossible. Information includes a knowledge of the principles on which any programme is based, the immediate objectives of such a programme in each specific case, and the ways in which the programme can be supported beyond treatment sessions. Passing on information is, therefore, of fundamental importance but not always easy to accomplish. Pressures on teacher time, demands from other clients, lack of confidence in the professional capability of those who have different training and different priorities, delays in correspondence, administrative failures and many other hazards can result in teachers remaining unaware of the helping strategies being devised by those outside the classroom and vice versa.

Changes in the educational, health and social services have not always helped easy communication. Staffing has been reduced; information goes straight into the computer; parental demands have increased; informal chatting does not appear to be cost-effective; job specifications direct attention elsewhere; crisis management dominates. However, because the time spent at school and at home is far greater than that spent in therapeutic sessions, teachers and parents have to find out what they can do to support specialized help and make efforts to ensure consistency of approach. Dismissing help as unlikely to succeed almost guarantees failure. The one who misses out when concerned adults fail to co-operate is the withdrawn or isolated individual. Reading about possible helping strategies may provide some basis for understanding and support, and can help to prevent the 'spiralling negative cycle' (Webster-Stratton and Herbert, 1994, p. 19) which some children experience.

COUNSELLING

Children and adolescents who are socially isolated, lonely, anxious or depressed may be given help and support in the form of counselling. The best setting for this is probably the school, where attention can be given not only to the individual needing help but also to the other members of his or her class or other group. However, relatively few schools have full-time qualified counsellors on their staffs. As Hughes (1989) points out, the attempt in the 1960s and 1970s to introduce full-time counsellors into secondary schools had only limited success. Even so, counselling is now widely recognized as a relevant and important area of activity for schools, most of which have some form of pastoral care provision which includes counselling.

Pastoral care, aspects of which have already been discussed in Chapter 7 (pp.107–8), is considered to be the concern of all teachers, but some members of staff, especially year tutors in secondary school who may well have taken relevant in-service courses, are given special responsibility for the general welfare of pupils in addition to their teaching duties. Individual or group counselling may also be provided by educational or clinical psychologists (within or outside the school), psychiatrists and other professionals such as social workers, as well as by independent practitioners and voluntary agencies.

Aims of counselling

According to Herbert (1988), the main aim of counselling with children is to produce constructive behaviour and positive personality change. However, Hamblin (1993) stresses that the task of the counsellor is not to bring about fundamental personality modification, but rather to increase self-knowledge and a change in behaviour; counselling aims to help pupils to find more effective ways of using their existing resources and strengths in respect of aptitudes and abilities. Murgatroyd (1985) sees the main aim of the counsellor as helping the individual to cope better with some stress or concern. In the case of children who are withdrawn or isolated, the main aims of counselling might be to increase their self-confidence, improve their self-image, allow them to discuss their worries and anxieties freely and help them to deal more effectively with their difficulties over social participation. Many withdrawn children have no-one to talk to, and the opportunities afforded by a warm and sympathetic counsellor to give expression to their feelings are a welcome source of relief.

Theoretical bases of counselling

Counselling is an umbrella term, encompassing a variety of theoretical standpoints and methods of approach. Models of counselling have evolved from psychotherapy, psychoanalysis, social and cognitive learning theory, developmental psychology and the study of interpersonal skills (Dryden, 1993). Woolfe, Dryden and Charles-Edwards (1989) see the key influences determining counselling philosophies and practices as (1) schools of psychoanalysis, especially Freudian; (2) Carl Rogers, with his emphasis on personal growth and humanistic psychology; and (3) behavioural and cognitive schools of psychology. Many counsellors select what they consider to be of value from a range of theoretical formulations, although Wheeler (1993) expresses reservations about eclectic approaches to counselling.

Strategies used in counselling

In view of the many influences bearing on the practice of counselling, it is not surprising that many different strategies are used by counsellors in their interactions with their clients. Those who are particularly attracted to the 'non-directive' (or, as it is now called, the 'person-centred') approach involve themselves in the painstaking exploration of problems, encouraging the client to discover alternative ways of describing and dealing with them through developing a relationship of trust and confidential conversations between counsellor and client (Herbert, 1988). Person-centred counselling, according to Mearns and Thorne (1988), stresses primarily the quality of the relationship between counsellor and client, the importance of the individual's subjective reality, and the need for clients to accept responsibility for their own lives.

Cognitive-behavioural counselling also puts an emphasis on thinking about feelings and problems, and clients are encouraged to talk and write about themselves, their views and their attitudes. In addition, they are encouraged and helped to improve their life-skills and carry out relevant tasks successfully (Wooster and Bird, 1979; Meichenbaum, 1983; Trower, Casey and Dryden, 1988). Children may be helped to learn new coping skills, reinforce their existing coping skills, or recover their ability to cope after failure (Murgatroyd, 1985). Nelson-Jones (1993) provides a detailed list of life-skills needed by the individual, as well as strategies likely to promote those skills; these include

- thinking skills (e.g. decision-making and managing problems);
- action skills (e.g. making relationships and social participation);
- feelings-related skills (e.g. confidence, self-acceptance).

Group counselling

Although most withdrawn and isolated children will benefit from an opportunity to talk to a counsellor on an individual and confidential basis about their situation, experiences and feelings, such pupils are also likely to gain from participation in group counselling activities. Ratigan (1989) asserts that the group is a powerful means for learning and therapy, though a group approach may not be suitable for some individuals, for example, those suffering from severe depression or psychotic illness. The group counsellor can use a variety of strategies, including discussions, games, simulations, role play and psychodrama.

Hamblin (1981, 1986, 1993) gives details of a wide range of group approaches that can be used by those involved in counselling and pastoral care. Themes covered in group counselling include self-presentation, dealing with peer pressure, facing up to disappointment, and coping with tension, threat and anxiety. An example of an activity suggested by Hamblin (1986) for first-year secondary school pupils on understanding and dealing with the experience of feeling isolated includes asking the pupils, who work in groups of three, to suggest ideas about (a) the kinds of behaviour that would allow them to help the lonely individual; (b) behaviour that could increase isolation; and (c) how they might adapt to new situations. These ideas can form the basis for discussion in the larger group, usually the whole class.

Effectiveness of counselling

There can be little doubt that most children experiencing loneliness and rejection derive support and comfort, at least in the short term, from easy access to a counsellor. Some of the limited number of evaluation studies that have been carried out have reported positive results from a period of counselling, with evidence for the efficacy of cognitive-behavioural counselling being more impressive than for other forms (Bolger, 1989). However, there are so many difficulties in the way of carrying out rigorous assessments of counselling, including the variety of approaches used and the unreliability of measures of outcome, that it is not possible to draw any firm conclusions about its effectiveness (Maguire, 1973; Bolger, 1989).

BEHAVIOUR MODIFICATION

Behavioural techniques have for some time now been accepted as effective in changing children's behaviour (see, for example, Herbert, 1987; Wheldall and Glynn, 1989). While they do present some problems to teachers wishing to implement them in their classrooms (a point which will be discussed later in this section), the main assumptions made by behavioural approaches, especially behaviour modification, can be incorporated into a teacher's basic repertoire, as well as providing the foundations of a specially devised programme.

Principles of behaviour modification

The assumptions underlying behaviour modification programmes are:

● behaviour will tend to be repeated (when similar circumstances recur) if it has proved 'rewarding' for the individual in the past, that is, if it has in some way reduced the individual's needs;

- desired behaviour can be established by rewarding it consistently (reinforcement) and by not rewarding the undesired behaviour;
- behaviour can be gradually 'shaped' through reinforcement, so that the individual is moved from an approximation of the desired behaviour to the actual desired behaviour through a series of pre-planned stages, all carefully identified and consistently rewarded.

With these assumptions in mind, it becomes clear that behavioural approaches involve careful analysis of existing behaviour (through observation), so that the programme can be constructed; judicious selection of 'rewards', so that the change in behaviour is worthwhile to the individual concerned; precise specification of programme objectives, so that the steps in the programme can be delineated and recorded; and consistency in rewarding the desired behaviour (or its approximation), so that there is no confusion in the mind of the learner and no reverting to previous behaviour patterns. More detailed discussion of behavioural techniques can be found in Poteet (1973); O'Leary and O'Leary (1977); Westmacott and Cameron (1981); Axelrod (1983); Harrop (1983); Herbert (1991) and Sundel and Sundel (1993).

Implementing behaviour modification programmes

As already noted, teachers are sometimes wary of using behavioural approaches in their classrooms because these programmes are based on detailed observation and planning. They can, therefore, seem very time-consuming. Some teachers feel that behavioural approaches manipulate learners in unacceptable ways; others feel that they involve giving too much attention to one pupil to the detriment of the others. It could be argued, however, that the time involved is well spent if the programmes lead to more appropriate behaviour, enhancement of learning, and the solution of class management problems. The learners may be considerably happier with their changed behaviour patterns than they were before and the manipulation involved is usually fairly short-term, the responsibility for their behaviour being handed back to the individuals concerned as soon as possible.

To illustrate how a behaviour modification approach could help withdrawn and isolated pupils, the difficulties of a new school entrant will be considered.

> *May* was just over 5 years of age when she came to school. Because she lived in a rather remote rural area, she had never been to nursery school or playgroup. She had two brothers considerably older than herself (14 and 18 years of age). Her father, mother and brothers were very involved in running the family farm and May, while certainly not neglected, spent a lot of time on her own. She was a silent child whose wishes were anticipated before she had to speak. Although her family tried to find time for her, there was not much chance to talk to May or read to her.

Going to school was not a successful venture for May. She found the presence of the other children overwhelming and badly missed her mother. She retreated as far as she could from the others and would cry if any approach were made. The rest of the class soon began to adjust to one another but May was left more and more isolated.

Realizing what was happening, her teacher began to observe May very carefully and noticed that she often watched one of the boys, Scott, who liked to play on his own with construction toys. She gave some of these to May who did begin, rather tentatively, to move them about, taking her cue from what Scott was doing. The teacher would smile encouragingly at May as she passed, and began to give verbal approval if May put some of the play material together. Then, without making any fuss, the teacher brought two spare items from Scott's collection and put them near May, who was engaged in making a farmyard. Scott came to see what was going on and began to add to May's construction. Rather unwillingly, she accepted his help.

With careful planning and a little luck, the teacher eventually managed to get May to work with Scott. He, too, was somewhat isolated from the other children but would talk to them and to May, who did occasionally reply or even make a remark to him. The teacher could then begin to plan a programme which would bring Scott and, through him, May more into contact with the other children. It was important not to force the pace and also not to let May become totally dependent on Scott. The aim was a widening of relationships, not just the establishment of a single relationship.

It is interesting to ask a number of questions about this example of behaviour management. What was the reward which reinforced May's initial withdrawn and isolated behaviour? Clearly, her withdrawal was defensive but it also preserved the absence of peer relationships and solitariness which May experienced at home. To move her forward socially, her teacher had, therefore, to begin to shape her behaviour while ignoring her current isolation. What could interfere with the programme? The quality of the reward, the strength of the existing behaviour, the consistency of the reward and the reactions of the other children could be considered among other possibilities. The action which the teacher took was successful in May's case. What could have been done if it had not succeeded? Would re-analysing May's existing behaviour have helped? How could May's teacher build on the beginnings of behavioural change?

May's withdrawal was not serious but could have become so if no action had been taken. It is true, of course, that May's social skills, especially those involving interactions with other children and the ability to make friends, were probably underdeveloped. One of the next steps for the teacher to take would be to implement some training in social skills, an objective which would be entirely appropriate for all the reception class children. Attention will be given to these programmes in the next section.

Help from others

It is often possible for teachers to carry out a specially-devised behaviour modification programme in the course of their normal classroom procedures. Help from others (e.g. educational psychologists, nursery assistants, support teachers, parents) may also be required. Educational psychologists have a particularly useful role to play here (see Chazan, Laing and Davies, 1991). They can:

- observe, record and chart existing behaviour;
- analyse the desired behaviour in order to indicate how shaping of approximate behaviour can be carried out;
- provide teachers with schedules which monitor individual behaviour patterns;
- enlist the help of others outside school (especially those at home) to co-operate in the programme;
- evaluate behavioural change and help in planning the next programme.

Other adults in the classroom can help by ensuring that the selected reward is given whenever the approximation of the desired behaviour occurs, as any delay can prevent the establishment of change. They can also continue to support individual children as the programme progresses, freeing the teacher to work with the other pupils. At the same time, the power of teacher approval as a reward must not be forgotten.

The various ways in which Behaviour Modification programmes can be used are discussed in Thompson and Dockens (1975) and Sheldon (1982), amongst others. Walker and Shea (1986) and Wheldall and Merrett (1989) are particularly concerned with practical classroom approaches, both formal and rather more informal, the latter authors dealing with the secondary stage. For teachers, as for parents, a realization of how behaviour is controlled by its consequences (feedback) and how it can be modified through reward and reinforcement is important, not just in the case of 'acting out' pupils but also for children who are becoming more and more remote from those around them.

STRATEGIES DESIGNED TO IMPROVE SOCIAL COMPETENCE

Social development is complex, highly personal, and always evolving and changing as situations and the people involved in them alter. Effective social adaptation, that is, the ability to show appropriate interpersonal reactions in any situation, is an important component of this development. Skilled interactive behaviour is, however, more than mere reflection of the behaviour or wishes of others. Socially well-developed individuals can take their own place competently and capably in interpersonal reactions and relationships.

Social skills training (SST)

What are the social skills which have to be acquired to achieve such social capability? The consensus from a number of different writers (Rinn and Markle, 1979; Oden, 1980; Spence, 1980; Ellis and Whittington, 1981, 1983; and Schroeder and Rakos, 1983) could be summarized as follows:

- *performance skills* (what individuals have to be able to do to interact effectively): show appropriate body language, eye contact and emotional reactions; listen to others; converse using a variety of registers (simple, complex, specific); be aware of another person's point of view; be sufficiently assertive without trying to dominate;
- *interpretative skills* (what individuals have to be able to do so that they can decode the behaviour of others and react effectively): perceive the body language and eye contact of others; appreciate peer values and norms; react to the mood of others and their displayed emotion; make adequate (and appropriate) verbal contributions; be able to lead as well as follow when necessary.

Ellis and Whittington (1981) suggest that socially 'unskilled' behaviour should be seen as requiring training at different levels – remedial, developmental and specialized. 'Remedial' work aims to help individuals to acquire skills they do not have; 'developmental' SST encourages the effective display of skills which individuals have, even in embryonic form, but either do not use or use inappropriately; 'specialized' training offers opportunities to develop and use sophisticated skills for specific situations (Davies, 1983).

The distinction which Ellis and Whittington (1981) make between 'remedial' and 'developmental' approaches to social skills deficits is an important one. It points to the need to ascertain, before implementing any programme, whether the skills have never been acquired (e.g. because of lack of opportunity) or whether the individual is failing to use them (e.g. because of inhibition). There may be difficulty in deciding on this point. In the case of *May* (see previous section), did she have some useful social skills when she came to school but could not adapt them to a new situation, or were there skills which she simply did not have? The distinction affects the programme to be implemented. With young children, it may be possible to encompass both areas at the same time; but with older pupils, basing a programme on assumed ignorance of skills, just because they are not displayed in class, for example, could be counter-effective.

Aims of SST

The listing at the beginning of this section of performance and interpretative skills tends to imply that there is agreement among workers in this field on what the skills are and what the aims of any programme should be. In fact, this is not entirely the case. 'Social competence' itself is so difficult to define with any degree of precision that there is little agreement on how it might be achieved. What individuals have to acquire is a whole set of value systems and beliefs about themselves and others, involving social knowledge, social functioning and sensitivity in relationships. Because this is a considerable undertaking, it is not surprising that people may be socially competent in some areas and not in others, at some times in their life and not at other times, and may be particularly vulnerable when affected by sudden or severe change.

Principles and practice of SST

A number of general principles on which SST programmes can be built have been put forward by Ellis and Whittington (1981). These involve an emphasis on the importance of sensitization, practise, feedback and transfer. Oden (1980), Herbert (1986) and Goddard and Cross (1987) are concerned with primary school children, while Rinn and Markle (1979), Goldstein *et al.* (1980), Spence (1980) and Furnham (1986) look at older children, adolescents and young adults. All seek to promote 'mutual positive feelings' (Herbert, 1986, p. 19), acceptance and 'appropriate' behaviour (i.e. relevant to a particular situation).

Because of the wealth of information given about it, the programme developed by Spence (1980) for use with older pupils will be looked at in a little more detail. Her programme is particularly useful because she provides:

- a series of assessment measures;
- a discussion of training techniques;
- a description of practical approaches, including specially devised games and the use of video;
- an example of a specific programme, giving details of the content of each of twelve sessions.

The programme makes use of typical SST strategies, namely instruction, behaviour rehearsal, modelling and role-play. It is built on, and uses, existing performance and interpretative skills and offers opportunities for further development of these as well as for practise and transfer of new skills. For example, in Session 3 the programme deals with personal appearance and eye contact. Discussion of appearance and posture is followed by some instruction as to what would be appropriate in this area at, for example, a job interview. Appropriate behaviours are modelled, rehearsed and practised. A similar procedure follows with regard to eye contact. Role-playing allows for further practise, with attention being directed to specific points which then become targets to be achieved.

Story-telling and puppetry are key strategies in many SST programmes. To these can be added the use of video (also helpful in the initial assessment of social functioning and in monitoring progress – see, for example, Cartledge and Milburn, 1980; Spence, 1980). While most people are happy to see themselves on video, it has to be remembered that withdrawn and isolated individuals may find watching their own behaviour extremely distressing. Kehle and Gonzales (1991) found that editing tapes, so that only desired behaviours (or their approximations) are seen, increased self-esteem in withdrawn and also depressed pupils. Wetton and Cansell (1993) comment on similar use of video tapes, along with other suggested strategies. If self-modelling remains unacceptable, modelling of appropriate behaviour by others or videotapes of classroom or playground incidents can promote discussion of effective interpersonal reactions.

Implementing SST programmes

Implementing social skills training programmes of the kind described above can present problems to teachers, especially at the secondary stage. As with Behaviour Modification programmes, teachers may need to call on support from other professionals, especially in the case of severe withdrawal and isolation. Daniels (1990), Siner (1993) and Morgan and Pearson (1994), for example, describe social skills training programmes carried out in schools by educational psychologists with small groups of children experiencing poor peer relationships. Some of the activities suggested may indeed be suitable for all class members, and teachers need to be aware of these so that they can implement them at appropriate times.

Effectiveness of SST programmes

Of all the aims of SST, that of transfer of skills is the most difficult to achieve as well as being probably the most important. A programme can be considered successful when the skills which have been demonstrated, discussed and practised are used appropriately in real situations rather than artificial programme sessions. The ability to join in and sustain conversations, for example, has to be shown outside treatment times as well as within them. Enlisting the help of peers can help to establish new patterns of social behaviour.

A further difficulty lies in the interpretation of the term 'appropriate', which has been used frequently throughout this section. What is seen as appropriate depends to no small extent on age, gender, societal and cultural considerations, as well as on individual characteristics. SST programmes, therefore, need to be relevant to specific learners and even to specific situations, while always offering opportunities for wider application. 'Package' approaches to training may be less effective than an individually-tailored programme based on a relevant assessment of each child's strengths and weaknesses (Tiffen and Spence, 1986).

In general, behavioural social skills programmes produce at least a short-term positive response to training, and suggest that such training has something to offer to children who have difficulty in making relationships with their peers (Michelson *et al.*, 1983; Frederickson and Simms, 1990). However, researchers have tended to report only limited success as a result of SST programmes. For example, Gottman, Gonso and Schuler (1976) stressed, in work with isolated children, the importance of selecting skills for training that discriminate such children from their non-isolated peers; but it is not easy to target specific skills components (Trower, 1984). La Greca and Santogrossi (1980) obtained positive results, in terms of improved social skills, from programmes carried out with children aged 9 to 12+ years with poor peer relationships, but did not find improved ratings of peer acceptance as a result of the skills training. Malik and Furman (1993) emphasize that it is important to include peers in the training or generalization sessions, as there is little evidence that training sessions with adults will generalize to interactions with peers. It is also important that if a class as a whole is the unit for social skills training, the programme provides sufficient learning experience for those children who are deficient in social skills.

Social cognitive training

Emphasis in the foregoing section has been on teaching social skills. But children cannot display these skills adequately in everyday situations without understanding the nature of the situations in which they find themselves, knowing when to apply which skill, and perceiving the effect which they have on others and which others have on them. These are cognitive skills. Effective interpersonal functioning depends on both social and cognitive abilities, and in practice nowadays social skills programmes pay attention to both kinds of abilities (Frederickson and Simms, 1990). In this section, the emphasis will be put on the cognitive aspects of social performance, with particular reference to withdrawn and isolated pupils.

Aims of social cognitive training

Social cognitive training focuses on improving the child's ability to think about possible solutions to problems rather than on discrete practical skills such as making eye contact or using an appropriate tone of voice. As Pellegrini and Urbain (1985) point out, interpersonal cognitive problem-solving (ICPS) approaches place explicit stress on training covert thinking *processes* (such as identifying problems and generating alternative solutions) rather than on cognitive *content*, i.e. what a child knows about effective social interaction.

Over the past two decades or so, a number of programmes aimed at developing ICPS skills have been devised, pioneered by D'Zurilla and Goldfried (1971) and Spivack and Shure (1974). Such training seeks to improve the individual's ability to think up different ways of solving problems, look ahead to possible outcomes of any action taken and plan a series of actions designed to achieve a particular goal. The adult does not suggest the most acceptable answer to a problem but rather acts as a guide, encouraging children to think up their own ideas of resolving a situation to everyone's satisfaction and devising ways around potential obstacles. The implicit philosophy on which the ICPS approach is based is that, if one wishes to change the behaviour of children, one must influence the thinking which controls the behaviour.

Implementing ICPS programmes

ICPS strategies can be carried out by teachers in the ordinary classroom context as well as by educational psychologists, clinicians and parents. Spivack and Shure (1974) and Spivack, Platt and Shure (1976) have emphasized the importance of developing the language skills necessary for thinking logically, particularly in young children, and also the need to promote awareness of others. With appropriate language skills and social understanding, children can be helped from the early years to solve hypothetical and real-life situations. Activities can be devised to encourage children to think in terms of (1) possible consequences of actions (how might the girl feel if the boy pushes her? Will she be sad, happy or angry?); and (2) possible solutions to problems (a boy would like to play a game of Lotto but all the children in the group are outside in the playground or in the Wendy House).

In the case of non-responding or shy young children, Spivack and Shure (1974) suggest that they should be placed near the teacher or assistant and encouraged to whisper in her ear. To encourage participation, initial activities might stress movement rather than verbalization as a response. After a time, the child is likely to be ready to respond to, for example, puppet stories, and should be stimulated to give an answer to simple verbal choices, to say something about his or her own feelings, the feelings of others and the consequences of behaving in a particular way. Children reluctant to take any part in group activities should be praised for the smallest step they take towards improved sociability, but should not be coerced in any way. For further examples of programmes aimed at developing interpersonal cognitive problem-solving skills, see Elardo and Caldwell (1979); Thacker (1983); Chazan *et al.* (1983); and Bash and Camp (1985).

Effectiveness of social cognitive training

A number of projects involving the application of social cognitive training strategies have been reported to show positive outcomes. Spivack and Shure (1974) and Spivack, Platt and Shure (1976) have demonstrated improvements in ICPS skills following their programmes, especially in the case of young children. Elardo and Caldwell (1979) examined the effects of Project Aware on role-taking, problem-solving and classroom adjustment in 9- and 10-year-old children in the USA. Project Aware used a special curriculum written by Elardo and Caldwell and influenced by the work of Spivack and Shure. Discussion periods were held twice weekly for 25 minutes for each class in the sample, from November to the following May. The results of the project indicated that the pupils involved gained in respect for others, the ability to generate alternative solutions to problem situations, creative expression, patience and self-reliance.

Camp *et al.* (1977) tested the effectiveness of the 'Think Aloud' programme, designed to improve self-control in 6- to 8-year-old boys (the programme now has several versions for different age ranges, up to 12+ years – see Bash and Camp, 1985). 'Think Aloud' includes activities suggested by Meichenbaum and Goodman (1971) and Spivack and Shure (1974). Essentially, the child learns to answer four questions in trying to solve a personal problem: 'What is my problem? What is my plan? Am I using my plan? How did I do?' Camp *et al.* obtained positive results from this approach, the children involved showing improvements in respect of a number of prosocial behaviours.

Mize and Ladd (1990) worked with primary school children seen as having low status among peers. These children were helped to develop four skills: leading peers, asking questions of peers, making comments to peers and supporting peers. Their work indicated that a cognitive learning approach to social skill training is valid in the case of children at risk of poor peer acceptance (see also Connor, 1994).

However, not all studies show positive gains for withdrawn and isolated children following social skills training which included cognitive strategies. For example, Tiffen and Spence (1986) did not find any specific beneficial effects as a result of 12 weekly sessions (50 minutes each) of such training provided for 50 isolated and rejected children aged 7–12 years. The training involved both practical social skills and social cognitive aspects (problem-solving skills such as these related to decision-making and dealing with group pressures). Other researchers, too, have failed to find clear-cut beneficial effects following IPCS programmes (McClure, Chinsky and Larcen, 1978; Weissberg *et al.*, 1981).

Comparing SST and ICPS approaches

Michelson *et al.* (1983) compared the outcomes of behavioural social skills training and interpersonal cognitive problem-solving strategies in the case of a sample of 61 socially maladjusted boys attending a child psychiatric outpatient department. The boys were given either SST or ICPS training for 12 weekly hour-long sessions and were followed up a year after the cessation of the programme. As compared with a control group, both approaches resulted in positive changes in social, emotional and scholastic functioning by the close of treatment. At the one-year follow-up, the behavioural approach had continued to show a modest improvement between treatment and follow-up, but the ICPS treatment showed a decline in progress, as did the control group. However, Michelson and colleagues point out that the sample consisted of inner-city children, and that the study was carried out in the context of a child psychiatric clinic rather than a school.

Spence (1983), Beck and Forehand (1984) and Frederickson and Simms (1990) argue in favour of combining SST and ICPS approaches, though this does not necessarily get over the difficulties of generalizing and maintaining the effects of treatment. As Bierman and Furman (1984) emphasize, it is important to supplement skill training with changes in the environment that maximize the probability that any new competencies which children acquire are recognized and accepted by others.

Pellegrini and Urbain (1985), in an evaluation of IPCS training with children, conclude that available data suggest that a wide variety of approaches are effective for teaching problem-solving skills to children. However, they caution that newly acquired cognitive skills do not translate automatically into more adaptive social behaviour, nor do they necessarily bring about an improvement in sociometric status. While ICPS training is sensible and appealing, outcome data indicate that its successful application is a matter of considerable complexity.

PSYCHOTHERAPY

As Jennings (1995) points out, the term 'psychotherapy' tends to be used in several senses, referring to psychoanalytic psychotherapy, psychological therapies in general or counselling. This section is particularly concerned with psychodynamic psychotherapy. Like counselling, psychotherapy of this kind aims to help individuals suffering from emotional difficulties, including loneliness, anxiety and depression. However, it is based largely on psychoanalytic schools of thought, and attempts to bring about more fundamental personality changes than counselling usually does.

According to Boston and Lush (1993), psychotherapists aim at bringing about internal changes in personality leading to a more positive approach to life, an increase in trust, a greater integration of different aspects of experience, higher self-esteem, and an improved ability to deal with anxieties and conflicts. Fernando (1993) states that the child psychotherapist seeks to understand the child's experience and how past events may be affecting present behaviour or have distorted the child's development and perception of him or herself and others.

Child psychotherapists may work on a one-to-one basis with clients or with groups of children. They also work with parents, some focusing on family therapy where the family is seen as the unit for treatment. Some give particular attention to cognitive conscious processes. Most psychotherapists see children once weekly or more frequently over a year or longer, though nowadays shorter-term therapy is not uncommon, perhaps in the form of brief focal therapy. In all forms of psychotherapy, the relationship between therapist and client is very important. Psychotherapy is mostly provided in clinical settings, though therapists also work in other contexts such as schools, day-care centres and units for adolescents.

Individual psychodynamic therapy

Child psychotherapists working with individual children along psychodynamic lines use both verbal and non-verbal means of communication with their clients. Play equipment and drawing materials are usually employed, especially with younger children, to encourage the free expression of feelings, thoughts and anxieties. The therapist uses interpretation as a way of giving structure, meaning and purpose to apparently meaningless utterances and non-verbal behaviour (Dale, 1996). Treatment involves a continual working through of past experiences, which are often re-enacted in less obvious ways (Fernando, 1993). Dale emphasizes that psychodynamic therapy should take account not only of the dynamic interplay between unconscious forces operating on the individual child, but also of the wider influences from family, friends and the environment.

The withdrawn, uncommunicative child may find it difficult to respond to psychotherapy on a one-to-one basis, although depressed children and adolescents may benefit from this approach. In general, it is not easy to reach any definite conclusions about the effectiveness of individual psychotherapy. Rachman (1971), reviewing studies of the effects of psychotherapy with children, concluded that convincing evidence was hard to find for the long-term beneficial outcomes of therapeutic interventions based on psychodynamic theory. However, there were indications that even brief supportive therapy may bring about positive changes in behaviour or at least accelerate the natural processes of recovery. Roughly two-thirds of poorly adjusted children receiving therapy of some kind do show improvement when followed up two years after treatment, but the same result is found in the case of children not receiving treatment. Rachman acknowledges that his review covers children presenting a variety of behavioural and emotional disorders and a wide range of psychotherapeutic approaches, so that the evidence is often difficult to interpret.

Since the time of Rachman's review, it has become even more difficult to make generalizations about the effectiveness of individual therapy based on psychodynamic principles. Therapists have broadened the focus of therapy from the traditional emphasis on the child's unconscious to include cognitive processes, observable behaviour, the family system, and the peer or social system (Schaefer and O'Connor, 1983; Rutter, 1986). Psychotherapy is now often only a part of the treatment of children, which may include trying to effect changes in school as well as family.

Cognitive psychotherapy

As McAdam and Gilbert (1985) explain, cognitive psychotherapy puts the emphasis on conscious rather than on unconscious processes, with the therapist taking a more active role than with the more traditional psychotherapies. This approach, which owes much to Kelly (1955) and Beck (1976), aims to help the client to understand his or her thinking processes better, gain insight into the connections between thoughts, mood and behaviour, and learn how distortions of thinking can be identified and corrected. Children who are lonely and isolated may well have negative and disturbing thoughts which can be modified by cognitive therapy (see McMullin, 1987; Persons, 1989 and Schuyler, 1991 for accounts of the practice of cognitive therapy).

Rhodes (1993) describes work in schools using solution-focused brief therapy (see Ajmal and Rhodes, 1995). This approach is concerned not only with the actions of clients, but their constructs and perceptions of the world. It encourages the child to use 'exceptions' to the problem (i.e. when it does not occur) as a basis for action, and to set goals, preferably small realistic steps, as a start of something new. Solution-focused brief therapy takes place for about 5–6 sessions of an hour each.

Group therapy

The practice of group therapy with children and adolescents, pioneered by Slavson (1943) in New York, has developed since that time, although group therapy is not as widely available in Britain as it seems to warrant. Group therapy can be organized to include a variety of therapeutic situations, and is conducted through play, activities such as painting, modelling and woodwork, and/or verbal interchange. The therapist may be active or passive, directive or non-directive; he or she may seek to interpret what the members of the group do and say, or refrain from interpretation. Group therapy may be provided in a clinical setting or in other contexts such as the school (Kolvin *et al.*, 1981).

Although the activities of the group may be structured or unstructured, planning is needed and the physical setting is of great importance. Play and activity materials should be chosen to facilitate the establishment of contact with each child and encourage insight and the expression of feelings. Groups need to be kept small, usually ranging from about 4 to 6 children, selected to achieve balance in the group.

Foulkes and Anthony (1965) showed how the group therapy setting can be adapted to meet the needs of different age groups, with verbal exchange being the predominant means of intercommunication in the case of older children. Axline (1989) describes the principles and practice of non-directive individual and group play therapy, based on the work of Carl Rogers (1951). The non-directive approach gives children the opportunity to play out their accumulated feelings of tension, frustration, fear and bewilderment.

Axline asserts that the group experience injects a very realistic element because the child lives in the world with other children and must consider the reactions and feelings of others. Both Axline (1989) and Ginott (1961) recommend group therapy as particularly suitable for withdrawn children, including those who are over-inhibited, shy, isolated and uncommunicative. Withdrawn children often find it difficult to relate to a therapist in individual treatment and are reached more readily in group therapy. The therapist should guard against overwhelming the withdrawn child who is reluctant to start playing, but should show acceptance of the child and leave it to him or her to become more active. Membership of a small group encourages the withdrawn child to thaw out, but the individual must remain the focus of treatment.

Studies of the effectiveness of group therapy have mostly been on too small a scale to do justice to the issue, often lacking reliable outcome measures, adequate sampling and controls, full descriptions of the treatment and long-term follow-ups (Kolvin *et al.*, 1981; Woolfe and Dryden, 1996). However, both research and clinical reports have indicated that play, activity and verbal group therapy can have beneficial results, including an increase in sociability, better acceptance by peers and improved self-concept (Schiffer, 1971; Kolvin *et al.*, 1981; Schaefer and O'Connor, 1983; Vinogradov and Yalom, 1989; Dwivedi, 1993; and Bergin and Garfield, 1994).

As generalization of treatment effects is not always found in real life situations, the work of Bierman (1989) is most promising. In this approach, rejected children take part in a highly structured therapy group. When ready, they move on to a highly structured naturalistic peer group (such as swimming lessons). Then step-by-step, they are encouraged to participate in social activities at different levels (see also Bierman, Miller and Stabb, 1987 and Malik and Furman, 1993). The organization of this staged approach to social participation may, of course, present practical difficulties.

Family therapy

A child's emotional and social difficulties are frequently related to a malfunctioning family environment. In such cases, family therapy may be considered appropriate, where the unit of treatment is the family group and all the family members may be seen together. Family therapy aims to help families change their deep-seated habits of behaving, and develop alternative ways of dealing with problems that occur (Herbert, 1988; Jenkins, 1990).

Family therapy encompasses a variety of approaches. Therapists may focus attention on the way in which a particular family is organized; challenge the beliefs within a family system which tend to inhibit the development of the children who are members of it; or emphasize the problem (e.g. withdrawn behaviour) and the patterns of exchange between family members who are connected with the problem (Treacher and Carpenter, 1984; Campion, 1985).

As it is easy for family therapy, once commenced, to go on for a considerable time, Bentovim and Kinston (1978) developed brief focal family therapy in treating children, so as to make this form of therapy more widely available. This strategy emphasizes seeing the whole family or marital couple, determining a number of dynamic hypotheses on the basis of history-taking and observations of family interaction, and then constructing a time-limited plan. The plan does not rest on any rigid theoretical ideas, but involves a defined contract and specific goals. The family is seen once weekly or more frequently, over a period of between three and nine months. Cases described by Kinston and Bentovim (1978) as dealt with through brief family therapy included a 10-year-old boy presenting fears, depression and school refusal, and an 11-year-old boy with separation anxiety and general fearfulness. Kinston and Bentovim found that brief focal family therapy had more impact on the children involved than on the families themselves – 87 per cent of children in 22 families improved to some extent, while only 50 per cent of the families showed positive change.

Campion (1985) asserts that it is always useful to try to interpret children's behaviour, in school as well as at home, in terms of their experiences within their own family system. Asen (1996), too, while recognizing that some parents cling on to their practices and beliefs and are reluctant to change them, considers that work with the family can alleviate the burden that children often carry on behalf of their families.

CONCLUSION

This chapter has considered four ways in which specialized help can be provided in the case of children and adolescents who are withdrawn or isolated: counselling, behaviour modification, social competence training and psychotherapy. These different kinds of help are not necessarily exclusive; they are often provided in combination. Which form of treatment is likely to be most effective can be determined only in the light of a careful assessment of the needs of the individual child in his or her family and school context, and many factors affect the outcome whatever strategy is used. However, because of the nature of the withdrawn child's difficulties, it would seem that treatment employing an approach which brings the child into contact with others in a specially planned group is likely to be appropriate, and that family work almost always usefully complements other forms of treatment.

Chapter 10

Conclusion

GENERAL DISCUSSION

Why is it important to help withdrawn and isolated pupils?

Herbert (1991) points out that the reduction in infectious diseases and other physical illnesses in young people has led to increased parental concern over emotional and social problems in their children. Education has always seen social-emotional development as one of its major aims. Children who display obvious behaviour difficulties are, therefore, likely to be the focus of attention of those with whom they come into contact. When the difficulties take the form of 'acting out', with pupils showing aggressive, disturbing behaviour, attention is immediately given. Withdrawal is not so visible. Those who find themselves on the perimeter of social relationships make few demands on those with whom they come into contact. In fact, they may spend time and energy on deliberately avoiding being noticed in any way.

With all the pressures in classrooms today, it is understandable that teachers do not go looking for behaviour problems. They may well feel they have more than enough to do when they try to cope with disruptive incidents. Yet withdrawn and isolated pupils also need help. Their inability to join with others in the educational experiences offered can retard their cognitive development, as well as making them feel apprehensive, tense and even stressed in class and miserable in the playground.

Low attainment and negative self-feelings are not the only potential consequences of inadequate interpersonal relationships. Feelings of loneliness can have far-reaching effects on personal interactions and on self-perception (Sletta *et al.*, 1996). Depression can precede or follow social withdrawal and lead to eating or sleeping disorders, poor physical health, apathy or even suicide. In addition, withdrawal does not always involve isolated or inhibited behaviour. It can present as conduct disorder, with the individual trying to force a way into personal relationships or to attack those existing between others.

Inhibition tends to be progressive and pervasive. While it is true that the 'self' is not a single entity (inasmuch as people behave differently and see themselves in a different light in various circumstances), there is a 'co-ordination between different contextual demands/resources' (Burnham and Harris, 1996, p. 136). Thus, inadequacy in classroom relationships can spread to the playground, the journey home and out-of-school activities, with the individuals concerned losing confidence in their social competence and missing out on opportunities for interaction with others. Children who can be distinguished from the majority of their peers, whether by reason of physical appearance, disability, communication difficulties or behaviour that is unexpected or inappropriate, are especially vulnerable to exclusion from groups. The benefits of friendship may be denied them (see next section) along with the damage to their self-esteem.

Where do the main problems lie?

It could be suggested that withdrawn and isolated pupils are deficient in social skills. This is not necessarily an accurate assumption. Some children possess the necessary skills but do not use them at all in certain situations; some have developed only immature responses to others, so that when more sophisticated interactions are called for (e.g. at school entry or adolescence), they fail where they have formerly succeeded; some have inadequate perceptual ability so that they do not 'read' social situations correctly and therefore respond ineffectively (Curran, 1979). Examples of these behaviours are to be found throughout this book. One more will be given here to reflect some of the considerations mentioned above.

Tommy is a 12-year-old Y7 pupil. He is a big, well-made boy whose major difficulties lie in his lack of maturity, which was also evident at the primary stage. In the later primary years, however, his immaturity (especially in speech) was accepted and even found quite endearing. However, at the secondary stage, the discrepancy between his appearance and his behaviour became more and more marked and the acceptance he had formerly enjoyed turned to hostility, with teasing and verbal abuse.

These changed reactions bewildered Tommy, who spent most of his first term in secondary school in tears. He also seemed to lack any organizational ability, so that he was forever lost in school. He mislaid important documents, such as timetables, homework diaries and exercise books, earning constant rebukes from staff which added to his finding school a very negative experience. His general learning difficulties did not help in this respect. Tommy has become increasingly depressed, with his mood moving between apathy and hysterical outbursts. He has also become reluctant to attend school at all, a reaction which may not be causing his teachers (or his peers) as much concern as it might.

Social adaptability is necessarily to be considered as a complex construct, incorporating social awareness, social confidence and emotional well-being. Problems in any of these areas may lead to inadequate adaptation to social situations and consequent isolation, as others reject any overtures or the individual ceases to make them. Withdrawn and isolated pupils fail to generate the 'shared understandings' (Youniss, 1992) which are essential for social adaptability.

These pupils may also miss out on the benefits of friendship and the social functions which friendship provides before and during formal schooling, especially at adolescence (Morris, 1968; Hartup, 1992). Maccoby (1980) comments: 'To become a socially mature person, the child must also share goals with others, and consider others' perspectives in order to arrive at co-operative plans' (p. 409). Friendships offer opportunities for achieving this necessary condition for social-emotional development. They enable children and young people to practise and refine their social skills in a climate of mutual understanding. Thus, child–child relationships have an important part to play in social understanding, a part which is rather different from child–adult relationships (Youniss and Volpe, 1978).

Members of groups interact with and influence one another. Groups also offer a basis for social comparison so that individuals can see how their behaviour and performance appear in the light of what others do and achieve (Hargie, Saunders and Dickson, 1994). The powerful effect of group norms is marked in late childhood and adolescence. Not to have access to these group experiences cuts individuals off from their peers and from the status and protection which the group can provide.

Inadequate social relationships, therefore, affect important aspects of an individual's social, emotional and cognitive development. While the whole concept of 'adequacy' in this complex area is open to debate, it can be said that if the individual feels inadequate in establishing and maintaining social relationships, then his or her self-esteem suffers, whatever interpersonal behaviour is displayed.

What can be done to help?

Teachers

Teachers are not unaware of those pupils in their class who are severely withdrawn and isolated, although they are often at a loss as to how best they can be helped. Assessment can also reveal others in the class whose problem may not be so acute but which is also deleterious to their psychological health. Especially in the early years at school, social skills training can help not just socially insecure class members but many of the others as well. Adolescents are more difficult to help, as they become increasingly sensitive to what may be seen as adult intrusion into personal or peer group matters. To establish a school climate conducive to shared behaviour, plan opportunities for group activities, be alert to changes in social behaviour and attend to what is happening outside the classroom as well as inside it, are important responsibilities for teachers, whatever the age of the pupil. Teachers are also the link between pupils and those outside school, in particular, parents.

Parents, sibling and peers

The parental contribution to their child's social development is considerable. But it is not one-way. The children themselves play an active part in constructing the interactions that develop, so that the process of child-rearing can change between one child and the next. Cultural, societal and gender considerations also affect both the interactions and the expectations within and beyond the family. Yet parents, like teachers, may be unaware of difficulties in social development unless they are marked. Children are reluctant to admit to even quite serious problems, such as bullying or name-calling, fearing that parental involvement could worsen the situation. It can be surprising how far children will go to conceal their negative relationships with their peers.

How parents can help withdrawn and isolated children cannot, therefore, be firmly stated. Rather, they need to be sensitive to their child's reactions to others, children and adults, and to his or her attitudes to school. Academic performance can also be a useful clue, especially if it suddenly deteriorates. As in school, there need to be opportunities in the home for children and young people to feel part of a corporate whole and realize their responsibilities and rights (Maccoby, 1980).

Where help is offered to promote their child's social expertise, parents can do a great deal to support any programme, even though it may not be easy for them to alter their established relationship with the child. They can also, of course, initiate requests for help from the school or other professionals, if need be.

Relationships between siblings is another sensitive area. Dunn (1988) has stressed how co-operative play between siblings can be observed from a very early age, although concern for self may well be dominant then and in later years. It is in the context of family relationships that children develop the social skills which they find to be effective in getting them what they want, and the cognitive understanding which accompanies and determines their social behaviour. The detail of how development comes about is still not fully known, and hence the reasons for individual differences are not easily accounted for. There is no questioning the importance of early family relationships, however, although parents, trying to cope with their own pressures, may find sibling rivalry aggravating rather than developmental. Help given to young children at crucial points in behavioural crises can prevent the adoption of negative viewpoints and promote social understanding.

Eisenberg and Mussen (1989) point out that the roots of prosocial, altruistic behaviour also lie in early family experiences and, while a relationship between prosocial behaviour and self-esteem has not been shown, such behaviour does help children to respond to others in peer group situations and establish friendships, a vital ingredient in positive social interactions.

As children grow older and become less family-centred, the importance of peer relationships increases. If the peer group continues to reject certain individuals because of what is seen as their negative attributes or inability to display expected social reactions, then social skills training programmes are unlikely to be wholly successful. This is a good reason for suggesting that training programmes should have a wider audience than just the individuals who seem to function inadequately when with others. All class members need to consider the feelings of others, and groups have to be structured in such a way that the positive strategies which are being indicated in classroom discussion are implemented in co-operative group work (see Cowie and Rudduck, 1990; Kutnick and Rogers, 1994).

Often because of the pressures under which they themselves are living, parents can take up an entrenched position which serves to perpetuate the behaviour difficulties their children are displaying. They may deny there is a problem at all; blame the school (as in the case of *Susan* – see pp.43–4); or be completely indifferent to the problem (as in the case of *Wayne* – see pp.76–7). On the other hand, they may be over-protective (as in the case of *Ewan* and *Eddie* – see pp.33 and 104–5) or be faced with quite different behaviour at home than that shown in school (as with *Daisy* and *Robin* – see pp.35 and 38–9). The importance of home and school working together is clear, just as is the need for changes in the reaction of siblings and peers if new interactional skills are to be introduced and maintained.

Help from others

In addition to the help which can be offered to withdrawn and isolated pupils by teachers, parents, siblings and peer groups, other professionals and non-professionals can be involved. Support or friendship can come from a wide range of people involved in some way with these children. Adults living or working in the neighbourhood, running various organizations, or sharing a common interest can provide the basis for a relationship which may give withdrawn individuals the interactional experiences they require. They also provide opportunities for the adults concerned to observe the child's behaviour, so that difficulties in adjustment are recognized and help sought from home or school as appropriate. Benign neglect of a worrying situation is not in anyone's best interests.

Support from professionals other than teachers is often vital in resolving interactional problems. Educational psychologists, child psychiatrists, counsellors, social workers, educational welfare officers, speech therapists and peripatetic teachers are amongst those whose contribution to the individual child's well-being is of great importance. In today's financial climate, where cuts are eating away the provision of these services, it is sometimes difficult to obtain professional support from outside sources for withdrawn and isolated pupils. Once again, their needs may be overlooked while attention is focused on crisis management, as schools feel they can only afford to fund support for disruptive and disrupting children. Yet, in terms of personal well-being, those who are withdrawn and isolated could also benefit considerably from such outside help.

AREAS REQUIRING FURTHER CONSIDERATION

Social competence training

While a number of training programmes to develop social strategies exist (see Chapters 7 and 9), their long-term effect is difficult to gauge. Children's behaviour changes with the circumstances in which they find themselves and their own growth and development. The effect of any programme on such a complex area could, therefore, be essential to such changes or of moderate or even minimal importance. Spence (1983) notes how inconclusive much of the research work on social skills training has been, and later studies have also found the development of interactional skills difficult to measure. Short-term gains can often be shown, but long-term gains are much more problematic in attribution.

For any training programme to be effective, there have to be opportunities for practising new skills in order to reinforce them. When pupils have acquired the reputation of being unresponsive to others, these opportunities may seldom be available. A programme has to be embedded in the display of more tolerant attitudes towards the withdrawn pupil on the part of other pupils, staff and those at home. This change of view is not easy to achieve, especially in older pupils.

It is also the case that experiences other than social strategies training can alter social standing (e.g. a change of teacher or school; the arrival of a new pupil in the class; a different approach to a subject or the opportunity to select subjects; a sudden growth spurt). Training programmes interact with these other changes. All in all, it is not surprising that programmes aimed at advancing social development offer promise rather than proof of lasting benefit.

The impact of the National Curriculum

Pressures on all school staff have seldom been greater. The sheer amount of academic content that has to be dealt with is taxing for teachers, especially as a range of subjects is involved, with national assessment in some of them. While all schools still strive to keep individual pupils and their development at the centre of the educational process, the balance has probably tipped towards cognitive aspects of this development rather than social, emotional, creative or even physical aspects. There are no SATs (Standard Assessment Tests) in social relationships. This may be a good thing but, inevitably, it can also mean that a lower priority may be given to social development than to academic performance.

Personal and social education is not, of course, neglected in schools, and individual achievements in a variety of fields are recognized. Yet, the emphasis on meeting targets, assessing understanding and even monitoring progress, essential though it is, can make pupils in their turn feel under pressure. Behaviour problems can ensue and the negative cycle of alienation from school and its perceived values may begin.

It is because of such unfortunate possibilities that attention to the acquisition of social skills is particularly important in the early years at school and at adolescence. Selecting socially enlightening experiences for young children which fit into required attainment targets is helpful to them, as are class management techniques that encourage the co-operation of all pupils. Discussion of individual differences, opportunities for creative productions and displays of physical prowess, taking on the part of others, or thinking about alternative solutions to imaginary or real situations, all promote self-understanding and social adaptability as well as skills in communication, co-ordination, writing and listening. The National Curriculum, therefore, is not antipathetic to the development of social skills in the early years.

Adolescence, on the other hand, can present problems in this area. There seems to be a divide between what enthusiasts in the field of personal-social skills can envisage happening and the ability of the ordinary form tutor to achieve these goals. Secondary school organization removes the close personal understanding that exists in primary schools between teachers and pupils. Constant changing of venue, staff expectations, routines and assessments puts pressures on withdrawn pupils which they cannot always deal with (see *Tommy* in this chapter). There often appears to be simply not enough time to unravel the history of the experiences which have led to the present negative attitude to others. Adolescence is also a time of personal sensitivity in which even well-meaning approaches can be resented.

It may be that teaching National Curriculum requirements in an interesting way which involves pupils, with well-planned work and clear organization, is the best way to counteract withdrawal or apathy in the later school years. A sense of positive achievement in class can enhance self-esteem and even change the views of others towards isolates. It remains to be seen what effect the current emphasis on quality control and opportunities for examination success will have on pupils who find establishing relationships within the classroom very difficult.

The management of learning

The transfer to schools themselves of much of what was formerly the responsibility of central management has made significant changes in the funding and organization of education. Whether it has done anything to bridge what Sayer (1993) sees as 'the gap between what is now expected of schools and the future needs of society' (p. 1) is open to question. It has certainly altered the role of headteachers and made them focus on running not so much a 'good' school as a financially viable one. It has also led teachers to accept 'quality assurance' targets which they themselves have not set and may not believe in. As Levačić (1995) remarks, these targets may be the equivalent to 'measuring company performance by the monetary value of sales' (p. 41). The attendant pressures on pupils to perform well on fairly short tests in specific areas could encourage teachers to concentrate on certain aspects of the curriculum, especially at the primary stage, and make it difficult for them to give time to pupils' individual needs. Differentiation is now an accepted concept, but what is achieved in its pursuit can be limited.

Teachers are aware of how little they may be able to offer those whose learning is not progressing as well as it might. The need for work tailored to each learner's need becomes a stressor for teachers rather than a means of encouraging co-operative learning in which all class members participate.

There are just too many other pressing concerns. It takes time to work out why a child is displaying negative behaviour towards others and diagnose whether there are interactional deficits (i.e. social skills are not known) or interpersonal inhibitions (i.e. social skills have been acquired but are not used). Concern for the process of learning can easily become lost in a plethora of committees and an avalanche of paper.

It is easy to say that the answer to many of these problems is more money. Finances are not unlimited and prudent spending has always been considered a virtue, if not a necessity. But constant pressures on schools to manage budgetary reductions can damage educational provision, especially at the primary stage where most of the budget is allocated to salaries and essential services such as heating, books, paper and maintenance. Easing financial restrictions would make it possible for schools to offer increased support to pupils who need it, rather than just to those who demand it.

At the same time, management of classrooms can still be carried out in ways that help withdrawn and isolated pupils. Whole-class teaching may be less stressful for them than group work; careful organization and planning can minimize opportunities for others to victimize them in passing, through pushing or taunting; and what is expected of them is immediately clear.

It will be interesting to see in the future how far what is going on in classrooms will come to reflect educational principles, governmental diktats, school aspirations and parental expectations. Withdrawn and isolated pupils are rather a good litmus paper for revealing how far the system is providing for individual learners. At the moment, it is sadly often true to say that their presence is scarcely registered.

Parental considerations

If teachers are facing increased stress in their job today, so are many parents. Some, indeed, are under acute pressures – financial, employment, housing. The prevalence of depression is rising and maternal depression in particular inhibits interest in and concern for the children. Family patterns are also changing, with a growing number of non-traditional families. Children are exposed more often than before to traumatic situations such as parental discord, separation and divorce. The media provide little respite.

The 'map of experience' which children create for themselves reflects the context in which they live and, therefore, involves their home circumstances to a large degree. Where they experience different cultural contexts in home and school, confusion can lead to emotional and behavioural difficulties. Some become aggressive towards the host community; others try to make themselves invisible so as not to invite aggression. A degree of isolation is likely to be a fairly common feeling when individuals find themselves in a minority and this will only be avoided when each ethnic group accepts the other, though cultural differences remain. 'Equality of opportunities' is once again being seen as an important educational objective, with schools drawing up policies to achieve this goal and attempting to implement them. If such an objective can be reached, the isolation felt by some pupils should be reduced and their self-esteem enhanced.

Parents may place more emphasis on how accepted their child feels at school than on how well he or she does academically (Hughes, Wikeley and Nash, 1994). Withdrawal, however, is often not considered by the home to be a problem. It may be equated with 'good' behaviour, seen as a matter of the child's own choice or even not recognized as existing. To involve parents in programmes to encourage positive relationships can, therefore, be ineffective unless they themselves change their views, perhaps as a result of training programmes of their own (Webster-Stratton and Herbert, 1994).

These training programmes, aimed to change 'the interpersonal antecedents and consequences that are eliciting and maintaining children's negative behaviours' (Webster-Stratton and Herbert, 1994, p. 23), have been shown to be fairly effective where they have been tried, especially with parents of younger children. They could be of use to depressed and isolated parents as well as to those who do not recognize any problem in their child. There will always remain a hard core of parents who cannot be reached by training sessions. Some of these might respond to other approaches, such as courses on stress management, financial planning, English as an additional language or marital communication. These could be offered by a whole variety of people and make use of videos, cartoon-like productions or other presentations appropriate to the local situation.

Pupils with special needs

Pupils with learning difficulties, whether of a cognitive or physical nature, are especially vulnerable to being overlooked as friends or group members and may even suffer rejection or hostility from others. Their reactions may be slow or unpredictable and their speech difficult to understand. They may fail to follow rules properly, to join in activities or to realize when an episode is over. They may have few suggestions as to how an activity can be continued or improved. Physical disabilities can lead to name-calling rather than appropriate support; cognitive disabilities can lead to others, children and adults, dismissing them as 'thick' or 'daft'.

Tolerance of others may be falling victim to the current emphasis on competition and self-interest. The antidote would seem to be to offer opportunities for children to get to know their fellow-pupils with special needs better (Madge and Fassam, 1982). Yet integration of pupils with learning difficulties into mainstream classes has not always proved successful. Those integrated may be over-reliant on adult support; they can present problems for the ordinary teacher, who may not always make allowances for their particular problem (e.g. deafness); they may appear to be accepted in the classroom but it may be a different story in the playground or on the bus on the way home.

Pupils with special educational needs have to work hard at developing interpersonal relationships. They are more likely to be successful in this area at the primary stage than at the secondary stage. Establishing real friendships is also problematic, especially amongst older pupils. If people with disabilities were to become more prominent in society in general or on the media, attitudes could begin to change. Unfortunately, at the moment teachers may find the presence of pupils with learning difficulties in their class an additional burden and even an obstacle to the achievement of high levels of performance by the school. Integration itself may be under threat.

There are other children whose withdrawal must also cause concern. These are the pupils whose behaviour changes because of adverse circumstances (e.g. child abuse or marital breakdown), because they have become involved in drug or substance abuse, or because all their energy is being expended on various forms of employment (see *Andy*, p.87). They, too, can become isolated from their fellow-pupils, not so much because they are rejected as because they themselves reject school and see it as having little meaning in their life other than as an occasional sanctuary. Pastoral care programmes can help to break down their isolation, where these are sensitively planned, and support should always be readily available.

A FINAL COMMENT

Probably more problems have been posed than have been solved by this book. Withdrawn behaviour is usually not difficult to identify, except in its early stages. Yet it is precisely in these early stages that help can be most usefully given. As with many other conditions, personal–social developmental difficulties need to be dealt with before they begin to affect other aspects of development. Various assessments are available to supplement school and parental observation and their use could aid early identification.

Being aware that an individual is showing withdrawn behaviour does not always promote remediation. Teachers and parents, even if they recognize that the child is not at ease in interpersonal relationships, may not know what to do about it, may not agree about what should be done, or may be under too much pressure from other sources to do what they know should be done.

If this book has succeeded in demonstrating that withdrawn behaviour exists, can be assessed, and can be helped in various ways by school staff, parents, siblings, peers and professionals other than teachers, it may have done something to alleviate individual isolation and alienation. Action may be time-consuming in the immediate term, but may save considerably more time in the future, and also enhance the well-being of the pupils concerned.

References

Achenbach, T. M. (1991) *Integrative Guide for the 1991 CBCL/4–18, YSR and TRF Profiles*. Burlington: University of Vermont.

Achenbach, T. M. and Edelbrock, C. S. (1983) *Manual for the Child Behaviour Checklist and Revised Behaviour Profile*. Burlington: University of Vermont Department of Psychiatry.

Achenbach, T. M. and Edelbrock, C. S. (1986) *Manual for the Teacher's Report Form and Teacher Version of the Child Behaviour Profile*. Burlington: University of Vermont Department of Psychiatry.

Achenbach, T. M. and Edelbrock, C. S. (1987) *Manual for the Youth Self-Report and Profile*. Burlington: University of Vermont Department of Psychiatry.

Achenbach, T. M., Verhulst, F. C., Baron, G. D. and Althaus, M. (1987a) A comparison of syndromes derived from the Child Behaviour Checklist for American and Dutch Boys aged 6–11 and 12–16. *Journal of Child Psychology and Psychiatry*, **28**, 437–53.

Achenbach, T. M., Verhulst, F. C., Edelbrock, C., Baron, G. D. and Akkerhuis, G. W. (1987b) Epidemiologic comparisons of American and Dutch children II: Behavioural/emotional problems reported by teachers for ages 6 to 11. *Journal of the American Academy of Child and Adolescent Psychiatry*, **26**, 326–32.

Ainsworth, M. D. S., Bell, S. M. and Stayton, D. J. (1974) Infant–mother attachment and social development. In M. P. M. Richards (ed.) *The Integration of a Child into a Social World*. Cambridge: Cambridge University Press.

Ajmal, Y. and Rhodes, J. (1995) Solution-focused brief therapy, EPs and schools. *Educational and Child Psychology*, **12**, 16–21.

Alden, L. E., Bieling, P. J. and Meleshko, K. G. A. (1995) An interpersonal comparison of depression and social anxiety. In K. D. Craig and K. S. Dobson (eds) *Anxiety and Depression in Adults and Children*. Thousand Oaks, CA: Sage.

Archer, J. (1992) Childhood gender roles. In H. McGurk (ed.) *Childhood Social Development: Contemporary Perspectives*. Hove: Lawrence Erlbaum.

Arkin, R. M., Lake, E. A. and Baumgardner, A. H. (1986) Shyness and self-presentation. In W. H. Jones, J. M. Cheek and S. R. Briggs (eds) *Shyness: perspectives on research and treatment*. New York: Plenum.

Asarnow, J. R. (1994) Annotation: childhood-onset schizophrenia. *Journal of Child Psychology and Psychiatry*, **55**, 1345–71.

Asen, K. E. (1996) Helping the families of problem children. In V. Varma (ed.) *Managing Children with Problems*. London: Cassell.

Asendorpf, J. (1986) Shyness in middle and late childhood. In W. H. Jones, J. M. Cheek and S. R. Briggs (eds) *Shyness: perspectives on research and Treatment*. New York: Plenum.

Asendorpf, J. (1991) Development of inhibited children's coping with unfamiliarity. *Child Development*, **62**, 1460–74.

Asendorpf, J. (1993) Abnormal shyness in children. *Journal of Child Psychology and Psychiatry*, **34**, 1069–81.

Asher, S. R. (1990) Recent advances in the study of peer rejection. In S. R. Asher and J. D. Coie (eds) *Peer Rejection in Childhood*. Cambridge: Cambridge University Press.

Asher, S. R. and Dodge, K. A. (1986) Identifying children who are rejected by their peers. *Developmental Psychology*, **22**, 444–9.

Asher, S. R. and Hymel, S. (1981) Children's social competence in peer relations: sociometric and behavioural assessment. In J. D. Wine and M. D. Syme (eds) *Social Competence*. New York: Guildford Press.

Asher, S. R., Hymel, S. and Renshaw, P. D. (1984) Loneliness in children. *Child Development*, **55**, 1456–64.

Asperger, H. (1944) Die autischen Psychopathen in Kindersalter. *Archiv fur Psychiatrie und Nervenkrankheiten*, **117**, 76–136.

Asperger, H. (1979) Problems of infantile autism. *Communication*, **13**, 45–52.

Axelrod, S. (1983) *Behaviour Modification for the Classroom Teacher* (2nd edn). New York: McGraw Hill.

Axline, V. M. (1989) *Play Therapy*. London: Churchill-Livingstone.

Bagley, C. A. (1992) In-service provision and teacher resistance to whole-school change. In D. Gill, B. Mayer and M. Blair (eds) *Racism and Education*. London: Sage Publications for the Open University.

Bailey, A., Phillips, W. and Rutter, M. (1996) Autism: towards an integration of clinical, genetic, neuropsychological and neurobiological perspectives. *Journal of Child Psychology and Psychiatry*, **37**, 89–126.

Baker, C., Davies, N. and Stallard, T. (1985) Prevalence of behaviour problems in primary school children in North Wales. *British Journal of Special Education*, **12**, 19–26.

Bannister, D. and Fransella, F. (1986) *Inquiring Man: Theory of Personal Constructs*. London: Routledge & Kegan Paul.

Barnes, P. (ed.) (1995) *Personal, Social and Emotional Development of Children*. Oxford: Blackwell for the Open University.

Bash, M. A. S. and Camp, B. W. (1985) *Think Aloud: increasing social and cognitive skills – a problem solving program for children*. Champaign, IL: Research Press.

Bastiani, J. and Wolfendale, S. (eds) (1996) *Home–School Work in Britain*. London: David Fulton.

Baumrind, D. (1971) Current patterns of parental authority. *Developmental Psychology Monographs*, **4** (1, Part 2).

Beail, N. (1985) *Repertory Grid Technique and Personal Constructs: applications in clinical and educational settings*. London: Routledge & Kegan Paul.

Beazley, S. and Moore, M. (1995) *Deaf Children, their Families and Professionals*. London: David Fulton.

Beck, A. T. (1976) *Cognitive Therapy and the Emotional Disorders*. New York: International Universities Press.

Beck, S. and Forehand, R. (1984) Social skills training for children: a methodological and clinical review of behaviour modification studies. *Behavioural Psychotherapy*, **12**, 17–45.

Behar, L. B. (1977) The Preschool Behaviour Questionnaire. *Journal of Abnormal Child Psychology*, **5**, 265–75.

Behar, L. B. and Stringfield, S. (1974) A behaviour rating scale for the preschool child. *Developmental Psychology*, **10**, 601–10.

Beidel, D. C., Neal, A. M. and Lederer, A. S. (1991) The feasibility and validity of a daily diary for the assessment of anxiety in children. *Behavior Therapy*, **22**, 505–17.

Bennett, N. and Dunne, E. (1992) *Managing Classroom Groups*. London: Simon & Schuster.

Bennett, N., Desforges, C., Cockburn, A. and Wilkinson, B. (1984) *The Quality of Pupil Learning Experiences*. London: Lawrence Erlbaum.

Bentovim, A. and Kinston, W. (1978) Brief focal family therapy when the child is the referred patient: 1. Clinical. *Journal of Child Psychology and Psychiatry*, **19**, 1–12.

Berden, G. F. M. G., Althaus, M. and Verhulst, F. C. (1990) Major life events and changes in the behavioural functioning of children. *Journal of Child Psychology and Psychiatry*, **31**, 949–60.

Bergin, A. E. and Garfield, S. L. (eds) (1994) *Handbook of Psychotherapy and Behaviour Change* (4th edn). New York: John Wiley.

Besag, B. (1989) *Bullies and Victims in Schools*. Milton Keynes: Open University Press.

Beveridge, S. (1993) *Special Educational Needs in Schools*. London: Routledge.

Bierman, K. L. (1989) Improving the peer relationships of peer rejected children. In B. Lahey and A. Kazdin (eds) *Advances in Clinical Child Psychology*, 12. New York: Plenum.

Bierman, K. L. and Furman, W. (1984) The effects of social skills training and peer involvement on the social adjustment of pre-adolescents. *Child Development*, **55**, 151–62.

Bierman, K. L., Miller, C. L. and Stabb, S. D. (1987) Improving the social behaviour and peer acceptance of rejected boys: effects of social skill training with instructions and prohibitions. *Journal of Consulting and Clinical Psychology*, **55**, 194–200.

Blagg, N. R. (1987) *School Phobia and its Treatment*. London: Croom Helm.

Blatchford, P. and Sharp, S. (eds) (1994) *Breaktime and the School*. London: Routledge.

Bolger, T. (1989) Research and evaluation in counselling. In W. Dryden, D. Charles-Edwards and R. Woolfe (eds) *Handbook of Counselling in Britain*. London: Routledge.

Bolton, F. and Bolton, S. R. (1987) *Working with Violent Families: a guide for clinical and legal practitioners*. Newbury Park, CA: Sage.

Booth, T. and Swann, W. (eds) (1987) *Including Pupils with Disabilities*. Milton Keynes: Open University Press.

Boston, M. and Lush, D. (1993) Can child psychotherapists predict and assess their own work? A research note. *Association of Child Psychology and Psychiatry Review and Newsletter*, **15**, 112–19.

Bottery, M. (1992) *The Ethics of Educational Management*. London: Cassell.

Boulton, M. J. (1995) Playground behaviour and peer interaction patterns of primary school boys classified as bullies, victims or not involved. *British Journal of Educational Psychology*, **65**, 165–77.

Boulton, M. J. (1996) Lunchtime supervisors' attitudes towards playful fighting, and ability to differentiate between playful and aggressive fighting: an intervention study. *British Journal of Educational Psychology*, **66**, 367–81.

Bowlby, J. (1953) *Child Care and the Growth of Love*. Harmondsworth:

Penguin Books.

Bowlby, J. (1969) *Attachment and Loss: attachment*. New York: Basic Books.

Bowlby, J. (1973) *Attachment and Loss: separation*. New York: Basic Books.

Bowlby, J. (1980) *Attachment and Loss: loss, sadness and depression*. New York: Basic Books.

Boyle, M. H. and Jones, S. C. (1985) Selecting measures of emotional and behavioural disorders for use in general populations. *Journal of Child Psychology and Psychiatry*, **26**, 137–60.

Breakwell, G. (1990) *Interviewing*. Leicester: BPS.

Brennan, T. (1982) Loneliness at adolescence. In L. A. Peplau and D. Perlman (eds) *Loneliness: a sourcebook of current theory, research and therapy*. New York: John Wiley.

Bronfenbrenner, U. (1974) *A Report on Longitudinal Evaluations of Pre-school Programs. Vol. 2: Is Early Intervention Effective?* Washington, DC: DHEW Publication (OHD).

Brooks-Gunn, J. and Paikoff, R. L. (1992) Changes in self-feeling during the transition towards adolescence. In H. McGurk (ed.) *Childhood Social Development: contemporary perspectives*. Hove: Lawrence Erlbaum.

Brown, G. and Desforges, C. (1979) *Piaget's Theory: a psychological critique*. London: Routledge & Kegan Paul.

Brown, S. and McIntyre, D. (1993) *Making Sense of Teaching*. Buckingham: Open University Press.

Brubacher, J. W., Case, C. W. and Reagan, T. G. (1994) *Becoming a Reflective Educator*. Thousand Oaks, CA: Corwin Press.

Bruner, J. S. (1974) The organisation of early skilled action. In P. M. Richards (ed.) *The Integration of a Child into a Social World*. London: Cambridge University Press.

Bruner, J. S., Jolly, A. and Sylva, K. (eds) (1976) *Play: its role in development and evolution*. New York: Basic Books.

Bryan, J. H. (1975) Children's co-operation and helping behaviours. In E. M. Hetherington (ed.) *Review of Child Development Research*. Chicago: University of Chicago Press.

Bryant, B. K. (1992) Conflict resolution strategies in relation to children's peer relations. *Journal of Applied Developmental Psychology*, **13**, 35–50.

Bull, S. L. and Solity, J. E. (1987) *Classroom Management: principles to practice*. London: Routledge.

Bulman, L. and Jenkins, D. (1988) *The Pastoral Curriculum*. Oxford: Basil Blackwell.

Burbach, D. J., Kashani, J. H. and Rosenberg, T. K. (1989) Parental bonding and depressive disorders in adolescents. *Journal of Child Psychology and Psychiatry*, **30**, 417–29.

Burgess-Macey, C. (1992) Tackling racism and sexism in the primary classroom. In D. Gill, B. Mayor and M. Blair (eds) *Racism and Education*. London: Sage Publications for the Open University.

Burgoyne, J., Ormrod, R. and Richards, M. (1987) *Divorce Matters*. Harmondsworth: Penguin Books.

Burnham, J. and Harris, Q. (1996) Emerging ethnicity: a tale of three cultures. In K. N. Dwivedi and V. P. Varma (eds) *Meeting the Needs of Ethnic Minority Children*. London: Jessica Kingsley.

Bushell, W. (1996) The immigrant (West Indian) child in school. In K. N. Dwivedi and V. P. Varma (eds) *Meeting the Needs of Ethnic Minority Children*. London: Jessica Kingsley.

Buss, A. H. (1984) A conception of shyness. In J. A. Daly and J. C. McCroskey (eds) *Avoiding Communication: shyness, reticence and communication apprehension*. London: Sage.

Buss, A. H. (1986) A theory of shyness. In W. H. Jones, J. M. Cheek and S. R. Briggs (eds) *Shyness: perspectives on research and treatment*. New York: Plenum.

Cairns, R. B., Cairns, B. D., Neckerman, H. J., Gest, S. D. and Gariépy, J-L. (1988) Social networks and aggressive behaviour: peer support or peer rejection. *Developmental Psychology*, **24**, 815–23.

Cairns, R. B., Leung, Man-Chi, Buchanan, L. and Cairns, B. D. (1995) Friendships and social networks in childhood and adolescence – fluidity, reliability and interrelations. *Child Development*, **66**, 1330–45.

Caldwell, B. J. and Spinks, J. M. (1992) *Leading the Self-Managing School*. London: The Falmer Press.

Camp, B., Blom, G. E., Herbert, F. and van Doorninck, W. J. (1977) 'Think Aloud': a program for developing self-control in young aggressive boys. *Journal of Abnormal Child Psychology*, **5**, 157–69.

Campion, J. (1985) *The Child in Context: family-systems theory in educational psychology*. London: Methuen.

Cangelosi, J. S. (1988) *Classroom Management Strategies*. New York: Longman.

Cantwell, D. P. (1990) Depression across the early life span. In M. Lewis and S. M. Miller (eds) *Handbook of Developmental Psychopathology*. New York: Plenum.

Cantwell, D. P. and Baker, L. (1985) Speech and language: development and disorders. In M. Rutter and L. Hersov (eds) *Child and Adolescent Psychiatry: modern approaches* (2nd edn). Oxford: Basil Blackwell.

Caplan, M. Z. and Hay, D. F. (1989) Preschoolers' responses to peers' distress and beliefs about bystander intervention. *Journal of Child Psychology and Psychiatry*, **30**, 231–42.

Carlson, G. A. (1984) Comparison by age of onset in adolescent depression. *Journal of Occupational Psychiatry*, **15**, 46–9.

Cartledge, G. and Milburn, J. F. (eds) (1980) *Teaching Social Skills to Children: Innovative Approaches*. London: Pergamon.

Case, R. (1985) *Intellectual Development: Birth to Adulthood*. New York: Academic Press.

Caspi, A., Elder, G. H. and Bern, D. J. (1988) Moving away from the world: life-course patterns of shy children. *Developmental Psychology*, **24**, 824–31.

Cattell, R. B. (1946) *The Description and Measurement of Personality*. New York: World Books.

Cattell, R. B. (1965) *The Scientific Analysis of Personality*. Chicago: Aldine Publishing.

Cattell, R. B., Eber, H. W. and Tatsuoka, M. M. (1970) *The 16 Factor Personality Questionnaire*. Champaign, IL: IPAT.

Cawthron, P., James, A., Dell, J. and Seagroatt, V. (1994) Adolescent onset psychosis: a clinical and outcome study. *Journal of Child Psychology and Psychiatry*, **35**, 1321–32.

Chapman, M., Zahn-Waxler, C., Cooperman, G. and Iannotti, R. (1987) Empathy and responsibility in the motivation of children's helping. *Developmental Psychology*, **23**, 140–5.

Chazan, M. (1992) The home and the school. In J. C. Coleman (ed.) *The School Years: current issues in the socialization of young people*. London: Routledge.

Chazan, M. and Jackson, M. S. (1971) Behaviour problems in the infant school. *Journal of Child Psychology and Psychiatry*, **12**, 191–210.

Chazan, M. and Jackson, M. S. (1974) Behaviour problems in the infant school: changes over two years. *Journal of Child Psychology and Psychiatry*, **15**, 33–46.

Chazan, M., Laing, A. F. and Davies, D. (1991) *Helping Five- to Eight-Year-Olds with Special Educational Needs*. Oxford: Basil Blackwell.

Chazan, M., Laing, A. and Jackson, M. S. (1971) *Just Before School*. Oxford: Basil Blackwell, for the Schools Council.

Chazan, M., Laing, A. F., Cox, T. and Jackson, M. S. (1977) *Studies of Infant School Children 2: Deprivation and Development*. Oxford: Basil Blackwell.

Chazan, M., Laing, A. F., Shackleton Bailey, M. and Jones, G. (1980) *Some of Our Children: the early education of children with special needs*. London: Open Books.

Chazan, M., Laing, A. F., Jones, J., Harper, G. C. and Bolton, J. (1983) *Helping Young Children with Behaviour Difficulties*. London: Croom Helm.

Cheek, J. M. and Buss, A. H. (1979) *Scales of Shyness, Sociability and Self-esteem and Correlations Among Them*. University of Texas: self-published.

Cheek, J. M. and Briggs, S. R. (1990) Shyness as a personality trait. In W. R. Crozier (ed.) *Shyness and Embarrassment: perspectives from social psychology*. Cambridge: Cambridge University Press.

Cillessen, A. H. N., van Ijzendoorn, H. W., van Lieshout, C. F. M. and Hartup, W. W. (1992) Heterogeneity among peer-rejected boys: subtypes and stabilities. *Child Development*, **63**, 893–905.

Clarke-Stewart, A. (1982) *Day Care*. London: Fontana.

Clegg, D. and Billington, S. (1994) *The Effective Primary Classroom*. London: David Fulton.

Cohen, D. (1983) *Piaget: critique and reassessment*. London: Croom Helm.

Cohen, P., Cohen, J., Kasen, S., Velez, C. N., Hartmark, C., Johnson, J., Rojas, M., Brook, J. and Streuning, E. L. (1993) An epidemiological study of disorders in late childhood and adolescence – I. Age- and gender-specific prevalence. *Journal of Child Psychology and Psychiatry*, **34**, 851–68.

Coie, J. D. and Dodge, K. A. (1983) Continuities and changes in children's social status: a five-year longitudinal study. *Merrill-Palmer Quarterly*, **29**, 261–82.

Coie, J. D., Dodge, K. A. and Coppotelli, H. (1982) Dimensions and types of social status: a cross-age perspective. *Developmental Psychology*, **18**, 557–70.

Coie, J. D., Dodge, K. A. and Kupersmidt, J. B. (1990) Peer group behaviour and social status. In S. R. Asher and J. D. Coie (eds) *Peer Rejection in Childhood*. Cambridge: Cambridge University Press.

Cole, M. and Walker, S. (1989) *Teaching and Stress*. Milton Keynes: Open University Press.

Coleman, J. C. (1980) *The Nature of Adolescence*. London: Methuen.

Colmar, S. (1988) A perspective on behaviour checklists. *Educational Psychology*, **8**, 117–21.

Conners, C. K. (1969) A teacher rating scale for use in drug studies with children. *American Journal of Psychiatry*, **126**, 884–8.

Connor, M. J. (1994) Peer relations and peer pressure. *Educational Psychology in Practice*, **9**, 207–15.

Cooper, P. and McIntyre, D. (1996) *Effective Teaching and Learning*. Buckingham: Open University Press.

Cooper, P., Smith, C. J. and Upton, G. (1994) *Emotional and Behavioural Difficulties*. London: Routledge.

Coopersmith, S. (1967) *The Antecedents of Self-Esteem*. San Francisco: Freeman.

Costello, A. J., Edelbrock, C. S., Dulcan, M. K., Kalas, R. and Klaric, S. H. (1984) *Report on the NIMH Diagnostic Interview Schedule for Children (DISC)*. Washington, DC: National Institute for Mental Health.

Coulby, J. and Coulby, D. (1990) Interviewing in junior classrooms. In J. Docking (ed.) *Education and Alienation in the Junior School*. London: The Falmer Press.

Cowen, E. L., Pedersen, A., Bagigian, H., Izzo, L. D. and Troot, M. A. (1973) Long-term follow-up of early detected vulnerable children. *Journal of Consulting and Clinical Psychology*, **41**, 438–46.

Cowie, H. (1995) Child care and attachment. In P. Barnes (ed.) *Personal, Social and Emotional Development of Children*. Oxford: Blackwell for the Open University.

Cowie, H. and Pecherek, A. (1994) *Counselling: approaches and issues in education*. London: David Fulton.

Cowie, H. and Rudduck, J. (1990) *Cooperative Learning Traditions and Transitions*. London: BP Educational Service for the Cooperative Group Work Project at Sheffield University.

Cowie, H. and Sharp, S. (eds) (1995) *Peer Counselling in Schools: a time to listen*. London: David Fulton.

Cox, A. D., Puckering, C., Pound, A. and Mills, M. (1987) The impact of maternal depression in young children. *Journal of Child Psychology and Psychiatry*, **28**, 917–28.

Craig, K. D. and Dobson, K. S. (1995) Perspectives on anxiety and depression in adults and children. In K. D. Craig and K. S. Dobson (eds) *Depression in Adults and Children*. Thousand Oaks, CA: Sage.

Crockenberg, S. B. (1981) Infant irritability, mother responsiveness and social support influences on the security of infant–mother attachment. *Child Development*, **52**, 857–65.

Croll, P. and Moses, D. (1985) *One in Five: the assessment and incidence of special educational needs*. London: Routledge & Kegan Paul.

Crozier, W. R. (1995) Shyness and self-esteem in middle childhood. *British Journal of Educational Psychology*, **65**, 85–95.

Crozier, W. R. and Burnham, M. (1990) Age-related differences in children's understanding of shyness. *British Journal of Developmental Psychology*, **8**, 179–85.

Cummings, E. M. and Davies, P. T. (1994) Maternal depression and child development. *Journal of Child Psychology and Psychiatry*, **35**, 73–112.

Curran, J. P. (1979) Social skills: methodological issues and future directions. In A. S. Bellack and M. Hersen (eds) *Research and Practice in Social Skills Training*. New York: Plenum.

Curry, N. E. and Arnaud, S. H. (1984) Play in developmental pre-school settings. In T. D. Yawkey and A. Pelligrini (eds) *Child's Play: developmental and applied*. Hillside, NJ: Lawrence Erlbaum.

Dale, F. (1996) The psychodynamic approach to children with problems. In V. Varma (ed.) *Managing Children with Problems*. London: Cassell.

Daniels, A. J. (1990) Social skills training for primary-aged children. *Educational Psychology in Practice*, **6**, 159–62.

Davies, G. (1983) An introduction to life and social skills training. *Maladjustment and Therapeutic Education*, **1**, 13–21.

Dean, J. (1989) *Special Needs in the Secondary School: the whole school approach*. London: Routledge.

Delamont, S. (1980) *Sex Roles and the School*. London: Methuen.

Denham, S. A. (1986) Social cognition, pro-social behaviour, and emotion in preschoolers: contextual evaluation. *Child Development*, **57**, 194–201.

DFE (Department for Education) (1994a) *Bullying: don't suffer in silence*. London: HMSO.

DFE (Department for Education) (1994b) *Code of Practice on Special Educational Needs*. London: Central Office of Information.

DES (Department of Education and Science) (1985) *Education For All* (The Swann Report). London: HMSO.

Docking, J. (ed.) (1990a) *Education and Alienation in the Junior School*. London: The Falmer Press.

Docking, J. (1990b) *Managing Behaviour in the Primary School*. London: David Fulton.

Dodge, K. A. (1983) Behavioural antecedents of peer social status. *Child Development*, **54**, 1386–99.

Dodge, K. A. and Feldman, E. (1990) Issues in social cognition and sociometric status. In S. R. Asher and J. D. Coie (eds) *Peer Rejection in Childhood*. Cambridge: Cambridge University Press.

Dodge, K. A., Coie, J. D. and Brakke, N. P. (1982) Behaviour patterns of socially rejected and neglected preadolescents: the roles of social approach and aggression. *Journal of Abnormal Child Psychology*, **10**, 389–410.

Dryden, W. (ed.) (1993) *Questions and Answers on Counselling in Action*. London: Sage.

Duck, S. (1991) *Friends For Life* (2nd edn). Hemel Hempstead: Harvester Wheatsheaf.

Dunham, J. (1992) *Stress in Teaching*. London: Routledge.

Dunn, J. (1984) *Sisters and Brothers*. London: Fontana.

Dunn, J. (1986) Growing up in a family world: issues in the study of social development in young children. In M. Richards and P. Light (eds) *Children of Social Worlds*. Cambridge: Polity Press.

Dunn, J. (1988) *The Beginnings of Social Understanding*. Oxford: Basil Blackwell.

Dunn, J. (1996) Children's relationships: bridging the divide between cognitive and social development. *Journal of Child Psychology and Psychiatry*, **37**, 507–18.

Dunn, J. and McGuire, S. (1992) Sibling and peer relationships in childhood. *Journal of Child Psychology and Psychiatry*, **33**, 67–105.

Dunne, E. and Bennett, N. (1990) *Talking and Learning in Groups*. Basingstoke: Macmillan Education.

Durkin, K. (1995) *Developmental Social Psychology*. Oxford: Basil Blackwell.

Dwivedi, K. N. (ed.) (1993) *Group Work with Children and Adolescents: a handbook*. London: Jessica Kingsley.

Dygdon, J. A. and Conger, A. J. (1990) A direct nomination method for the identification of neglected members in children's peer groups. *Journal of Abnormal and Child Psychology*, **18**, 55–74.

D'Zurilla, T. J. and Goldfried, M. R. (1971) Problem-solving and behaviour modification. *Journal of Abnormal Psychology*, **78**, 107–26.

Edelbrock, C., Costello, A. J., Dulcan, M. K., Conover, N. C. and Kalas, R. (1986) Parent–child agreement on child psychiatric symptoms assessed via structured interview. *Journal of Child Psychology and Psychiatry*, **27**, 181–90.

Edwards, T. (1995) Uncertain knowledge and indeterminate practice. In J. Ruddock (ed.) *An Education that Empowers*. Clevedon: Multilingual Matters.

Egeland, B., Kalkoske, M., Gottesman, N. and Erickson, M. F. (1990) Preschool behaviour problems: stability and factors accounting for change. *Journal of Child Psychology and Psychiatry*, **31**, 891–909.

Eggers, C. (1978) Course and prognosis of childhood schizophrenia. *Journal of Autism and Childhood Schizophrenia*, **8**, 21–36.

Ehlers, S. and Gillberg, C. (1993) The epidemiology of Asperger syndrome: a total population study. *Journal of Child Psychology and Psychiatry*, **34**, 1327–50.

Eisenberg, N. and Mussen, P. H. (1989) *The Roots of Prosocial Behaviour in Children*. Cambridge: Cambridge University Press.

Elardo, P. T. and Caldwell, B. M. (1979) The effects of an experimental social development program on children in the middle childhood period. *Psychology in the Schools*, **16**, 93–100.

Elizur, J. (1986) The stress of school entry: parental coping behaviors and children's adjustment to school. *Journal of Child Psychology and Psychiatry*, **27**, 625–38.

Elkind, D. and Bowen, R. (1979) Imaginary audience behaviour in children and adolescents. *Developmental Psychology*, **15**, 38–44.

Ellis, R. and Whittington, D. (1981) *A Guide to Social Skill Training*. London: Croom Helm.

Ellis, R. and Whittington, D. (eds) (1983) *New Directions in Social Skill Training*. London: Croom Helm.

Ernst, C. and Angst, J. (1983) *Birth Order: its influence on personality*. Berlin: Springer Verlag.

Erwin, P. (1993) *Friendship and Peer Relations in Children*. Chichester: John Wiley.

Esser, G., Schmidt, M. H. and Woerner, W. (1990) Epidemiology and course of psychiatric disorders in school-age children – results of a longitudinal study. *Journal of Child Psychology and Psychiatry*, **31**, 243–63.

Evans, E. D. and McCandless, B. R. (1978) *Children and Youth: psychosocial development* (2nd edn). New York: Holt, Rinehart & Winston.

Eysenck, H. J. (1970) *The Structure of Human Personality*. London: Methuen.

Eysenck, H. J. and Eysenck, S. B. G. (1975) *Eysenck Personality Questionnaire (Junior)*. London: Hodder & Stoughton.

Eysenck, S. B. G. and Eysenck, H. J. (1963) The validity of questionnaires and rating assessments of extraversion and neuroticism and factorial validity. *British Journal of Psychology*, **54**, 51–62.

Faulkner, D. (1995) Play, self and the social world. In P. Barnes (ed.) *Personal, Social and Emotional Development of Children*. Oxford: Blackwell for the Open University.

Fawcett, M. (1996) *Learning Through Child Observation*. London: Jessica Kingsley.

Fell, G. (1994) You're only a dinner lady: a case study of the 'SALVE' lunchtime organiser project. In P. Blatchford and S. Sharp (eds) *Breaktime and the School*. London: Routledge.

Fergusson, D. M. and Lynskey, M. T. (1996) Adolescent resiliency to family adversity. *Journal of Child Psychology and Psychiatry*, **37**, 281–92.

Fernando, D. (1993) Working as a child psychotherapist at the Cassel Hospital. *Therapeutic Care and Education*, **2**, 343–50.

Field, T., Healy, B., Goldstein, S., Perry, S., Bendell, D., Schanberg, S., Zimmerman, E. A. and Kuhn, C. (1988) Infants of depressed mothers show depressed behaviour even with non-depressed adults. *Child Development*, **59**, 1569–97.

Finch, A. J., Jr. and Belter, R. W. (1993) Projective techniques. In T. H. Ollendick and M. Hersen (eds) *Handbook of Child and Adolescent Assessment*. Boston: Allyn & Bacon.

Finnie, V. and Russell, A. (1988) Preschool children's social status and their mothers' behavior and knowledge in their supervisory role.

Developmental Psychology, **24**, 789–801.

Fitton, J. B. (1972) Use of the Rutter Behaviour Scales. *Journal of Association of Educational Psychologists*, **3**, 45–7.

Flavell, J. H. (1963) *The Developmental Psychology of Jean Piaget*. Princeton, NJ: D. Van Nostrand.

Fontana, D. (1994) *Managing Classroom Behaviour* (2nd edn). Leicester: British Psychological Society.

Foot, H. C., Morgan, M. J. and Shute, R. H. (eds) (1990) *Children Helping Children*. New York: John Wiley.

Forman, E. A., Minick, M. and Stone, C. A. (1993) *Contexts for Learning: sociocultural dynamics in children's development*. Corby: Oxford University Press.

Foulkes, S. H. and Anthony, E. J. (1965) *Group Psychotherapy: the psychoanalytic approach* (2nd edn). Harmondsworth: Penguin Books.

Frederickson, N. (1991) Children can be so cruel – helping the rejected child. In G. Lindsay and A. Miller (eds) *Psychological Services for Primary Schools*. London: Longman.

Frederickson, N. and Simms, J. (1990) Teaching social skills to children: towards an integrated approach. *Educational and Child Psychology*, **7**, 5–17.

Frith, U. (1989) *Autism: explaining the enigma*. Oxford: Basil Blackwell.

Frosh, S. (1983) Children and teachers in schools. In S. Spence and G. Shepherd (eds) *Developments in Social Skills Training*. London: Academic Press.

Frosh, S. J. and Callias, M. M. (1980) Social skills training in an infant school setting. *Behavioural Psychology*, **8**, 69–79.

Fullan, M. (1991) *The New Meaning of Educational Change*. London: Cassell.

Furman, W., Rahe, D. F. and Hartup, W. W. (1979) Rehabilitation of socially withdrawn preschool children through mixed-age and same-age socialization. *Child Development*, **50**, 915–22.

Furnham, A. (1986) Social skills training with adolescents and young adults. In C. R. Hollin and P. Trower (eds) *Handbook of Social Skills Training Vol. 1: Applications across the Life Span*. Oxford: Pergamon.

Galloway, D. (1990) *Pupil Welfare and Counselling*. London: Longman.

Galloway, D., Leo, E. L., Rogers, C. and Armstrong, D. (1995) Motivational styles in English and mathematics among children identified as having special educational needs. *British Journal of Educational Psychology*, **65**, 477–87.

Galloway, F. (1989) *Personal and Social Education in the Primary School*. Exeter: Pergamon Educational Productions.

Galton, M., Simon, B. and Croll, P. (1980) *Inside the Primary Classroom*.

London: Routledge & Kegan Paul.

Garber, J., Kruss, M. R., Koch, M. and Lindholm, L. (1988) Recurrent depression in adolescents: a follow-up study. *Journal of the American Academy of Children and Adolescent Psychiatry*, **27**, 49–54.

Garforth, F. W. (1985) *Aims, Values and Education*. Hull: Christygate Press.

Garmezy, N. (1985) Stress-resistant children: the search for protective factors. In J. E. Stevenson (ed.) *Recent Research in Developmental Psychopathology*. Oxford: Pergamon.

Garmezy, N. and Rutter, M. (eds) (1983) *Stress, Coping and Development in Children*. New York: McGraw-Hill.

Gascoigne, E. (1995) *Working with Parents as Partners in SEN*. London: David Fulton.

Geen, R. G. (1994) Social motivation. In B. Parkinson and A. M. Colman (eds) *Emotion and Motivation*. London: Longman.

Gillberg, C. and Gillberg, I. C. (1989) Asperger syndrome – some epidemiological considerations: a research note. *Journal of Child Psychology and Psychiatry*, **30**, 631–8.

Gillberg, I. C., Hellgren, L. and Gillberg, C. (1993) Psychotic disorders diagnosed in adolescence: outcome at age 30 years. *Journal of Child Psychology and Psychiatry*, **34**, 1173–85.

Gillborn, D. (1995) *Racism and Antiracism in Real Schools*. Buckingham: Open University Press.

Ginott, H. G. (1961) *Group Psychotherapy with Children*. New York: McGraw-Hill.

Goddard, S. and Cross, J. (1987) A social skills training approach to dealing with disruptive behaviour in the primary school. *Maladjustment and Therapeutic Education*, **5**, 24–9.

Goldstein, A. P., Sprafkin, R. P., Gershaw, N. J. and Klein, P. (1980) Social skills training through structured learning. In G. Cartledge and J. F. Milburn (eds) *Teaching Social Skills to Children*. Oxford: Pergamon.

Goodman, R. (1994) A modified version of the Rutter parent questionnaire including extra items on children's strengths: a research note. *Journal of Child Psychology and Psychiatry*, **35**, 1483–94.

Goodyer, I. M. (1995) *The Depressed Child and Adolescent: developmental and clinical perspectives*. Cambridge: Cambridge University Press.

Goodyer, I. M., Wright, C. and Altham, P. M. E. (1990) Recent achievements and adversities in anxious and depressed school age children. *Journal of Child Psychology and Psychiatry*, **31**, 1063–78.

Goodyer, I. M., Ashby, L., Altham, P. M. E., Vize, C. and Cooper, P. J. (1993) Temperament and major depression in 11–16 year olds. *Journal of Child Psychology and Psychiatry*, **34**, 1409–24.

Gordon, P. (1992) Racial incidents in Britain 1988–90: a survey. *Runnymede Bulletin*, **254**, 7–9.

Gottman, J., Gonso, J. and Schuler, P. (1976) Teaching social skills to isolated children. *Journal of Abnormal Child Psychology*, **4**, 177–97.

Gottman, J. M. (1977) Towards a definition of social isolation in children. *Child Development*, **48**, 513–17.

Graham, P. and Rutter, M. (1968) The reliability and validity of the psychiatry assessment of the child, II: Interview with the parent. *British Journal of Psychiatry*, **114**, 581–92.

Gray, H. and Freeman, A. (1988) *Teaching Without Stress*. London: Paul Chapman.

Green, K. D., Forehand, R., Beck, S. J. and Vosk, B. (1980) An assessment of the relationship among measures of children's social competence and children's academic achievement. *Child Development*, **51**, 1149–56.

Gresham, F. M. and Little, S. G. (1993) Peer-referenced assessment strategies. In T. H. Ollendick and M. Hersen (eds) *Handbook of Child and Adolescent Assessment*. Boston: Allyn & Bacon.

Guralnick, M. J. (1990) Peer interactions and the development of handicapped children's social and communicative competence. In H. C. Foot, M. J. Morgan and R. H. Shute (eds) *Children Helping Children*. New York: John Wiley.

Gurney, P. (1990) The enhancement of self esteem in junior classrooms. In J. Docking (ed.) *Education and Alienation in the Junior School*. London: The Falmer Press.

Hamblin, D. (ed.) (1981) *Problems and Practice of Pastoral Care*. Oxford: Basil Blackwell.

Hamblin, D. (1986) *A Pastoral Programme*. Oxford: Basil Blackwell.

Hamblin, D. (1993) *The Teacher and Counselling* (2nd edn). Hemel Hempstead: Simon & Schuster.

Hammen, C. (1995) The social context of risk for depression. In K. D. Craig and K. S. Dobson (eds) *Anxiety and Depression in Adults and Children*. Thousand Oaks, CA: Sage.

Harber, C. and Meighan, R. (1989) *The Democratic School: educational management and the practice of democracy*. Ticknall, Derbyshire: Education Now.

Hargie, O., Saunders, C. and Dickson, D. (1994) *Social Skills in Interpersonal Communication* (3rd edn). London: Routledge.

Hargreaves, A. (1994) *Changing Teachers, Changing Times*. London: Cassell.

Hargreaves, A., Baglin, E., Henderson, P., Leeson, P. and Tossell, T. (1988) *Personal and Social Education: choices and challenges*. Oxford: Basil Blackwell.

Hargreaves, D. H. and Hopkins, D. (1991) *The Empowered School*. London: Cassell.

Hargreaves, D. H., Hestor, S. and Mellor, F. (1975) *Deviance in Classrooms*. London: Routledge & Kegan Paul.

Harrington, R. and Wood, A. (1995) Validity and classification of child and adolescent depressive disorders. Review of the field circa 1995. In G. Forrest (ed.) *Childhood Depression*. London: Association for Child Psychology and Psychiatry, Occasional Papers No. 11.

Harrington, R., Brenden Kamp, D., Groothues, C., Rutter, M., Fudge, H. and Pickles, A. (1994) Adult outcomes of childhood and adolescent depression III: Links with suicidal behaviours. *Journal of Child Psychology and Psychiatry*, **35**, 1309–19.

Harris, J., Tyre, C. and Wilkinson, C. (1993) Using the Child Behaviour Checklist in ordinary primary school. *British Journal of Educational Psychology*, **63**, 245–60.

Harris, P. L. (1989) *Children and Emotion: the development of psychological understanding*. Oxford: Basil Blackwell.

Harrop, A. (1983) *Behaviour Modification in the Classroom*. London: Hodder & Stoughton.

Harter, S. (1985) Manual for the Self-Perception Profile for Children. University of Denver (unpublished MS).

Hartup, W. W. (1978) Children and their friends. In H. McGurk (ed.) *Issues in Childhood Social Development*. London: Methuen.

Hartup, W. W. (1983) Peer relations. In P. H. Mussen (ed.) *Handbook of Child Psychology, Vol. IV: Socialization, personality and social development*. New York: John Wiley.

Hartup, W. W. (1989) Social relationships and their developmental significance. *American Psychologist*, **44**, 120–6.

Hartup, W. W. (1992) Friendships and their developmental significance. In H. McGurk (ed.) *Childhood Social Development*. Hove: Lawrence Erlbaum.

Hartup, W. W. (1996) The company they keep: friendships and their developmental significance. *Child Development*, **67**, 1–13.

Hartup, W. W., Laursen, B., Stewart, M. A. and Easterson, A. (1988) Conflict and the friendship relations of young children. *Child Development*, **59**, 1590–1600.

Hay, D. F. (1994) Prosocial development. *Journal of Child Psychology and Psychiatry*, **35**, 29–72.

Hegarty, S. and Pocklington, K. with Lucas, D. (1981) *Educating Pupils with Special Needs in the Ordinary School*. Windsor: NFER-Nelson.

Henshall, C. and McGuire, J. (1986) Gender development. In M. Richards and

P. Light (eds) *Children of Social Worlds*. Cambridge: Polity Press & Basil Blackwell.

Herbert, M. (1974) *Emotional Problems of Development in Children*. London: Academic Press.

Herbert, M. (1986) Social skills training with children. In C. R. Hollin and P. Trower (eds) *Handbook of Social Skills Training (Vol. 1)*. Oxford: Pergamon.

Herbert, M. (1987) *Behavioural Treatment of Children with Problems: a practice manual* (2nd edn). London: Academic Press.

Herbert, M. (1988) *Working with Children and their Families*. London: British Psychological Society/Routledge.

Herbert, M. (1991) *Clinical Child Psychology: social learning, development and behaviour*. Chichester: John Wiley.

Herjanic, B. and Reich, W. (1982) Development of a structured psychiatric interview: agreement between child and parent on individual symptoms. *Journal of Abnormal Child Psychology*, **10**, 307–24.

Hersov, L. (1985) School refusal. In M. Rutter and L. Hersov (eds) *Child and Adolescent Psychiatry: modern approaches* (2nd edn). Oxford: Basil Blackwell.

Hersov, L. and Berg, I. (eds) (1980) *Out of School: modern perspectives in truancy and school refusal*. Chichester: John Wiley.

Hetherington, E. M., Reiss, D. and Plomin, R. (1994) *Separate Social Worlds of Siblings*. Hillsdale, NJ: Lawrence Erlbaum.

Hightower, A. D., Work, W. C., Cowen, E. L., Lotyczewski, B. S., Spinell, A. P., Guare, J. C. and Rohrbeck, C. A. (1986) The Teacher–Child Rating Scale: a brief objective measure of elementary school children's problem behaviors and competencies. *School Psychology Review*, **15**, 393–409.

Hinde, R. A. (1976) On describing relationships. *Journal of Child Psychology and Psychiatry*, **17**, 1–19.

Hinde, R. A. (1979) *Towards Understanding Relationships*. London: Academic Press.

Hitchfield, E. M. (1973) *In Search of Promise*. London: Longman.

Hodges, K. (1993) Structured interviews for assessing children. *Journal of Child Psychology and Psychiatry*, **34**, 49–68.

Hodges, K. (1994) Reply to David Shaffer: structured interviews for assessing children. *Journal of Child Psychology and Psychiatry*, **35**, 785–8.

Hodges, K. and Zeman, J. (1993) Interviewing. In T. H. Ollendick and M. Hersen (eds) *Handbook of Child and Adolescent Assessment*. Boston: Allyn & Bacon.

Hodges, K., Gordon, Y. and Lennon, M. (1990) Parent–child agreement on symptoms assessed via a clinical research interview for children: the Child Assessment Schedule (CAS). *Journal of Child Psychology and Psychiatry*, **31**, 427–36.

Hodges, K., McKnew, D., Cytryn, L., Stern, L. and Kline, J. (1982) The Child Assessment Schedule (CAS) Diagnostic Interview: a report on reliability and validity. *Journal of the American Academy of Child Psychiatry*, **21**, 468–73.

Holly, L. (ed.) (1989) *Girls and Sexuality: teaching and learning.* Milton Keynes: Open University Press.

Holly, P. (1994) Striving for congruence: the properties of a learning system. In C. Bayne-Jardine and P. Holly (eds) *Developing Quality Schools.* London: The Falmer Press.

Hops, H. and Lewinsohn, P. M. (1995) A course for the treatment of depression among adolescents. In K. D. Craig and K. S. Dobson (eds) *Anxiety and Depression in Adults and Children.* Thousand Oaks, CA: Sage.

Howlin, P. (1986) An overview of social behaviour in autism. In E. Schopler and G. Mesibov (eds) *Social Behaviour in Autism.* New York: Plenum.

Howlin, P. and Rutter, M. (1987) *Treatment of Autistic Children.* Chichester: John Wiley.

Hughes, M., Pinkerton, G. and Plewis, I. (1979) Children's difficulties on starting infant school. *Journal of Child Psychology and Psychiatry*, **20**, 187–96.

Hughes, M., Wikely, F. and Nash, T. (1994) *Parents and their Children's Schools.* Oxford: Basil Blackwell.

Hughes, P. (1989) Counselling in education (primary and secondary). In W. Dryden, D. Charles-Edwards and R. Woolfe (eds) *Handbook of Counselling in Britain.* London: Routledge.

Hutt, C. (1978) Sex-role differentiation in social development. In H. McGurk (ed.) *Issues in Childhood Social Development.* London: Methuen.

Hymel, S. and Franke, S. (1985) Children's peer relations: assessing self-perceptions. In B. Schneider, K. Rubin and J. Ledingham (eds) *Children's Peer Relations: issues in assessment and intervention.* New York: Springer.

Hymel, S., Rubin, K. H., Rowden, R. and LeMare, L. (1990) Children's peer relationships: longitudinal prediction of internalizing and externalizing problems from middle to late childhood. *Child Development*, **61**, 2004–21.

Jackson, S. (1993) *Adolescence and its Social Worlds.* Hove: Lawrence Erlbaum.

Jahoda, G. (1959) Development of the perception of social difference in children from 6 to 10. *British Journal of Psychology*, **50**, 159–75.

James, J., Charlton, T., Leo, E. and Indoe, D. (1991) A peer to listen. *Support for Learning*, **6**, 165–9.

Jeffrey, P. (1984) *Rogers Personal Adjustment Inventory: revised.* Windsor: NFER-Nelson.

Jelinek, M. M. and Brittan, E. M. (1975) Multiracial education – 1. Inter-ethnic friendship patterns. *Educational Research*, **18**, 44–53.

Jenkins, H. (1990) Annotation – Family Therapy: developments in thinking and practice. *Journal of Child Psychology and Psychiatry*, **31**, 1015–26.

Jennings, C. (1995) Child educational psychologists and the changing contexts of child and adolescent mental health. *Educational and Child Psychology*, **12**, 5–15.

John, R., Mednick, S. and Schulsinger, F. (1982) Teacher reports as a predictor of schizophrenia and borderline schizophrenia: a Bayesian decision analysis. *Journal of Abnormal Psychology*, **91**, 399–413.

Johnson, J. H. (1986) *Life Events as Stressors in Childhood and Adolescence.* Newbury Park, CA: Sage.

Johnson, K. (1989) *Trauma in the Lives of Children.* Basingstoke: Macmillan.

Jowett, S. and Baginsky, M. with MacNeil, M. M. (1991) *Building Bridges.* Windsor: NFER-Nelson.

Kagan, J. and Moss, H. A. (1982) *Birth to Maturity.* New York: John Wiley.

Kahn, J. H., Nursten, J. P. and Carroll, H. C. M. (1981) *Unwillingly to School: school phobia or school refusal – a psycho-social problem.* Oxford: Pergamon.

Kandel, D. B. (1986) Adult sequelae of adolescent depressive symptoms. *Archives of General Psychiatry*, **43**, 255–64.

Kane, B. (1979) Children's concept of death. *Journal of Genetic Psychology*, **134**, 141–53.

Kauffman, J. M., Lloyd, J. W. and McGee, K. A. (1989) Adaptive and maladaptive behaviour: teachers' attitudes and their technical assistance needs. *Journal of Learning Disabilities*, **21**, 19–22.

Kazdin, A. E. (1990) Childhood depression. *Journal of Child Psychology and Psychiatry*, **31**, 121–60.

Kehle, T. J. and Gonzales, F. (1991) Self-modeling for children's emotional and social concerns. In P. W. Dowrick (ed.) *Practical Guide to Using Video in the Behavioural Sciences.* New York: John Wiley.

Keller, M. B., Beardslee, W., Lavon, P. W., Wunder, J., Samuelson, D. L. and Samuelson, H. (1988) Course of major depression in non-referred adolescents: a retrospective study. *Journal of Affective Disorders*, **15**, 235–43.

Kellmer Pringle, M. L. (1970) *Able Misfits.* London: Longman.

Kelly, G. (1955) *The Psychology of Personal Constructs.* New York: Norton.

Kelvin, R. G., Goodyer, I. M. and Altham, P. M. E. (1996) Temperament and psychopathology amongst siblings of probands with depressive and anxiety disorders. *Journal of Child Psychology and Psychiatry*, **37**, 543–50.

Kendall, P. C. and Brady, E. U. (1995) Comorbidity in the anxiety disorders of childhood: implications for validity and clinical significance. In K. D. Craig and K. S. Dobson (eds) *Anxiety and Depression in Adults and Children*. Thousand Oaks, CA: Sage.

Kennedy, E., Spence, S. H. and Hensley, R. (1989) An examination of the relationships between childhood depression and social competence amongst primary school children. *Journal of Child Psychology and Psychiatry*, **30**, 561–73.

Kent, L., Vostanis, P. and Feehan, C. (1995) Teacher reported characteristics of children with depression. *Educational and Child Psychology*, **12**, 62–70.

Kimmel, D. C. (1985) *Adolescence: a developmental transition*. Hillsdale, NJ: Lawrence Erlbaum.

King, R. (1978) *All Things Bright and Beautiful? – a sociological study of infants' classrooms*. Chichester: John Wiley.

Kinston, W. and Bentovim, A. (1978) Brief focal family therapy when the child is the referred patient. II: Methodology and Results. *Journal of Psychology and Psychiatry*, **19**, 119–43.

Kitzinger, S. and Kitzinger, C. (1989) *Talking with Children about Things that Matter*. London: Pandora Press.

Kline, P. (1993) *The Handbook of Psychological Testing*. London: Routledge.

Knight, D., Hensley, V. R. and Waters, B. (1988) A validation of the Children's Depression Scale and the Children's Depression Inventory with a prepubertal sample. *Journal of Child Psychology and Psychiatry*, **29**, 853–63.

Kolko, D. J. and Kazdin, A. E. (1993) Emotional/behavioral problems in clinic and nonclinic children: correspondence among child, parent and teacher reports. *Journal of Child Psychology and Psychiatry*, **34**, 991–1006.

Kolvin, I. and Fundudis, T. (1981) Elective mute children: psychological development and background factors. *Journal of Child Psychology and Psychiatry*, **22**, 219–32.

Kolvin, I., Garside, R. F., Nicol, A. R., MacMillan, A., Wolstenholme, F. and Leitch, I. F. (1977) Familial and social correlates of behavioural and sociometric deviance in 8 year old children. In P. J. Graham (ed.) *Epidemiological Approaches in Child Psychiatry*. London: Academic Press.

Kolvin, I., Garside, R. F., Nicol, A. R., MacMillan, A., Wolstenholme, E. and Leitch, I. F. (1981) *Help Starts Here*. London: Tavistock Publications.

Kovacs, M. (1978) *Interview Schedule for Children (ISC) (10th revision)*. University of Pittsburg School of Medicine.

Kovacs, M. (1985) The Children's Depression Inventory. *Psychopharmacology Bulletin*, **21**, 995–8.

Kovacs, M. and Gatsonis, C. (1989) Stability and change in childhood-onset depressive disorders: longitudinal course as a diagnostic validator. In L. N. Robins and J. E. Barrett (eds) *The Validity of Psychiatric Diagnosis*. New York: Raven.

Kovacs, M., Feinberg, T. L., Crouse-Novak, M. A., Paulauskas, S. L. and Finkelstein, R. (1984a) Depressive disorders in childhood I: a longitudinal prospective study of characteristics and recovery. *Archives of General Psychiatry*, **41**, 229–237.

Kovacs, M., Feinberg, T. L., Crouse-Novak, M. A., Paulauskas, S. L., Pollock, M. and Finkelstein, R. (1984b) Depressive disorders in childhood II: a longitudinal study of the risk for a subsequent major depression. *Archives of General Psychiatry*, **41**, 643–9.

Kupersmidt, J. B. and Coie, J. D. (1990) Preadolescent peer status, aggression and school adjustment as predictors of externalizing problems in adolescence. *Child Development*, **61**, 1350–62.

Kupersmidt, J. B., Coie, J. D. and Dodge, K. A. (1990) The role of poor peer relationships in the development of disorder. In S. R. Asher and J. D. Coie (eds) *Peer Rejection in Childhood*. Cambridge: Cambridge University Press.

Kurtz, Z., Thornes, R. and Wolkind, S. (1996) Educational psychology and the educational sector in mental health services for children and young people: findings from recent national research. *Educational and Child Psychology*, **13**, 52–9.

Kutnick, P. and Rogers, C. (eds) (1994) *Groups in Schools*. London: Cassell.

Kyriacou, C. (1986) *Effective Teaching in Schools*. Hemel Hempstead: Simon & Schuster.

Ladd, G. W. (1990) Having friends, keeping friends, and being liked by peers in the classroom: predictors of children's early school adjustment? *Child Development*, **61**, 1081–1100.

Ladd, G. W. and Golter, B. S. (1988) Parents' management of preschoolers' peer relations: is it related to children's social competence? *Developmental Psychology*, **24**, 109–17.

Ladd, G. W., Muth, S. and Hart, C. H. (1991) Parents' management of children's peer relationships: facilitating and supervising children's activities in the peer culture. In R. D. Parke and G. W. Ladd (eds) *Family–peer Relationships: modes of linkage*. Hillsdale, NJ: Lawrence Erlbaum.

La Greca, A. M. and Santogrossi, D. A. (1980) Social skills training with elementary school students: a behavioral group approach. *Journal of Consulting and Clinical Psychology*, **48**, 220–8.

Laing, A. F. and Chazan, M. (1987) *Teachers' Strategies in Coping with Behaviour Difficulties in First Year Junior School Children*, Maidstone: Association of Workers for Maladjusted Children.

Lambert, N. M. and Bower, E. M. (1961) *A Process For In-school Screening of Children with Emotional Handicaps*. Princeton, NJ: Educational Testing Service.

Lang, M. and Tisher, M. (1978) *Children's Depression Scale*. Victoria, Australia: Australian Council for Educational Research.

Lang, M. and Tisher, M. (1983) *Children's Depression Scale – 2nd Research Edition*. Victoria, Australia: Australian Council for Educational Research.

Lang, P. (1990) Responding to disaffection: talking about pastoral care in the primary school. In J. Docking (ed.) *Educational and Alienation in the Junior School*. London: The Falmer Press.

Langner, T. S., Gersten, J. C., McCarthy, E. D. and Eisenberg, J. G. (1976) A screening inventory for assessing psychiatric impairment in children 6 to 18. *Journal of Consulting Clinical Psychology*, **44**, 286–96.

Lansdown, R. (1992) The child's concept of death. In C. Kaplan (ed.) *Bereaved Children*. London: Association for Child Psychology and Psychiatry, Occasional Papers No. 7.

Latane, B. and Darley, J. M. (1970) *The Unresponsive Bystander: why doesn't he help?* Englewood Cliffs, NJ: Prentice Hall.

Latane, B. and Nida, S. (1981) Ten years of research on group size and helping. *Psychological Bulletin*, **89**, 308–24.

Lau, A. (1996) Family therapy and ethnic minorities. In K. N. Dwivedi and V. P. Varma (eds). *Meeting the Needs of Ethnic Minority Children*. London: Jessica Kingsley.

Lawrence, B. and Bennett, S. (1992) Shyness and education: the relationship between shyness, social class and personality variables in adolescents. *British Journal of Educational Psychology*, **62**, 257–63.

Lazarus, P. J. (1982) Incidence of shyness in elementary school age children. *Psychological Reports*, **51**, 904–6.

Ledingham, J. E. and Schwartzman, A. E. (1984) Developmental patterns of aggressive and withdrawn behavior in childhood: preliminary findings. *Journal of Abnormal and Child Psychology*, **12**, 157–68.

Leech, N. and Wooster, A. D. (1986) *Personal and Social Skills*. Oxford: Pergamon.

Lefkowitz, M. M. and Tesiny, E. P. (1985) Depression in children: prevalence and correlates. *Journal of Consulting and Clinical Psychology*, **53**, 647–56.

Levačić, R. (1995) *Local Management of Schools: analysis and practice.* Buckingham: Open University Press.

Lewis, A. and Lewis, V. (1988) Young children's attitudes, after a period of integration, towards peers with severe learning difficulties. *European Journal of Special Needs Education*, **3**, 161–71.

Leyden, S. (1985) *Helping the Child of Exceptional Ability.* London: Croom Helm.

Light, P. (1979) *The Development of Social Sensitivity.* Cambridge: Cambridge University Press.

Lindsay, G. and Peake, A. (eds) (1989) Child sexual abuse. *Educational and Child Psychology*, **6**, 1.

Lindsay, G. and Wedell, K. (1982) The early identification of educationally 'at risk' children revisited. *Journal of Learning Disabilities*, **15**, 212–17.

Lollis, S. P., Ross, H. S. and Tate, E. (1991) Parents' regulation of children's peer interactions. In R. D. Parke and G. W. Ladd (eds) *Family–peer Relationships: modes of linkage.* Hillsdale, NJ: Lawrence Erlbaum.

Lord, C. (1984) The development of peer relationships in children with autism. In F. Morrison, F. McHale, C. Lord and D. Keating *Applied Developmental Psychology I.* New York: Academic Press.

McAdam, E. and Gilbert, P. (1985) Cognitive psychotherapy. *Association of Child Psychology and Psychiatry Newsletter*, **7**, 19–27.

McCabe, M. and Marwit, S. J. (1993) Depressive symptomatology, perceptions of attractiveness, and body image in children. *Journal of Child Psychology and Psychiatry*, **34**, 1117–24.

McCaffery, J. and Lyons, E. (1993) Teaching children to be good friends – developmental groupwork with vulnerable children. *Educational and Child Psychology*, **10**, 75–7.

McCandless, B. R. and Marshall, H. R. (1957) A picture sociometric technique for pre-school children and its relation to teacher judgements of friendship. *Child Development*, **28**, 139–47.

McClure, L. F., Chinsky, J. M. and Larcen, S. W. (1978) Enhancing social problem solving performance in an elementary school setting. *Journal of Educational Psychology*, **70**, 504–13.

Maccoby, E. E. (1980) *Social Development.* New York: Harcourt Brace Jovanovich.

MacDonald, K. and Parke, R. D. (1984) Bridging the gap: parent–child play interaction and peer interactive competence. *Child Development*, **55**, 1265–77.

Macfarlane, J. W., Allen, L. and Honzik, M. P. (1954) *A Developmental Study of the Behaviour Problems of Normal Children between Twenty-one Months and Fourteen Years.* University of California Publications on Child Development, 2. Berkeley: University of California Press.

McGee, R. and Stanton, W. R. (1992) Sources of distress among New Zealand adolescents. *Journal of Child Psychology and Psychiatry*, **33**, 999–1010.

McGee, R., Silva, P. A. and Williams, S. (1984) Behaviour problems in a population of seven year old children: prevalence, stability and types of disorder – a research report. *Journal of Child Psychology and Psychiatry*, **25**, 251–60.

McGrew, W. C. (1972) *An Ethological Study of Children's Behaviour.* New York: Academic Press.

McGuire, J. and Richman, N. (1986) The prevalence of behavioural problems in three types of preschool group. *Journal of Child Psychology and Psychiatry*, **27**, 455–72.

McGurk, H. (1992) *Childhood Social Development: contemporary perspectives.* Hove: Lawrence Erlbaum.

McKinney, J. P., Fitzgerald, H. E. and Strommen, E. A. (1977) *Developmental Psychology: the adolescent and young adult.* Homewood, IL: Dorsey Press.

McMullin, R. E. (1987) *Handbook of Cognitive Therapy Techniques.* London: Norton.

McNiff, J. (1985) *Personal and Social Education: a teacher's handbook.* Cambridge: Hobsons.

Madge, N. and Fassam, M. (1982) *Ask the Children: experiences of physical disability in the school years.* London: Batsford.

Maguire, U. (1973) Counselling effectiveness: a critical discussion. *British Journal of Guidance and Counselling*, **1**, 38–51.

Malek, M. (1996) *Home–School Work* (Highlight No. 145). London: National Children's Bureau.

Malik, N. M. and Furman, W. (1993) Problems in children's peer relations: what can the clinician do? *Journal of Child Psychology and Psychiatry*, **34**, 1303–26.

Marcoen, A. and Goosens, L. (1993) Loneliness, attitude towards aloneness and solitude: age differences and developmental significance during adolescence. In S. Jackson and H. Rodriguez-Tomé (eds) *Adolescence and its Social Worlds.* Hove: Lawrence Erlbaum.

Marks, I. (1987) The development of normal fear: a review. *Journal of Child Psychology and Psychiatry*, **28**, 667–97.

Martlew, M. and Hodson, J. (1991) Children with mild learning difficulties in an integrated and in a special school: comparisons of behaviour, teasing and teachers' attitudes. *British Journal of Educational Psychology*, **61**, 355–72.

Masten, A. S., Morison, P. and Pellegrini, D. S. (1985) A revised class play method of peer assessment. *Developmental Psychology*, **21**, 523–33.

Matsuura, M., Okubo, Y., Kojima, T., Takahashi, R., Wang, Y.-F., Shen, Y.-C. and Lee, C. K. (1993) A cross-national prevalence study of children with emotional and behavioural problems – a WHO collaborative study in the Western Pacific Region. *Journal of Child Psychology and Psychiatry*, **34**, 307–15.

Mays, W. (1982) Piaget's sociological theory. In S. Modgil and C. Modgil (eds) *Jean Piaget: consensus and controversy*. London: Holt, Rinehart & Winston.

Meadows, S. (1986) *Understanding Child Development*. London: Hutchinson.

Meadows, S. (1993) *The Child as Thinker*. London: Routledge.

Mearns, D. and Thorne, B. (1988) *Person-centred Counselling in Action*. London: Sage.

Meichenbaum, D. (1983) Cognitive behaviour modification with exceptional children: a promise yet unfulfilled. *Exceptional Children Quarterly*, **1**, 83–8.

Meichenbaum, D. H. and Goodman, J. (1971) Training impulsive children to talk to themselves: a means of developing self-control. *Journal of Abnormal Psychology*, **77**, 115–26.

Melhuish, E. C., Lloyd, E., Martin, S. and Mooney, A. (1990a) Type of child care at 18 months – 2: relations with cognitive and language development. *Journal of Child Psychology and Psychiatry*, **31**, 861–70.

Melhuish, E. C., Mooney, A., Martin, S. and Lloyd, E. (1990b) Type of child care at 18 months – 1: differences in interactional experience. *Journal of Child Psychology and Psychiatry*, **31**, 849–60.

Mellsop, G. W. (1972) Psychiatric patients seen as children and adults: childhood predictors of adult illness. *Journal of Child Psychology and Psychiatry*, **13**, 91–101.

Merikangas, K. R. and Angst, J. (1995) The challenge of depressive disorders in adolescence. In M. Rutter (ed.) *Psychosocial Disturbances in Young People: challenge for prevention*. Cambridge: Cambridge University Press.

Merrett, F. and Wheldall, K. (1984) Classroom behaviour problems which junior school teachers find most troublesome. *Educational Studies*, **10**, 87–91.

Michelson, L., Mannarino, A. P., Marchione, K. E., Stern, M., Figueroa, J. and Beck, S. (1983) A comparative outcome study of behavioural social-skills training, interpersonal-problem solving and non-directive control treatments with child psychiatric patients. *Behaviour Research and Therapy*, **21**, 545–56.

Miller, L. C. (1967) Louisville Behaviour Checklist for Males (6–12). *Psychological Reports*, **21**, 885–96.

Mitchell, J. (1990) Students' perceptions of difference among their peers. Paper presented at International Special Education Congress, Cardiff, Wales, July 1990.

Mitchell, S. (1991) *The PSE Staff Development Manual*. Lancaster: Framework Press.

Mize, J. and Ladd, G. (1990) A cognitive–social learning approach to social skill training. *Developmental Psychology*, **26**, 388–97.

Mooney, A., Creeser, R. and Blatchford, P. (1991) Children's views on teasing and fighting in junior schools. *Educational Research*, **33**, 103–12.

Mooney, R. L. and Gordon, L. V. (1950) *Mooney Problem Check List*. New York: Psychological Corporation.

Moran, S., Smith, P. K., Thompson, D. and Whitney, I. (1993) Ethnic differences in experiences of bullying: Asian and white children. *British Journal of Educational Psychology*, **63**, 431–40.

Morgan, V. and Pearson, S. (1994) Social skills training in a junior school setting. *Educational Psychology in Practice*, **10**, 99–103.

Morris, J. F. (1968) Social learning and perspectives in adolescence. In E. A. Lunzer and J. F. Morris (eds) *Development in Human Learning*. London: Staples Press.

Mortimore, P. (1986) *The Junior School Project Part C: Understanding School Effectiveness*. London: ILEA Research and Statistics Branch.

Moses, D. (1982) Special educational needs: the relationship between teacher assessment, test scores and classroom behaviour. *British Educational Research Journal*, **8**, 111–22.

Mosley, J. (1993) *Turn Your School Around*. Wisbech: LDA.

Murfitt, J. and Thomas, J. B. (1983) The effects of peer counselling on the self-concept and reading attainment of secondary-aged slow learning pupils. *Remedial Education*, **18**, 73–4.

Murgatroyd, S. (1985) *Counselling and Helping*. London: British Psychological Society/Methuen.

Murray, L. (1992) The impact of post-natal depression on infant development. *Journal of Child Psychology and Psychiatry*, **33**, 543–61.

Musun-Miller, L. (1990) Sociometrics with pre-school children: agreement between different strategies. *Journal of Applied Developmental Psychology*, **11**, 195–207.

Nabuzoka, D. and Smith, P. K. (1993) Sociometric status and social behaviour of children with and without learning difficulties. *Journal of Child*

Psychology and Psychiatry, **34**, 1435–48.

Neeper, R. and Lahey, B. B. (1988) *Comprehensive Behaviour Rating Scale for Children (CBRSC)*. Sidcup: Psychological Corporation.

Nelson-Jones, R. (1993) *Practical Counselling and Helping Skills*. London: Cassell.

Newcomb, A. F. and Bukowski, W. M. (1984) A longitudinal study of the utility of social preference and social impact of sociometric classification schemes. *Child Development*, **55**, 1434–47.

Newcomb, A. F., Bukowski, W. M. and Pattee, L. (1993) Children's peer relations: a meta-analytic review of popular, rejected, neglected, controversial and average sociometric status. *Psychological Bulletin*, **113**, 99–128.

Newson, J. and Newson, E. (1963) *Infant Care in an Urban Community*. London: Allen & Unwin.

Newson, J. and Newson, E. (1968) *Four Years Old in an Urban Community*. London: Allen & Unwin.

Newson, J. and Newson, E. (1976) *Seven Years Old in the Home Environment*. London: Allen & Unwin.

Nowicki, S., Jr. and Strickland, B. R. (1973) A locus of control scale for children. *Journal of Consulting and Clinical Psychology*, **40**, 148–54.

Oden, S. (1980) A child's social isolation: origins, prevention, intervention. In G. Cartledge and J. F. Milburn (eds) *Teaching Social Skills to Children*. Oxford: Pergamon.

O'Leary, K. D. and O'Leary, S. G. (1977) *Classroom Management: the successful use of behaviour modification*. New York: Pergamon.

Ollendick, T. H. (1983) Reliability and validity of the Revised Fear Survey Schedule for Children (FSSC-R). *Behavior Research and Therapy*, **21**, 685–92.

Ollendick. T. H. (1995) Assessment of anxiety and phobic disorders in children. In K. D. Craig and K. S. Dobson (eds) *Anxiety and Depression in Adults and Children*. Thousand Oaks, CA: Sage.

Ollendick, T. H. and Hersen, M. (eds) (1993) *Handbook of Child and Adolescent Assessment*. Boston: Allyn & Bacon.

Ollendick, T. H., King, N. J. and Frary, R. B. (1989) Fears in children and adolescents: reliability and generalizability across gender, age and nationality. *Behaviour Research and Therapy*, **27**, 19–26.

Ollendick, T. H., Yule, W. and Ollier, K. (1991) Fears in British children and their relationship to manifest anxiety and depression. *Journal of Child Psychology and Psychiatry*, **32**, 321–31.

Ollendick, T. H., Greene, R. W., Francis, G. and Baum, C. G. (1991) Sociometric status: its stability and validity among neglected, rejected and unpopular children. *Journal of Child Psychology and Psychiatry*, **32**, 525–34.

Olweus, D. (1991) Bully/victim problems among schoolchildren: basic facts and effects of a school-based intervention programme. In D. Pepler and K. Rubin (eds) *Development and Treatment of Childhood Aggression*. Hillsdale, NJ: Lawrence Erlbaum.

Olweus, D. (1993) *Bullying at School: what we know and what we can do*. Oxford: Basil Blackwell.

Osborn, A. F., Butler, N. R. and Morris, A. (1984) *The Social Life of Britain's Five-year-olds*. London: Routledge & Kegan Paul.

Ostrov, E. and Offer, D. (1978) Loneliness and the adolescent. In S. C. Feinstein and P. L. Giovacchini (eds) *Adolescent Psychiatry, Vol. VI*. Chicago: University of Chicago Press.

Paisey, A. (1981) *Organization and Management in Schools*. London: Longman.

Parke, R. D. and Bhavnagri, N. P. (1988) Parents as managers of children's peer relationships. In D. Belle (ed.) *Children's Social Networks and Social Supports*. New York: John Wiley.

Parker, J. G. and Asher, S. R. (1987) Peer relations and later personal adjustment: are low-accepted children at risk? *Psychological Bulletin*, **102**, 357–89.

Parkhurst, S. T. and Asher, S. R. (1992) Peer rejection in middle school: subgroup differences on behaviour, loneliness and interpersonal concerns. *Developmental Psychology*, **28**, 231–41.

Parkinson, B. and Colman, A. M. (eds) (1994) *Emotion and Motivation*. London: Longman.

Parten, M. (1932/3) Social participation among pre-school children. *Journal of Abnormal and Social Psychology*, **27**, 243–69.

Pearce, J. (1977) Depressive disorder in childhood. *Journal of Child Psychology and Psychiatry*, **18**, 79–84.

Pellegrini, D. S. and Urbain, E. S. (1985) An evaluation of interpersonal cognitive problem-solving training with children. *Journal of Child Psychology and Psychiatry*, **26**, 17–41.

Peplau, L. A. and Perlman, D. (eds) (1982) *Loneliness: a sourcebook of current theory, research and therapy*. New York: John Wiley.

Perlman, D. and Peplau, L. A. (1981) Toward a social psychology of loneliness. In R. Gilmour and S. Duck (eds) *Personal Relationships: Vol. 3, Relationships in Disorder*. London: Academic Press.

Perry, D. G., Kusel, S. J. and Perry, L. C. (1988) Victims of peer aggression. *Developmental Psychology*, **24**, 807–14.

Persons. J. B. (1989) *Cognitive Therapy in Practice*. London: Norton.

Pervin, L. P. (1980) *Personality: theory, assessment and research*. New York: John Wiley.

Peters, R. S. (1973) *Authority, Responsibility and Education* (3rd edn). London: George Allen & Unwin.

Phillips, J. L., Jr. (1975) *The Origins of Intellect: Piaget's Theory* (2nd edn). San Francisco: W. H. Freeman & Co.

Piaget, J. (1951) *Play, Dreams and Imitation in Childhood*. London: Routledge & Kegan Paul.

Pierce, J. W. and Wardle, J. (1993) Self esteem, parental appraisal and body size in children. *Journal of Child Psychology and Psychiatry*, **34**, 1125–36.

Pilkonis, P. A. (1977) Shyness, public and private, in its relationship to other measures of social behavior. *Journal of Personality*, **45**, 585–95.

Pilling, D. and Pringle, M. K. (1978) *Controversial Issues in Child Development*. London: Paul Elek.

Pollard, A. and Tann, S. (1987) *Reflective Teaching in the Primary School*. London: Cassell.

Porter, R. B. and Cattell, R. B. (1968) *Children's Personality Questionnaire*. Los Angeles, CA: Western Psychological Services.

Poteet, J. A. (1973) *Behaviour Modification: a practical guide for teachers*. University of London Press.

Povey, R. (ed.) (1980) *Educating the Gifted Child*. London: Harper & Row.

Preedy, M. (ed.) (1993) *Managing the Effective School*. London: Paul Chapman for the Open University.

Pring, R. (1984) *Personal and Social Education in the Curriculum*. London: Hodder & Stoughton.

Puckering, C., Cox, A. D., Mills, M. and Pound, A. (1995) The effects of family background, marriage and maternal depression on children's emotional modulation. In G. Forrest (ed.) *Childhood Depression*. London: ACPP Occasional Papers No. 11.

Putallaz, M. (1987) Maternal behaviour and children's sociometric status. *Child Development*, **58**, 324–40.

Putallaz, M. and Gottman, J. (1981) Social relationship problems in children: an approach to interventions. *Advances in Clinical Child Psychology, 6*. New York: Plenum.

Putallaz, M. and Heflin, A. H. (1990) Parent–child interaction. In S. R. Asher and J. D. Coie (eds) *Peer Rejection in Childhood*. Cambridge: Cambridge University Press.

Quay, H. C. and Peterson, D. R. (1979) *Manual for the Behavior Problem Checklist*. New Brunswick, NJ: Rutgers State University.

Quay, H. C. and Peterson, D. R. (1987) *Manual for the Revised Behavior Problem Checklist (RBPC)*. Coral Gables, FL: Self-published.

Rachman, S. (1971) *The Effects of Psychotherapy*. Oxford: Pergamon.

Ratigan, B. (1989) Counselling in groups. In W. Dryden, D. Charles-Edwards and R. Woolfe (eds) *Handbook of Counselling in Britain*. London: Routledge.

Reynolds, C. R. and Paget, K. D. (1983) National normative and reliability data for the Revised Children's Manifest Anxiety Scale. *School Psychology Review*, **12**, 324–36.

Reynolds, C. R. and Richmond, B. O. (1978) What I think and feel: a revised measure of children's manifest anxiety. *Journal of Abnormal Child Psychology*, **6**, 271–80.

Rhodes, J. (1993) The use of solution-focused brief therapy in schools. *Educational Psychology in Practice*, **9**, 27–34.

Richards, M. (1974) First steps in becoming social. In M. Richards (ed.) *The Integration of a Child into a Social World*. London: Cambridge University Press.

Richards, M. (1986) Introduction. In M. Richards and P. Light (eds) *Children of Social Worlds*. Cambridge: Polity Press.

Richman, N. (1977) Is a behaviour check-list for pre-school children useful? In P. J. Graham (ed.) *Epidemiological Approaches to Child Psychiatry*. London and New York: Academic Press.

Richman. N., Stevenson, J. and Graham, P. J. (1982) *Pre-school to School: a behavioural study*. London: Academic Press.

Rinn, R. C. and Markle, A. (1979) Modification of social skills deficit in children. In A. S. Bellack and M. Hersen (eds) *Research and Practice in Social Skills Training*. New York: Plenum.

Ritvo, E. R., Freeman, B. J., Ornitz, E. M. and Tanguay, P. E. (1976) *Autism: diagnosis, current research and management*. New York: Spectrum.

Roberts, I. (1994) Achieving a clear focus: whole school planning. In C. Bayne-Jardine and P. Holly (eds) *Developing Quality Schools*. London: The Falmer Press.

Robins, L. N. (1972) Follow-up studies of behavior disorders in children. In H. C. Quay and J. S. Werry (eds) *Psychopathological Disorders of Childhood*. New York: John Wiley.

Robins, L. N. and Rutter, M. (eds) (1992) *Straight and Devious Pathways from Childhood to Adulthood*. Cambridge: Cambridge University Press.

Rodgers, B. (1990) Behaviour and personality in childhood as predictors of adult psychiatric disorder. *Journal of Child Psychology and Psychiatry*, **31**, 393–414.

Roffey, S., Tarrant, T. and Majors, K. (1994) *Young Friends: schools and friendship*. London: Cassell.

Rogers, C. (1982) *A Social Psychology of Schooling*. London: Routledge &

Kegan Paul.

Rogers, C. R. (1951) *Client-centred Therapy*. Boston: Houghton-Mifflin.

Rogers, C. R. (1961) *Personal Adjustment Inventory*. New York: Association Press.

Roopnarine, J. L. and Adams, G. R. (1987) The interactional teaching patterns of mothers and fathers with their popular, moderately popular, or unpopular children. *Journal of Abnormal Child Psychology*, **15**, 125–36.

Ross, C. and Ryan, A. (1990) *Can I Stay in Today, Miss? Improving the School Playground*. Stoke-on-Trent: Trentham.

Ross, C. and Ryan, A. (1994) Changing playground society: a whole school approach. In P. Blatchford and S. Sharp (eds) *Breaktime and the School*. London: Routledge.

Ross, H. S., Tesla, C., Kenyon, B. and Lollis, S. (1991) Maternal intervention in toddler peer conflict: the socialization of principles of justice. *Developmental Psychology*, **26**, 994–1003.

Rossman, B. B. R. and Rosenberg, M. S. (1992) Family stress and functioning in children: the moderating effects of children's beliefs about their control over parental conflict. *Journal of Child Psychology and Psychiatry*, **33**, 699–716.

Rotenberg, K. J. and Whitney, P. (1992) Loneliness and disclosure processes in preadolescence. *Merrill-Palmer Quarterly*, **38**, 401–16.

Rubin, K. H. (1993) The Waterloo Longitudinal Project: correlates and consequences of social withdrawal from childhood to adolescence. In K. H. Rubin and J. B. Asendorpf (eds) *Social Withdrawal, Inhibition and Shyness in Childhood*. Hillsdale, NJ: Lawrence Erlbaum.

Rubin, K. H. and Mills, R. S. L. (1988) The many faces of social isolation in childhood. *Journal of Consulting and Clinical Psychology*, **56**, 916–24.

Rubin, K. H., Hymel, S. and Mills, R. S. L. (1989) Sociability and social withdrawal in childhood: stability and outcomes. *Journal of Personality*, **57**, 237–55.

Rubin, K. H., LeMare, L. J. and Lollis, S. (1990) Social withdrawal in childhood: developmental pathways to peer rejection. In S. R. Asher and J. D. Coie (eds) *Peer Rejection in Childhood*. Cambridge: Cambridge University Press.

Rubin, Z. and Sloman, J. (1984) How parents influence their children's friendships. In M. Lewis (ed.) *Beyond the Dyad*. New York: Plenum Press.

Russell, A. and Finnie, V. (1990) Preschool children's social status and maternal instructions to assist group entry. *Developmental Psychology*, **26**, 603–11.

Rutter, M. (1967) A children's behaviour questionnaire for completion by teachers. *Journal of Child Psychology and Psychiatry*, **8**, 1–11.

Rutter, M. (1972) *Maternal Deprivation Reassessed*. Harmondsworth: Penguin Books.

Rutter, M. (1983) Stress, coping and development: some issues and some questions. In N. Garmezy and M. Rutter (eds) *Stress, Coping and Development in Children*. New York: McGraw-Hill.

Rutter, M. (1986) Child psychiatry: looking 30 years ahead. *Journal of Child Psychology and Psychiatry*, **27**, 803–40.

Rutter, M. (1989) Pathways from childhood to adult life. *Journal of Child Psychology and Psychiatry*, **30**, 23–51.

Rutter, M. and Garmezy, N. (1983) Developmental psychopathology. In P. H. Mussen (ed.) *Handbook of Child Psychology, Vol. IV: Socialization, personality and social development*. New York: John Wiley.

Rutter, M. and Graham, P. (1968) The reliability and validity of the psychiatric assessment of the child. I. Interview with the child. *British Journal of Psychiatry*, **114**, 563–79.

Rutter, M., Tizard, J. and Whitmore, K. (eds) (1970) *Education, Health and Behaviour*. London: Longman.

Rutter, M., Graham, P., Chadwick, D. F. D. and Yule, W. (1976) Adolescent turmoil: fact or fiction. *Journal of Child Psychology and Psychiatry*, **17**, 35–56.

Rutter, M., Maughan, B., Mortimore, P. and Ouston, J. (1979) *Fifteen Thousand Hours*. London: Open Books.

Rutter, M., Cox, A., Tupling, C., Berger, M. and Yule, W. (1975) Attainment and adjustment in two geographical areas: I – The prevalence of psychiatric disorder. *British Journal of Psychiatry*, **126**, 493–509.

Ryder, J. and Campbell, L. (1988) *Balancing Acts in Personal, Social and Health Education*. London: Routledge.

Safran, S. P. (1989) Australian teachers' views of their effectiveness in behaviour management. *International Journal of Disability, Development and Education*, **36**, 15–27.

Safran, S. P. and Safran, J. S. (1987) Teachers' judgements of problem behaviors. *Exceptional Children*, **54**, 240–4.

Sandow, S. (ed.) (1994) *Whose Special Need? Some perceptions of special educational needs*. London: Paul Chapman.

Sandow, S., Stafford, D. and Stafford, P. (1987) *An Agreed Understanding? Parent–professional communication and the 1981 Education Act*. Windsor: NFER-Nelson.

Sanson, A., Oberklaid, F., Pedlow, R. and Prior, M. (1991) Risk indicators: assessment of infancy predictors of pre-school behavioural maladjustment. *Journal of Child Psychology and Psychiatry*, **32**,

609–26.

Sarason, S. B., Davidson, K. S., Lighthall, F. E., Waite, R. R. and Ruebush, B. K. (1960) *Anxiety in Elementary School Children*. New York: John Wiley.

Sawyer, M. G., Baghurst, P. and Mathias, J. (1992) Differences between informants' reports describing emotional and behavioural problems in community clinic-referred children: a research note. *Journal of Child Psychology and Psychiatry*, **33**, 441–9.

Sayer, J. (1993) *The Future Governance of Education*. London: Cassell.

Scarlett, W. G. (1980) Social isolation from agemates among nursery school children. *Journal of Child Psychology and Psychiatry*, **21**, 231–40.

Schaefer, C. E. and O'Connor, K. J. (eds) (1983) *Handbook of Play Therapy*. New York: John Wiley.

Schaffer, H. R. (1977) *Mothering*. London: Fontana/Open Books.

Schaffer, H. R. (1992) Joint involvement episodes as context for development. In H. McGurk (ed.) *Childhood Social Development: contemporary perspectives*. Hove: Lawrence Erlbaum.

Scherer, M. (1988) *Schools Skills Checklist* (see Chapter 5 in M. Scherer, I. Gersch and L. Fry (1990) *Meeting Disruptive Behaviour: assessment, intervention and partnership*). London: Macmillan.

Schiffer, M. (1971) *The Therapeutic Play Group*. London: Allen & Unwin.

Schinke, S. P., Botvin, G. J. and Orlandi, M. A. (1991) *Substance Abuse in Children and Adolescents: evaluation and intervention*. Newbury Park, CA: Sage.

Schroeder, H. E. and Rakos, R. F. (1983) The identification and assessment of social skills. In R. Ellis and D. Whittington (eds) *New Directions in Social Skill Training*. London: Croom Helm.

Schuyler, D. (1991) *A Practical Guide to Cognitive Therapy*. London: Norton.

Sears, R., Maccoby, E. E. and Levin, H. (1957) *Patterns of Child Rearing*. Evanston, IL: Row Peterson.

Seed, P. (1988) *Children with Profound Handicaps: parents' views and integration*. London: The Falmer Press.

Selman, R. L. and Hickey Schultz, L. (1990) *Making a Friend in Youth: developmental therapy and pair therapy*. Chicago: University of Chicago Press.

Semeonoff, B. (1981) Projective techniques. In F. Fransella (ed.) *Personality: theory, measurement and research*. London: Methuen.

Shaffer, D. (1994) Structured interviews for assessing children. *Journal of Child Psychology and Psychiatry*, **35**, 783–4.

Shapiro, S. B. and Sobel, M. (1981) Two multinominal random sociometric voting models. *Journal of Educational Statistics*, **6**, 287–310.

Sharp, D., Hay, D. F., Pawlby, S., Schmücker, G., Allen, H. and Kumar, R. (1995) The impact of postnatal depression on boys' intellectual development. *Journal of Child Psychology and Psychiatry*, **36**, 1315–36.

Sharp, S. (1994) Training schemes for lunch time supervisors in the United Kingdom: an overview. In P. Blatchford and S. Sharp (eds) *Breaktime and the School*. London: Routledge.

Sharp, S. (1996) The role of peers in tackling bullying in schools. *Educational Psychology in Practice*, **11**, 17–22.

Sharp, S. and Smith, P. K. (eds) (1994) *Tackling Bullying in Your School: a practical handbook for teachers*. London: Routledge.

Sheldon, B. (1982) *Behaviour Modification: theory, practice and philosophy*. London: Tavistock Publications.

Shepherd, G. (1983) Introduction. In S. Spence and G. Shepherd (eds) *Developments in Social Skills Training*. London: Academic Press.

Sherif, M. and Sherif, C. W. (1964) *Reference Groups: exploration into conformity and deviation of adolescents*. New York: Harper & Row.

Shipman, M. (1990) *In Search of Learning*. Oxford: Basil Blackwell.

Simpson, A. E. and Stevenson, J. (1985) Temperamental characteristics of three- to four-year-old boys and girls and child–family interactions. *Journal of Child Psychology and Psychiatry*, **26**, 43–53.

Siner, J. (1993) Social competence and co-operative learning. *Educational Psychology in Practice*, **9**, 170–80.

Slavson, S. R. (1943) *Introduction to Group Therapy*. New York: The Commonwealth Fund.

Sletta, O., Valås, H., Skaalvik, E. and Søbstad, F. (1996) Peer relations, loneliness and self-perceptions in school-aged children. *British Journal of Educational Psychology*, **66**, 431–45.

Smetana, J. G. (1989) Toddlers' social interactions in the context of moral and conventional transgressions in the home. *Developmental Psychology*, **25**, 499–508.

Smilansky, S. (1968) *The Effects of Sociodramatic Play on Disadvantaged Preschool Children*. London: John Wiley.

Smith, G. (1992) The unbearable traumatogenic past: child sexual abuse. In V. P. Varma (ed.) *The Secret Life of Vulnerable Children*. London: Routledge.

Smith, P. K. (1984) *Play in Animals and Humans*. Oxford: Basil Blackwell.

Smith, P. K. and Cowie, H. (1991) *Understanding Children's Development* (2nd edn). Oxford: Basil Blackwell.

Smith, P. K. and Sharp, S. (eds) (1994) *School Bullying: insights and perspectives*. London: Routledge.

Solity, J. (1992) *Special Education*. London: Cassell.

Sotto, E. (1994) *When Teaching Becomes Learning*. London: Cassell.

Spence, S. H. (1980) *Social Skills Training with Children and Adolescents: a counsellor's manual*. Windsor: NFER-Nelson.

Spence, S. H. (1983) Teaching social skills to children. *Journal of Child Psychology and Psychiatry*, **24**, 621–7.

Spivack, G. and Shure, M. B. (1974) *Social Adjustment of Young Children*. San Francisco: Jossey Bass.

Spivack, G., Platt, J. and Shure, M. B. (1976) *The Problem Solving Approach to Adjustment*. San Francisco: Jossey Bass.

Stafford-Clark, D. and Smith, A. C. (1983) *Psychiatry for Students* (6th edn). London: Allen & Unwin.

Stefanek, M. E., Ollendick, T. H., Baldock, W. P., Francis, G. and Yaeger, N. J. (1987) Self-statements in aggressive, withdrawn and popular children. *Cognitive Therapy and Research*, **2**, 229–39.

Steinberg, D. (1985) Psychotic and other severe disorders in adolescence. In M. Rutter and L. Hersov (eds) *Child and Adolescent Psychiatry: modern approaches* (2nd edn). Oxford: Basil Blackwell.

Steinberg, L. (1986) Latchkey children and susceptibility to peer pressure: an ecological analysis. *Developmental Psychology*, **22**, 433–9.

Stephan, W. G. (1985) Intergroup relations. In G. Linzey and E. Aronson (eds) *Handbook of Social Psychology* (3rd edn). New York: Random House.

Stern, A. E., Lynch, D. L., Oates, R. K., O'Toole, B. I. and Cooney, G. (1995) Self esteem, depression, behaviour and family functioning in sexually abused children. *Journal of Child Psychology and Psychiatry*, **36**, 1077–90.

Stevenson, J., Richman, N. and Graham, P. (1985) Behaviour problems and language abilities at three years and behavioural deviance at eight years. *Journal of Child Psychology and Psychiatry*, **26**, 215–30.

Stevenson-Hinde, J. and Shouldice, A. (1995) 4.5 to 7 years: fearful behaviour, fears and worries. *Journal of Child Psychology and Psychiatry*, **36**, 1027–38.

Stocker, C. M. (1994) Children's perceptions of relationships with siblings, friends and mothers: compensatory processes and links with adjustment. *Journal of Child Psychology and Psychiatry*, **35**, 1447–59.

Stott, D. H. (1963) *The Social Adjustment of Children (Manual of the Bristol Social Adjustment Guides)*. London: University of London Press.

Stott, D. H. (1974) *The Social Adjustment of Children: Manual of the Bristol Social Adjustment Guides* (5th edn). London: University of London Press.

Stott, D. H. and Marston, N. C. (1971) *Bristol Social Adjustment Guides: the Child in School* (2nd edn). London: Hodder & Stoughton.

Strauss, C. C., Forehand, R., Smith, K. and Frame, C. L. (1986) The association between social withdrawal and internalizing problems of children. *Journal of Abnormal Child Psychology*, **14**, 525–36.

Strauss, J. S. and Carpenter, W. T. (1972) The prediction of outcome in schizophrenia, 1: Characteristics of outcome. *Archives of General Psychiatry*, **27**, 739–46.

Strommen, E. A., McKinney, J. P. and Fitzgerald, H. E. (1977) *Developmental Psychology: the school-aged child.* Homewood, IL: Dorsey Press.

Sundel, S. S. and Sundel, M. (1993) *Behaviour Modification in the Human Services: an introduction to concepts and applications* (3rd edn). London: Sage.

Swanson, H. L. and Watson, B. L. (1982) *Educational and Psychological Assessment of Exceptional Children: theories, strategies and applications.* St. Louis: C. V. Mosby Co.

Szatmari, P., Brenner, R. and Nagy, J. (1989) Asperger's syndrome: a review of clinical features. *Canadian Journal of Psychiatry*, **34**, 554–60.

Tann, S. (1981) Grouping and group work. In B. Simon and J. Willcocks *Research and Practice in the Primary Classroom.* London: Routledge & Kegan Paul.

Tantam, D. (1988) Asperger's Syndrome. *Journal of Child Psychology and Psychiatry*, **29**, 245–55.

Tattum, D. (ed.) (1993) *Understanding and Managing Bullying.* Oxford: Heinemann.

Taylor, A. R., Asher, S. R. and Williams, G. A. (1987) The social adaptation of mainstreamed and mildly retarded children. *Child Development*, **58**, 1321–34.

Taylor, E. and Sandberg, S. (1984) Classroom behaviour problems and hyperactivity: a questionnaire study in English schools. *Journal of Abnormal Child Psychology*, **12**, 143–56.

Taylor, J. A. (1951) The relationship of anxiety to the conditioned eyelid response. *Journal of Experimental Psychology*, **42**, 183–8.

Thacker, J. (1983) *Steps to Success: an interpersonal problem solving approach for children.* Windsor: NFER-Nelson.

Thomas, A. and Chess, S. (1977) *Temperament and Development.* New York: Brunner/Mazel.

Thompson, R. J., Jr., Merritt, K. A., Keith, B. R., Murphy, L. B. and Johndrow, D. A. (1993) Mother–child agreement on the Child Assessment Schedule with non-referred children. *Journal of Child Psychology and Psychiatry*, **34**, 813–20.

Thompson, T. and Dockens, W. S. (eds) (1975) *Applications of Behaviour Modification.* New York: Academic Press.

Tiffen, K. and Spence, S. H. (1986) Responsiveness of isolated versus rejected children to social skills training. *Journal of Child Psychology and Psychiatry*, **27**, 343–57.

Tizard, B. and Hughes, M. (1984) *Young Children Learning*. London: Fontana.

Tomlinson, S. (1980) *Multicultural Education in White Schools*. London: Batsford.

Tomlinson, S. (1983) *Ethnic Minorities in British Schools: a review of the literature, 1960–82*. London: Heinemann.

Topping, K. (1988) *The Peer Tutoring Handbook*. London: Croom Helm.

Topping, K. (1995) *Paired Reading, Spelling and Writing. The Handbook for Teachers and Parents*. London: Cassell.

Tough, J. (1984) How young children develop and use language. In D. Fontana (ed.) *The Education of the Young Child*. Oxford: Basil Blackwell.

Treacher, A. and Carpenter, J. (eds) (1984) *Using Family Therapy*. Oxford: Basil Blackwell.

Trower, P. (ed.) (1984) *Radical Approaches to Social Skills Training*. London: Croom Helm.

Trower, P., Casey, A. and Dryden, W. (1988) *Cognitive-Behavioural Counselling*. London: Sage.

Troyna, B. and Hatcher, R. (1992) *Racism in Children's Lives*. London: Routledge.

Venables, P. H., Fletcher, R. P., Dalais, J. C., Mitchell, D. A., Schulsinger, F. and Mednick, S. A. (1983) Factor structure of the Rutter 'Children's Behaviour Questionnaire' in a primary school population in a developing country. *Journal of Child Psychology and Psychiatry*, **24**, 213–22.

Verhulst, F. C. and Akkerhuis, G. W. (1989) Agreement between parents' and teachers' ratings of behavioural/emotional problems of children aged 4 to 12. *Journal of Child Psychology and Psychiatry*, **30**, 123–36.

Verhulst, F. C. and van der Ende, J. (1992) Agreement between parents' reports and adolescents' self-reports of problem behaviour. *Journal of Child Psychology and Psychiatry*, **33**, 1011–23.

Verma, G. K. (1989) *Education For All: a landmark in pluralism*. London: The Falmer Press.

Vikan, A. (1985) Psychiatric epidemiology in a sample of 1510 10-yr-old children – 1. Prevalence. *Journal of Child Psychology and Psychiatry*, **26**, 55–75.

Vinogradov, S. and Yalom, I. (1989) *Group Psychotherapy*. Washington, DC: American Psychiatric Press.

Vitaro, F., Tremblay, R. E., Gagnon, C. and Boivin, M. (1992) Peer rejection from kindergarten to Grade 2: outcomes, correlates, and prediction.

Merrill-Palmer Quarterly, **38**, 382–400.

Vrugt, A. (1994) Perceived self-efficacy, social comparison, affective reactions and academic performance. *British Journal of Educational Psychology*, **64**, 465–72.

Vygotsky, L. S. (1976) Play and its role in the mental development of the child. In J. S. Bruner, A. Jolly and K. Sylva (eds) *Play: its role in development and evolution*. New York: Basic Books.

Wade, B. and Moore, M. (1993) *Experiencing Special Education*. Buckingham: Open University Press.

Waldrop, M. F., Bell, R. Q. and Goering, J. D. (1976) Minor physical anomalies and inhibited behaviour in elementary school girls. *Journal of Child Psychology and Psychiatry*, **17**, 113–22.

Walker, J. E. and Shea, T. M. (1986) *Behaviour Management: a practical approach for educators* (3rd edn). Columbus, OH: Charles E. Merrill.

Wallbank, S. (1992) The secret world of bereaved children. In V. P. Varma (ed.) *The Secret Life of Vulnerable Children*. London: Routledge.

Walsh, P. (1991) *Education and Meaning: philosophy in practice*. London: Cassell.

Warburton, F. W. (1969) The Assessment of Personality Traits. In J. F. Morris and E. A. Lunzer (eds) *Development in Learning. Vol. 3: Contexts of Education*. London: Staples Press.

Wasserman, G. A. and Allen, R. (1985) Maternal withdrawal from handicapped toddlers. *Journal of Child Psychology and Psychiatry*, **26**, 381–7.

Waterhouse, P. (1990) *Classroom Management*. Stafford: Network Educational Press.

Watkins, C. (1995) Personal–social education and the whole curriculum. In R. Best, P. Lang, C. Lodge and C. Watkins (eds) *Pastoral Care and Personal–Social Development*. London: Cassell.

Webster-Stratton, C. and Herbert, M. (1994) *Troubled Families – Problem Children*. Chichester: John Wiley.

Weir, K. and Duveen, G. (1981) Further development and validation of the prosocial behaviour questionnaire for use by teachers. *Journal of Child Psychology and Psychiatry*, **22**, 357–74.

Weissberg, R. P., Geston, E. L., Rapkin, B. D., Cowen, E. L., Davidson, E., Flores de Apodaca, R. and McKim, B. J. (1981) Evaluation of a social problem-solving training program for surburban and inner-city third-grade children. *Journal of Consulting and Clinical Psychology*, **49**, 251–61.

Weisz, J. R., Suwanlert, S., Chaiyasit, W., Weiss, B. and Jackson, E. W. (1991) Adult attitudes toward over- and undercontrolled child problems: urban and rural parents and teachers from Thailand and the United States.

Journal of Child Psychology and Psychiatry, **32**, 645–54.

Weisz, J. R., Suwanlert, S., Chaiyasit, W., Weiss, B., Achenbach, T. M. and Trevathan, D. (1989) Epidemiology of behavioural and emotional problems among Thai and American children: teacher reports for ages 6–11. *Journal of Child Psychology and Psychiatry*, **30**, 471–84.

Westmacott, E. V. S. and Cameron, R. J. (1981) *Behaviour Can Change*. Basingstoke: Globe Education (Macmillan Education Ltd).

Wetton, N. and Cansell, P. (1993) *Feeling Good: raising self-esteem in the primary school*. London: Forbes Publications.

Wheeler, S. (1993) Reservations about eclectic and integrative approaches to counselling. In W. Dryden (ed.) *Questions and Answers on Counselling in Action*. London: Sage.

Wheldall, K. and Glynn, T. (1989) *Effective Classroom Learning: a behavioural interactionist approach to teaching*. Oxford: Basil Blackwell.

Wheldall, K. and Merrett, F. (1989) *Positive Teaching in the Secondary School*. London: Paul Chapman.

Whitaker, P. (1995) *Managing to Learn*. London: Cassell.

White, B. L. (1979) *The Origins of Human Competence*. Lexington, MA.: Heath.

White, D. and Woollett, A. (1992) *Families: a context for development*. London: The Falmer Press.

Whitehead, L. (1979) Sex differences in children's responses to family stress: a re-evaluation. *Journal of Child Psychology and Psychiatry*, **20**, 247–54.

Willey, R. (1984) *Race, Equality and Schools*. London: Methuen.

Williams, B. T. R. and Gilmour, J. D. (1994) Annotation: sociometry and peer relationships. *Journal of Child Psychology and Psychiatry*, **35**, 997–1013.

Wiltshire Education Department Psychological and Advisory Services (1989) *WASP: Wiltshire Adjustment Support Preparation*. Cheltenham: Cheltenham and Gloucester College of Higher Education.

Wing, L. (1980) *Autistic Children: guide for parents*. London: Constable.

Wing, L. (1988) The continuum of autistic characteristics. In E. Schopler and G. B. Mesibov (eds) *Diagnosis and Assessment in Autism*. New York: Plenum.

Wing, L. and Attwood, A. (1987) Syndromes of autism and atypical development. In D. Cohen and A. Donnellan (eds) *Handbook of Autism and Pervasive Developmental Disorders*. New York: John Wiley.

Wing, L. and Gould, J. (1979) Severe impairments of social interaction and associated abnormalities in children: epidemiology and classification. *Journal of Autism and Childhood Schizophrenia*, **9**, 11–29.

Winter, D. (1994) *Personal Construct Psychology in Clinical Practice: theory, research and application.* London: Routledge.

Wolff, S. (1981) *Children Under Stress* (2nd edn). Harmondsworth: Penguin Books.

Wood, M. E. (1981) *The Development of Personality and Behaviour in Children.* London: Harrap.

Woodhead, M., Barnes, P., Miell, D. and Oates, J. (1995) Developmental perspectives on emotion. In P. Barnes (ed.) *Personal, Social and Emotional Development in Children.* Oxford: Blackwell for the Open University.

Woods, P. (1990) *The Happiest Days?* Basingstoke: The Falmer Press.

Woolfe, R. and Dryden, W. (1996) *Handbook of Counselling Psychology.* London: Sage.

Woolfe, R., Dryden, W. and Charles-Edwards, D. (1989) The nature and range of counselling practice. In W. Dryden, D. Charles-Edwards, and R. Woolfe (eds) *Handbook of Counselling in Britain.* London: Routledge.

Wooster, A. and Bird, E. (1979) Meeting pupils: strategies for the pastoral care tutor. *Therapeutic Education,* **7**, 44–7.

Wragg, E. C. (1994) *An Introduction to Classroom Observation.* London: Routledge.

Younger, A. J., Schwartzman, A. E. and Ledingham, J. E. (1985) Grade-related changes in children's perceptions of aggression and withdrawal in their peers. *Developmental Psychology,* **21**, 70–5.

Youniss, J. (1980) *Parents and Peers in Social Development.* Chicago: University of Chicago Press.

Youniss, J. (1992) Parent and peer relations in the emergence of cultural competence. In H. McGurk (ed.) *Childhood Social Development: contemporary perspectives.* Hove: Laurence Erlbaum.

Youniss, J. and Volpe, J. (1978) A relational analysis of children's friendships. In W. Damon (ed.) *Social Cognition.* San Francisco: Jossey Bass.

Zatz, S. and Chassin, L. (1983) Cognitions of text-anxious children. *Journal of Consulting and Clinical Psychology,* **51**, 526–34.

Zeitlin, H. (1990) Annotation: current interests in child–adult psychopathological continuities. *Journal of Child Psychology and Psychiatry,* **31**, 1145–60.

Zimbardo, P. G. (1977) *Shyness.* New York: Addison-Wesley.

Zimbardo, P. G. and Radl, S. L. (1981) *The Shy Child.* New York: Doubleday.

Zimbardo, P. G., Pilkonis, P. A. and Norwood, R. M. (1975) The social disease called shyness. *Psychology Today,* **8**, 68–72.

Ziv, A. (1970) Children's behaviour problems as viewed by teachers, psychologists and children. *Child Development,* **41**, 871–9.

Index of Case Histories of Children

Andy   87, 163

Christopher   111–12
Claire   32, 36, 90

Daisy   35, 70, 157

Eddie   104–5, 157
Ewan   33, 82, 157

Harry   42
Helen   31, 82, 83
Henry   47

James   40–1, 81, 91
Jamie   24
Jane   63–4
Joe   42, 91

Laura   40, 90
Lynne   44–5

May   138–9, 141

Peter   76, 107

Robin   38–9, 90, 116, 157

Stanley   46
Susan   43–4, 73, 91, 157

Tina   31
Tommy   154–5

Wayne   76–7, 111, 157

Name Index

Achenbach, T. M.   4, 5, 53, 54, 56, 96, 165
Adams, G. R.   126, 194
Ainsworth, M. D. S.   22, 165
Ajmal, Y.   149, 166
Akkerhuis, G. W.   5, 96, 165, 201
Alden, L. E.   34, 166
Allen, H.   74, 197
Allen, L.   98, 187
Allen, R.   74, 202
Altham, P. M. E.   77, 97, 178, 183
Althaus, M.   97, 168
Angst, J.   23, 100, 176, 189
Anthony, E. J.   150, 177
Archer, J.   19, 166
Arkin, R. M.   33, 166
Armstrong, D.   84, 177
Arnaud, S. H.   21, 173
Asarnow, J. R.   102, 166
Asen, K. E.   152, 166
Asendorpf, J.   33, 34, 35, 166
Ashby, L.   77
Asher, S. R.   11, 39, 57, 60, 88, 92, 95, 99, 103, 166, 192, 200
Asperger, H.   46, 166
Attwood, A.   45, 203
Axelrod, S.   138, 166
Axline, V. M.   150, 166

Baghurst, P.   54, 56, 196
Bagigian, H.   92, 95, 173
Baginsky, M.   106, 183
Bagley, C. A.   106, 166
Baglin, E.   115, 179
Bailey, A.   45, 167

Baker, C.   7, 167
Baker, L.   48, 170
Baldock, W. P.   67, 199
Bannister, D.   50, 167
Barnes, P.   16, 17, 74, 167, 203
Baron, G. D.   96, 165
Bash, M. A. S.   146, 167
Bastiani, J.   122, 167
Baum, C. G.   10, 11, 60, 94, 99, 191
Baumgardner, A. H.   33, 166
Baumrind, D.   75, 167
Beail, N.   50, 167
Beardslee, W.   100, 183
Beazley, S.   79, 167
Beck, A. T.   149, 167
Beck, S.   90, 144, 147, 167, 179, 189
Behar, L. B.   52, 53, 54, 167
Beidel, D. C.   67, 167
Bell, R. Q.   11, 202
Bell, S. M.   22, 165
Belter, R. W.   50, 176
Bendell, D.   74, 176
Bennett, N.   111, 167
Bennett, S.   57, 186
Bentovim, A.   151, 152, 167, 184
Berden, G. F. M. G.   97, 168
Berg, I.   43, 181
Berger, M.   8, 196
Bergin, A. E.   151, 168
Bern, D. J.   94, 96, 98, 171
Besag, B.   80, 168
Beveridge, S.   83, 168
Bhavnagri, N. P.   123,

192
Bieling, P. J.   34, 166
Bierman, K. L.   147, 151, 168
Billington, S.   105, 172
Bird, E.   136, 204
Blagg, N. R.   43, 65, 168
Blatchford, P.   112, 113, 168, 190
Blom, G. E.   146, 170
Boivin, M.   95, 201
Bolger, T.   137, 168
Bolton, F.   75, 168
Bolton, J.   63, 65, 146, 171
Bolton, S. R.   75, 168
Booth, T.   80, 168
Boston, M.   148, 168
Bottery, M.   110, 168
Botvin, G. J.   78, 86, 197
Boulton, M. J.   28, 80, 113, 168
Bowen, R.   34, 57, 175
Bower, E. M.   61, 186
Bowlby, J.   22, 168, 169
Boyle, M. H.   53, 169
Brady, E. U.   42, 44, 184
Brakke, N. P.   37, 39, 63, 174
Breakwell, G.   65, 169
Brenden Kamp, D.   100, 180
Brennan, T.   91, 169
Brenner, R.   46, 200
Briggs, S. R.   11, 172
Brittan, E. M.   26, 183
Bronfenbrenner, U.   22, 169

Brook, J.   9, 45, 172
Brooks-Gunn, J.   73, 169
Brown, G.   15, 169
Brown, S.   109, 169
Brubacher, J. W.   106, 169
Bruner, J. S.   27, 169
Bryan, J. H.   128, 169
Bryant, B. K.   126, 127, 169
Buchanan, L.   11, 190
Bukowski, W. M.   37, 60, 93, 99, 190, 191
Bull, S. L.   111, 169
Bulman, L.   108, 169
Burbach, D. J.   66, 169
Burgess-Macey, C.   117, 170
Burgoyne, J.   75, 170
Burnham, J.   70, 154, 170
Burnham, M.   10, 34, 88, 89, 173
Bushell, W.   20, 170
Buss, A. H.   34, 57, 170, 171
Butler, N. R.   6, 192

Cairns, B. D.   11, 42, 170
Cairns, R. B.   11, 42, 170
Caldwell, B. J.   110, 170
Caldwell, B. M.   146, 175
Callias, M. M.   68, 177
Cameron, R. J.   138, 202
Camp, B. W.   146, 167, 170
Campbell, L.   116, 196
Campion, J.   151, 152, 170

Cangelosi, J. S. 110, 170
Cansell, P. 143, 202
Cantwell, D. P. 48, 101, 170
Caplan, M. Z. 128, 170
Carlson, G. A. 100, 171
Carpenter, J. 151, 201
Carpenter, W. T. 102, 199
Carroll, H. C. M. 43, 183
Cartledge, G. 143, 171
Case, C. W. 106, 169
Case, R. 15, 171
Casey, A. 136, 201
Caspi, A. 94, 96, 98, 171
Cattell, R. B. 55, 71, 171, 193
Cawthorn, P. 102, 171
Chadwick, D. F. D. 8, 45, 196
Chaiyasit, W. 4, 54, 202
Chapman, M. 128, 171
Charles-Edwards, D. 135, 204
Charlton, T. 130, 131, 182
Chassin, L. 67, 204
Chazan, M. 2, 6, 7, 20, 63, 65, 83, 122, 140, 144, 171, 185
Cheek, J. M. 11, 57, 171, 172
Chess, S. 16, 72, 200
Chinsky, J. M. 147, 187
Cillessen, A. H. N. 39, 40, 93, 95, 172
Clarke-Stewart, A. 22, 172
Clegg, D. 105, 172
Cockburn, A. 111, 167
Cohen, D. 15, 172
Cohen, J. 9, 45, 172
Cohen, P. 9, 45, 172
Coie, J. D. 37, 39, 41, 60, 61, 63, 93, 96, 99, 172, 174, 185
Cole, M. 105, 172
Coleman, J. C. 85, 172
Colman, A. M. 84, 192
Colmar, S. 50, 172
Conger, A. J. 36, 61, 175
Conners, C. K. 53, 172
Connor, M. J. 146, 172

Conover, N. C. 5, 66, 175
Cooney, G. 77, 199
Cooper, P. 77, 109, 110, 172, 178
Cooperman, G. 128, 171
Coopersmith, S. 57, 172
Coppotelli, H. 41, 60, 61, 172
Costello, A. J. 5, 66, 172, 175
Coulby, D. 106, 173
Coulby, J. 106, 173
Cowen, E. L. 53, 92, 95, 147, 173, 181, 202
Cowie, H. 22, 89, 90, 91, 107, 126, 130, 131, 157, 173, 198
Cox, A. D. 8, 74, 75, 173, 193, 196
Cox, T. 20, 171
Craig, K. D. 10, 173
Creeser, R. 113, 190
Crockenberg, S. B. 74, 173
Croll, P. 20, 83, 111, 173, 177
Cross, J. 142, 178
Crouse-Novak, M. A. 101, 185
Crozier, W. R. 10, 11, 33, 34, 57, 88, 89, 173
Cummings, E. M. 74, 173
Curran, J. P. 154, 173
Curry, N. E. 21, 173
Cytryn, L. 67, 182

Dalais, J. C. 52, 201
Dale, F. 148, 174
Daniels, A. J. 143, 174
Darley, J. M. 129, 186
Davidson, E. 147, 202
Davidson, K. S. 73, 196
Davies, D. 6, 83, 140, 171
Davies, G. 141, 174
Davies, N. 7, 167
Davies, P. T. 74, 173
Dean, J. 80, 174
Delamont, S. 17, 174
Dell, J. 102, 171
Denham, S. A. 128, 174
Department for Education (DFE)

49, 68, 106, 174
Department of Education and Science (DES) 20, 174
Desforges, C. 15, 111, 167, 169
Dickson, D. 155, 179
Dobson, K. S. 10, 173
Dockens, W. S. 140, 200
Docking, J. 83, 106, 110, 174
Dodge, K. A. 37, 39, 40, 41, 60, 61, 63, 64, 93, 96, 99, 166, 172, 174, 185
Dryden, W. 135, 136, 151, 174, 201, 204
Duck, S. 130, 174
Dulcan, M. K. 5, 66, 172, 175
Dunham, J. 79, 108, 174
Dunn, J. 1, 10, 11, 15, 16, 17, 21, 22, 23, 24, 89, 96, 100, 122, 123, 126, 156, 174, 175
Dunne, E. 111, 167
Durkin, K. 120, 175
Duveen, G. 52, 202
Dwivedi, K. N. 151, 175
Dygdon, J. A. 36, 61, 175
D'Zurilla, T. J. 145, 175

Easterson, A. 127, 180
Eber, H. W. 55, 171
Edelbrock, C. S. 5, 53, 54, 56, 66, 96, 165, 172, 175
Edwards, T. 106, 175
Egeland, B. 95, 175
Eggers, C. 102, 175
Ehlers, S. 47, 175
Eisenberg, J. G. 25, 28, 54, 175, 186
Elardo, P. T. 146, 175
Elder, G. H. 94, 96, 98, 171
Elizur, J. 32, 175
Elkind, D. 34, 57, 175
Ellis, R. 114, 141, 142, 175
Erickson, M. F. 95, 175
Ernst, C. 23, 176
Erwin, P. 1, 9, 36, 176

Esser, G. 7, 9, 45, 100, 176
Evans, E. D. 1, 176
Eysenck, H. J. 55, 71, 72, 176
Eysenck, S. B. G. 55, 72, 176

Fassam, M. 79, 163, 188
Faulkner, D. 20, 176
Fawcett, M. 63, 176
Feehan, C. 44, 184
Feinberg, T. L. 101, 185
Feldman, E. 40, 174
Fell, G. 113, 176
Fergusson, D. M. 78, 176
Fernando, D. 148, 176
Field, T. 74, 176
Figueroa, J. 144, 147, 189
Finch, A. J. 50, 176
Finkelstein, R. 101, 185
Finnie, V. 122, 124, 125, 176, 195
Fitton, J. B. 52, 176
Fitzgerald, H. E. 90, 91, 188, 199
Flavell, J. H. 15, 177
Fletcher, R. P. 52, 201
Flores de Apodaca, R. 147, 202
Fontana, D. 113, 114, 177
Foot, H. C. 12, 177
Forehand, R. 90, 147, 167, 179, 199
Forman, E. A. 1, 177
Foulkes, S. H. 150, 177
Frame, C. L. 90, 199
Francis, G. 10, 11, 60, 67, 94, 99, 191, 199
Franke, S. 88, 182
Fransella, F. 50, 167
Frary, R. B. 43, 191
Frederickson, N. 40, 60, 99, 144, 147, 177
Freeman, A. 108, 179
Freeman, B. J. 101, 194
Frith, U. 101, 177
Frosh, S. J. 67, 68, 177
Fudge, H. 100, 180
Fullan, M. 106, 177
Fundudis, T. 48, 102, 184

Furman, W.   1, 10, 12, 37, 39, 60, 95, 96, 99, 122, 129, 130, 144, 147, 151, 188
Furnham, A.   142, 177

Gagnon, C.   95, 201
Galloway, D.   84, 108, 177
Galloway, F.   116, 177
Galton, M.   111, 177
Garber, J.   100, 177
Garfield, S. L.   151, 168
Garforth, F. N.   106, 178
Gariépy, J. L.   42, 170
Garmezy, N.   92, 94, 97, 102, 178, 196
Garside, R. F.   126, 150, 151, 184
Gascoigne, E.   122, 178
Gatsonis, C.   101, 185
Geen, R. G.   84, 178
Gershaw, N. J.   142, 178
Gerston, J. C.   54, 186
Gest, S. D.   42, 170
Geston, E. L.   147, 202
Gilbert, P.   149, 187
Gillberg, C.   46, 47, 102, 175, 178
Gillberg, I. C.   46, 102, 178
Gillborn, D.   86, 178
Gilmour, J. D.   10, 11, 39, 41, 60, 61, 203
Ginott, H. G.   150, 178
Glynn, T.   137, 203
Goddard, S.   142, 178
Goering, J. D.   11, 202
Goldfried, M. R.   145, 175
Goldstein, A. P.   142, 178
Goldstein, S.   74, 176
Golter, B. S.   124, 185
Gonso, J.   144, 178
Gonzales, F.   143, 183
Goodman, J.   146, 189
Goodman, R.   52, 178
Goodyer, I. M.   44, 77, 88, 97, 178, 183
Goosens, L.   9, 32, 38, 58, 188
Gordon, L. V.   56, 190
Gordon, P.   97, 178
Gordon, Y.   5, 181
Gottesman, N.   95, 175
Gottman, J. M.   37, 38,

144, 178, 179
Gould, J.   45, 203
Graham, P. J.   7, 8, 45, 54, 66, 71, 92, 95, 96, 194, 196, 199
Gray, H.   108, 179
Green, K. D.   90, 179
Greene, R. W.   10, 11, 60, 94, 99, 191
Gresham, F. M.   60, 62, 179
Groothues, C.   100, 180
Guare, J. C.   53, 181
Guralnick, M. J.   11, 179
Gurney, P.   107, 179

Hamblin, D.   108, 118, 130, 135, 136, 137, 179
Hammen, C.   100, 179
Harber, C.   110, 179
Hargie, O.   155, 179
Hargreaves, A.   109, 115, 179
Hargreaves, D. H.   25, 106, 179
Harper, G. C.   63, 65, 146, 171
Harrington, R.   77, 100, 180
Harris, J.   53, 180
Harris, P. L.   89, 180
Harris, Q.   70, 154, 170
Harrop, A.   138, 180
Hart, C. H.   124, 185
Harter, S.   57, 180
Hartmark, C.   9, 45, 172
Hartup, W. W.   12, 25, 26, 27, 39, 40, 60, 90, 93, 95, 97, 127, 129, 155, 172, 180
Hatcher, R.   86, 201
Hay, D. F.   25, 74, 97, 128, 170, 180, 197
Healy, B.   74, 176
Heflin, A. H.   123, 193
Hegarty, S.   80, 180
Hellgren, L.   102, 178
Henderson, P.   115, 179
Henshall, C.   17, 180
Hensley, R.   44, 59, 184
Herbert, F.   146, 170
Herbert, M.   2, 74, 75, 102, 114, 134, 135, 136, 137, 138, 142, 151, 153, 162, 180, 181, 202

Herjanic, B.   65, 66, 181
Hersen, M.   50, 191
Hersov, L.   43, 100, 181
Hestor, S.   25, 129
Hetherington, E. M.   71, 181
Hickey Schultz, L.   130, 197
Hightower, A. D.   53, 181
Hinde, R. A.   10, 25, 181
Hitchfield, E. M.   83, 181
Hodges, K.   5, 65, 66, 67, 181, 182
Hodson, J.   80, 188
Holly, L.   77, 182
Holly, P.   109, 182
Honzik, M. P.   98, 187
Hopkins, D.   106, 179
Hops, H.   9, 182
Howlin, P.   45, 46, 101, 182
Hughes, M.   7, 19, 32, 122, 162, 182, 200
Hughes, P.   135, 182
Hutt, C.   17, 18, 182
Hymel, S.   57, 60, 88, 95, 96, 99, 166, 182, 195

Iannotti, R.   128, 171
Indoe, D.   130, 131, 182
Izzo, L. D.   92, 95, 173

Jackson, E. W.   54, 202
Jackson, M. S.   6, 7, 20, 171
Jackson, S.   1, 182
Jahoda, G.   19, 182
James, A.   102, 171
James, J.   130, 131, 182
Jeffrey, P.   56, 182
Jelinek, M. M.   26, 183
Jenkins, D.   108, 169
Jenkins, H.   151, 183
Jennings, C.   148, 183
John, R.   96, 183
Johndrow, D. A.   5, 200
Johnson, J.   9, 45, 172
Johnson, J. H.   75, 78, 183
Johnson, K.   105, 183
Jolly, A.   27, 169
Jones, G.   6, 171

Jones, J.   63, 65, 146, 171
Jones, S. C.   53, 169
Jowett, S.   106, 183

Kagan, J.   100, 183
Kahn, J. H.   43, 183
Kalas, R.   5, 66, 172, 175
Kalkoske, M.   95, 175
Kandel, D. B.   100, 183
Kane, B.   78, 183
Kasen, S.   9, 45, 172
Kashani, J. H.   66, 169
Kauffman, J. M.   3, 183
Kazdin, A. E.   5, 44, 59, 101, 183, 184
Kehle, T. J.   143, 183
Keith, B. R.   5, 200
Keller, M. B.   100, 183
Kellmer Pringle, M. L.   83, 183
Kelly, G.   149, 183
Kelvin, R. G.   77, 183
Kendall, P. C.   43, 44, 184
Kennedy, E.   44, 184
Kent, L.   44, 184
Kenyon, B.   127, 195
Kimmel, D. C.   9, 38, 184, 187
King, N. J.   43, 191
King, R.   25, 184
Kinston, W.   151, 152, 167, 184
Kitzinger, C.   78, 184
Kitzinger, S.   78, 184
Klaric, S. H.   66, 172
Klein, P.   142, 178
Kline, J.   67, 182
Kline, P.   55, 56, 184
Knight, D.   59, 184
Koch, M.   100, 177
Kojima, T.   4, 188
Kolko, D. J.   5, 184
Kolvin, I.   48, 102, 126, 150, 151, 184
Kovacs, M.   59, 67, 101, 184, 185
Kruss, M. R.   100, 177
Kuhn, C.   74, 176
Kumar, R.   74, 197
Kupersmidt, J. B.   37, 39, 96, 99, 172, 185
Kurtz, Z.   3, 185
Kusel, S. J.   88, 192
Kutnick, P.   157, 185
Kyriacou, C.   109, 185

Ladd, G. W.   89, 124,

146, 185, 190
LaGreca, A. M. 144, 185
Lahey, B. B. 53, 190
Laing, A. F. 2, 6, 20, 63, 65, 83, 140, 146, 171, 185
Lake, E. A. 33, 166
Lambert, N. M. 61, 186
Lang, M. 59, 186
Lang, P. 108, 186
Langner, T. S. 54, 186
Lansdown, R. 78, 186
Larcen, S. W. 147, 187
Latane, B. 129, 186
Lau, A. 86, 186
Laursen, B. 127, 180
Lavon, P. W. 100, 183
Lawrence, B. 57, 186
Lazarus, P. J. 34, 35, 36, 90, 186
Lederer, A. S. 67, 167
Ledingham, J. E. 94, 95, 186, 204
Lee, K. K. 4, 189
Leech, N. 115, 186
Leeson, P. 115, 179
Lefkovitz, M. M. 45, 61, 186
Leitch, I. F. 126, 150, 151, 184
Le Mare, L. 88, 95, 98, 99, 103, 125, 182, 195
Lennon, M. 5, 181
Leo, E. L. 84, 130, 131, 177, 182
Leung, Man-Chi 11, 190
Levačić, R. 160, 186
Levin, H. 75, 197
Lewinsohn, P. M. 9, 182
Lewis, A. 11, 186
Lewis, V. 11, 186
Leyden, S. 83, 187
Light, P. 23, 187
Lighthall, F. E. 73, 196
Lindholm, L. 100, 177
Lindsay, G. 77, 94, 187
Little, S. G. 60, 62, 179
Lloyd, E. 22, 189
Lloyd, J. W. 3, 183
Lollis, S. P. 98, 99, 103, 123, 125, 127, 187, 195
Lord, C. 46, 101, 187
Lotyczewski, B. S. 53,

181
Lucas, D. 80, 180
Lush, D. 148, 168
Lynch, D. L. 77, 199
Lynskey, M. T. 78, 176
Lyons, E. 129, 187

McAdam, E. 149, 187
McCabe, M. 80, 187
McCaffery, J. 129, 187
McCandless, B. R. 1, 60, 176, 187
McCarthy, E. D. 54, 186
McClure, L. F. 147, 187
Maccoby, E. E. 73, 75, 155, 156, 187, 197
MacDonald, K. 123, 187
MacFarlane, J. W. 98, 187
McGee, K. A. 3, 8, 183, 188
McGee, R. 9, 96, 187, 188
McGrew, W. C. 32, 38, 188
McGuire, J. 4, 17, 96, 100, 122, 123, 175, 180, 188
McGuire, S. 10, 11, 175
McGurk, H. 1, 188
McIntyre, D. 109, 169, 172
McKim, B. J. 147, 202
McKinney, J. P. 90, 91, 188, 199
McKnew, D. 67, 182
MacMillan, A. 126, 150, 151, 184
McMullin, R. E. 149, 188
MacNeil, M. M. 106, 183
McNiff, J. 116, 188
Madge, N. 79, 163, 188
Maguire, U. 137, 188
Majors, K. 115, 119, 194
Malek, M. 122, 188
Malik, N. M. 1, 10, 12, 37, 39, 60, 95, 96, 99, 122, 130, 144, 151, 188
Mannarino, A. P. 144, 147, 189
Marchione, K. E. 144, 147, 189

Marcoen, A. 9, 32, 38, 58, 188
Markle, A. 141, 142, 194
Marks, I. 100, 188
Marshall, H. R. 60, 187
Marston, N. C. 33, 34, 51, 199
Martin, S. 22, 189
Martlew, M. 80, 188
Marwit, S. J. 80, 187
Masten, A. S. 62, 188
Mathias, J. 54, 56, 198
Matsuura, M. 4, 188
Maughan, B. 20, 113, 196
Mays, W. 16, 189
Meadows, S. 15, 17, 23, 189
Mearns, D. 136, 189
Mednick, S. 52, 96, 183, 201
Meichenbaum, D. 136, 146, 189
Meighan, R. 110, 179
Meleshko, K. G. A. 34, 166
Melhuish, E. C. 22, 189
Mellor, F. 25, 179
Mellsop, G. W. 92, 96, 189
Merikangas, K. R. 100, 189
Merrett, F. 7, 8, 140, 189, 203
Merritt, K. A. 5, 200
Michelson, L. 144, 147, 189
Miell, D. 16, 203
Milburn, J. F. 143, 171
Miller, C. L. 151, 168
Miller, L. C. 54, 189
Mills, M. 74, 75, 173, 193
Mills, R. S. L. 38, 64, 96, 195
Minick, M. 1, 177
Mitchell, D. A. 52, 201
Mitchell, J. 11, 189
Mitchell, S. 117, 190
Mize, J. 146, 190
Mooney, A. 22, 113, 189, 190
Mooney, R I. 56, 190
Moore, M. 79, 82, 167, 201
Moran, S. 97, 190
Morgan, M. J. 12, 177

Morgan, V. 143, 190
Morison, P. 62, 188
Morris, A. 6, 192
Morris, J. F. 26, 155, 190
Mortimore, P. 20, 113, 190, 196
Moses, D. 2, 20, 83, 173, 190
Mosley, J. 129, 190
Moss, H. A. 100, 183
Murfitt, J. 131, 190
Murgatroyd, S. 135, 136, 190
Murphy, L. B. 5, 200
Murray, L. 74, 190
Mussen, P. H. 25, 28, 157, 175
Musun-Miller, L. 60, 190
Muth, S. 124, 185

Nabuzoka, D. 11, 67, 190
Nagy, J. 46, 200
Nash, T. 122, 162, 182
Neal, A. M. 67, 167
Neckerman, H. J. 42, 170
Neeper, R. 53, 190
Nelson-Jones, R. 136, 190
Newcomb, A. F. 37, 60, 93, 99, 190, 191
Newson, E. 7, 8, 19, 191
Newson, J. 7, 8, 19, 191
Nicol, A. R. 126, 150, 151, 184
Nida, S. 129, 186
Norwood, R. M. 35, 204
Nowicki, S., Jr 57, 191
Nursten, J. P. 43, 183

Oates, J. 16, 203
Oates, R. K. 77, 199
Oberklaid, F. 94, 196
O'Connor, K. J. 149, 151, 197
Oden, S. 114, 141, 142, 191
Offer, D. 9, 38, 192
Okubo, Y. 4, 188
O'Leary, K. D. 138, 191
O'Leary, S. G. 138, 191
Ollendick, T. H. 10, 11, 43, 50, 53, 58,

60, 63, 65, 67, 94, 99, 191, 199
Ollier, K.   43, 191
Olweus, D.   12, 82, 88, 191
Omrod, R.   75, 180
Orlandi, M. A.   78, 86, 197
Ornitz, E. M.   101, 194
Osborn, A. F.   6, 192
Ostrov, E.   9, 38, 192
O'Toole, B. I.   77, 199
Ouston, J.   20, 113, 196

Paikoff, R. L.   73, 169
Paisey, A.   110, 192
Parke, R. D.   123, 187, 192
Parker, J. G.   92, 95, 99, 103, 192
Parkhurst, S. T.   39, 88, 95, 99, 192
Parkinson, B.   84, 192
Parten, M.   63, 192
Pattee, L.   37, 60, 92, 191
Paulauskas, S. L.   100, 185
Pawlby, S.   74, 197
Peake, A.   77, 187
Pearce, J.   44, 192
Pearson, S.   143, 190
Pecherek, A.   107, 173
Pedersen, A.   92, 95, 173
Pedlow, R.   94, 196
Pellegrini, D. S.   62, 145, 147, 188, 192
Peplau, L. A.   58, 192
Perlman, D.   58, 192
Perry, D. G.   88, 192
Perry, L. C.   88, 192
Perry, S.   74, 176
Persons, J. B.   149, 192
Pervin, L. P.   50, 192
Peters, R. S.   105, 106, 192
Peterson, D. R.   53, 193
Phillips, J. L., Jr   15, 192
Phillips, W.   45, 167
Piaget, J.   27, 192
Pickles, A.   100, 180
Pierce, J. W.   80, 193
Pilkonis, P. A.   35, 57, 193, 204
Pilling, D.   22, 193
Pinkerton, G.   7, 32, 182
Platt, J.   68, 114, 145,

146, 198
Plewis, I.   7, 32, 182
Plomin, R.   71, 181
Pocklington, K.   80, 180
Pollard, A.   105, 112, 193
Pollock, M.   101, 185
Porter, R. B.   55, 193
Poteet, J. A.   138, 193
Pound, A.   74, 75, 173, 193
Povey, R.   83, 193
Preedy, M.   110, 193
Pring, R.   114, 193
Pringle, M. K.   22, 193
Prior, M.   94, 196
Puckering, C.   74, 75, 173, 193
Putallaz, M.   123, 124, 193

Quay, H. C.   53, 193

Rachman, S.   149, 193
Radl, S. L.   35, 91, 204
Rahe, D. F.   129, 177
Rakos, R. F.   141, 197
Rapkin, B. D.   147, 202
Ratigan, B.   136, 193
Reagan, T. G.   106, 169
Reich, W.   65, 66, 181
Reiss, D.   71, 181
Renshaw, P. D.   57, 166
Reynolds, C. R.   58, 194
Rhodes, J.   149, 166, 194
Richards, M.   22, 75, 170, 194
Richman, N.   4, 7, 8, 54, 66, 71, 92, 95, 96, 194, 199
Richmond, B. D.   58, 194
Rinn, R. C.   141, 142, 194
Ritvo, E. R.   101, 194
Roberts, I.   106, 194
Robins, L. N.   92, 100, 194
Rodgers, B.   92, 100, 194
Roffey, S.   115, 119, 194
Rogers, C.   25, 84, 157, 177, 185, 194
Rogers, C. R.   56, 150, 194
Rohrbeck, C. A.   53, 181

Rojas, M.   9, 45, 172
Roopnarine, J. L.   126, 194
Rosenberg, M. S.   97, 195
Rosenberg, T. K.   66, 169
Ross, C.   112, 113, 195
Ross, H. S.   123, 127, 187, 195
Rossman, B. B. R.   97, 195
Rotenberg, K. J.   91, 195
Rowden, R.   88, 95, 99, 182
Rubin, K. H.   38, 64, 88, 95, 96, 98, 99, 103, 122, 125, 182, 195
Rubin, Z.   122, 195
Rudduck, J.   157, 173
Ruebush, B. K.   73, 195
Russell, A.   122, 124, 125, 176, 195
Rutter, M.   5, 6, 8, 20, 22, 44, 45, 52, 54, 66, 92, 94, 97, 98, 100, 102, 113, 149, 178, 180, 182, 195, 196
Ryan, A.   112, 113, 195
Ryder, J.   116, 196

Safran, J. S.   3, 196
Safran, S. P.   3, 196
Samuelson, D. L.   100, 183
Samuelson, H.   100, 183
Sandberg, S.   53, 200
Sandow, S.   82, 196
Sanson, A.   94, 196
Santogrossi, D. A.   144, 185
Sarason, S. B.   73, 196
Saunders, C.   155, 179
Sawyer, M. G.   54, 56, 196
Sayer, J.   160, 197
Scarlett, W. G.   10, 37, 63, 197
Schaefer, C. E.   149, 197
Schaffer, H. R.   22, 27, 151, 197
Schanberg, S.   74, 176
Scherer, M.   68, 197
Schiffer, M.   151, 197
Schinke, S. P.   78, 86,

197
Schmidt, M. H.   7, 9, 45, 100, 176
Schmückler, G.   74, 197
Schroeder, H. E.   141, 197
Schuler, P.   144, 178
Schulsinger, F.   52, 96, 183, 201
Schuyler, D.   149, 197
Schwartzmann, A. E.   94, 95, 186, 204
Seagroatt, V.   102, 171
Sears, R.   75, 197
Seed, P.   82, 197
Selman, R. L.   130, 197
Semeonoff, B.   50, 197
Shackleton Bailey, M.   6, 171
Shaffer, D.   66, 197
Shapiro, S. B.   62, 197
Sharp, D.   74, 197
Sharp, S.   12, 106, 112, 113, 126, 129, 130, 131, 168, 173, 197, 198
Shea, T. M.   140, 202
Sheldon, B.   140, 198
Shen, Y.-C.   4, 188
Shepherd, G.   67, 198
Sherif, C. W.   28, 198
Sherif, M.   28, 198
Shipman, M.   110, 198
Shouldice, A.   43, 64, 199
Shure, M. B.   68, 114, 145, 146, 198
Shute, R. H.   12, 177
Silva, P. A.   8, 96, 188
Simms, J.   144, 147, 177
Simon, B.   111, 177
Simpson, A. E.   96, 198
Siner, J.   143, 198
Skaalvik, E.   154, 198
Slavson, S. R.   150, 198
Sletta, O.   154, 198
Sloman, J.   122, 195
Smetana, J. G.   127, 198
Smilansky, S.   27, 198
Smith, A. C.   47, 199
Smith, C. J.   110, 172
Smith, G.   77, 198
Smith, K.   90, 199
Smith, P. K.   11, 12, 27, 67, 89, 90, 91, 97, 106, 190, 198

Sobel, M.   62, 197
Søbstad, F.   154, 198
Solity, J. E.   83, 111, 169, 198
Sotto, E.   109, 110, 198
Spence, S H.   44, 67, 114, 141, 142, 143, 144, 146, 147, 158, 184, 198, 200
Spinell, A. P.   53, 181
Spinks, J. M.   110, 170
Spivack, G.   68, 114, 145, 146, 198
Sprafkin, R. P.   142, 178
Stabb, S. D.   151, 168
Stafford, D.   82, 196
Stafford, P.   82, 196
Stafford-Clark, D.   47, 199
Stallard, T.   7, 167
Stanton, W. R.   9, 187
Stayton, D. J.   22, 165
Stefanek, M. E.   67, 199
Steinberg, D.   47, 102, 199
Steinberg, L.   124, 199
Stephan, W. G.   97, 199
Stern, A. E.   77, 199
Stern, L.   67, 182
Stern, M.   144, 147, 189
Stevenson, J.   7, 8, 54, 66, 71, 92, 95, 96, 194, 198, 199
Stevenson-Hinde, J.   43, 64, 199
Stewart, M. A.   127, 190
Stocker, C. M.   1, 11, 58, 59, 199
Stone, C. A.   1, 177
Stott, D. H.   7, 33, 34, 51, 199
Strauss, C. C.   90, 199
Strauss, J. S.   102, 199
Streuning, E. L.   9, 45, 172
Strickland, B. R.   57, 191
Stringfield, S.   52, 54, 167
Strommen, E. A.   90, 91, 188, 199
Sundel, M.   138, 200
Sundel, S. S.   138, 200
Suwanlert, S.   4, 54, 202
Swann, W.   80, 168
Swanson, H. L.   56, 200

Sylva, K.   27, 169
Szatmari, P.   46, 200

Takahashi, R.   4, 188
Tanguay, P. E.   101, 194
Tann, S.   105, 111, 112, 193, 200
Tantam, D.   46, 200
Tarrant, T.   115, 119, 194
Tate, E.   123, 187
Tatskoka, M. M.   55, 171
Tattum, D.   106, 200
Taylor, A. R.   11, 200
Taylor, E.   53, 200
Taylor, J. A.   58, 200
Tesiny, E. P.   45, 61, 186
Tesla, C.   127, 195
Thacker, J.   146, 200
Thomas, A.   16, 72, 200
Thomas, J. B.   131, 190
Thompson, D.   97, 190
Thompson, R. J., Jr   5, 200
Thompson, T.   140, 200
Thorne, B.   136, 189
Thornes, R.   3, 185
Tiffen, K.   144, 146, 200
Tisher, M.   59, 186
Tizard, B.   19, 196, 200
Tizard, J.   5, 6, 8, 52, 54, 196
Tomlinson, S.   20, 200
Topping, K.   112, 201
Tossell, T.   115, 179
Tough, J.   18, 201
Treacher, A.   151, 201
Tremblay, R. E.   95, 201
Trevathan, D.   4, 202
Troot, M. A.   92, 95, 173
Trower, P.   136, 144, 201
Troyna, B.   86, 201
Tupling, C.   8, 196
Tyne, C.   53, 180

Upton, G.   110, 172
Urbain, E. S.   145, 147, 192

Valås, H.   154, 198
van der Ende, J.   5, 201
van Doorninck, W. J.

146, 170
van Ijzendoorn, H. W.   39, 40, 93, 95, 172
van Lieshout, C. F. M.   39, 40, 93, 95, 172
Velez, C. N.   9, 45, 172
Venables, P. H.   52, 201
Verhulst, F. C.   5, 96, 97, 165, 168, 201
Verma, G. K.   20, 201
Vikan, A.   4, 201
Vinogradov, S.   151, 201
Vitaro, F.   95, 201
Vize, C.   77, 178
Volpe, J.   155, 204
Vosk, B.   90, 179
Vostanis, P.   44, 184
Vrugt, A.   84, 201
Vygotsky, L. S.   27, 201

Wade, B.   82, 201
Waite, R. R.   73, 196
Waldrop, M. F.   11, 202
Walker, J. E.   140, 202
Walker, S.   105, 172
Wallbank, S.   79, 202
Walsh, P.   106, 202
Wang, Y. F.   4, 188
Warburton, F. W.   72, 202
Wardle, J.   80, 193
Wasserman, G. A.   74, 202
Waterhouse, P.   110, 202
Waters, B.   59, 184
Watkins, C.   118, 202
Watson, B. L.   56, 200
Webster-Stratton, C.   74, 75, 134, 162, 202
Wedell, K.   94, 187
Weir, K.   52, 202
Weiss, B.   4, 54, 202
Weissberg, R. P.   147, 202
Weisz, J. R.   4, 54, 202
Westmacott, E. V. S.   138, 202
Wetton, N.   143, 202
Wheeler, S.   136, 203
Wheldall, K.   7, 8, 137, 140, 189, 203
Whitaker, P.   120, 203
White, B. L.   22, 203
White, D.   75, 77, 79, 203
Whitehead, L.   97, 203
Whitmore, K.   5, 6, 8,

52, 54, 196
Whitney, I.   97, 190
Whitney, P.   91, 195
Whittington, D.   114, 141, 142, 175
Wikely, F.   122, 162, 182
Wilkinson, B.   111, 167
Wilkinson, C.   53, 180
Willey, R.   20, 203
Williams, B. T. R.   10, 39, 41, 60, 61, 203
Williams, G. A.   11, 200
Williams, S.   8, 10, 96, 188
Wiltshire Education Dept.   114, 203
Wing, L.   45, 101, 203
Winter, D.   50, 203
Woerner, W.   7, 9, 45, 100, 176
Wolfendale, S.   122, 167
Wolff, S.   72, 79, 203
Wolkind, S.   3, 185
Wolstenholme, F.   126, 150, 151, 184
Wood, A.   77, 180
Wood, M. E.   27, 203
Woodhead, M.   16, 203
Woods, P.   111, 204
Woolfe, R.   135, 151, 204
Woollett, A.   75, 77, 79, 203
Wooster, A. D.   115, 136, 186, 204
Work, W. C.   53, 181
Wragg, E. C.   63, 204
Wright, C.   97, 178
Wunder J.   100, 183

Yaeger, N. J.   67, 199
Yalom, I.   151, 201
Younger, A. J.   95, 204
Youniss, J.   127, 155, 204
Yule, W.   8, 43, 45, 191, 196

Zahn-Waxler, C.   128, 171
Zatz, S.   67, 204
Zeitlin, H.   100, 102, 204
Zeman, J.   65, 181
Zimbardo, P. G.   35, 57, 91, 204
Zimmerman, E. A.   74, 176
Ziv, A.   3, 204

Subject Index

abuse of children 76, 77, 81, 121
see also substance abuse
Achenbach and Edelbrock Child Behaviour Checklists 5, 53, 54
adolescence 5, 8–9, 25, 27–8, 29, 32, 38, 39–40, 43, 44, 45, 73, 76, 78, 85–6, 91, 100–1, 102, 116, 123, 124, 130–1, 155, 156, 160 *and passim*
anxiety 2, 10, 11, 33, 34, 54, 58, 72, 73, 101, 148, 152 *and passim*
consequences of 101
test anxiety 73
see also phobic behaviour
Asperger's syndrome 46–7
assessment 49–69, 93–4, 156
behaviour checklists 50–9
difficulties in 93–4
interviewing 65–7
observation 62–4
peer-referenced 59–62

purpose of 50
self-monitoring 67
for social skills training 67–8
see also self-reports
attachment 22
autism 45–6, 101

behaviour modification strategies 64, 137–40
implementation of 138–40
principles of 137–8
role of educational psychologists in 140
behaviour schedules/checklists 50–1
Achenbach and Edelbrock Child Behaviour Checklists 5, 53, 54
Behar and Stringfield Preschool Behaviour Questionnaire 54
Bristol Social Adjustment Guide 33–4, 50–2, 63

Conners Teachers Rating Scale 53
Langner Screening Inventory 54
Louisville Behaviour Checklist 54
Neeper and Lahey Comprehensive Behaviour Rating Scale 53
Quay and Peterson Revised Behaviour Problem Checklist 53
Richman Behaviour Check List 54
Rutter Child Behaviour Scales 6–7, 8, 44, 52–3, 54, 62
see also general assessment; interviewing; self-reports; social skills training
bereavement 78
Bristol Social Adjustment Guides 33–4, 50–2, 63
bullying 12, 33, 80, 82, 88, 94, 106, 129, 156

causes of
    withdrawal/isolation
        70–87
    abuse 77
    anxiety 72
    child-rearing practices
        75
    disability 79–82
    family adversity 75–6,
        79
    maternal depression
        73–4
    neglect in family 76–7
    school factors 80–5
    temperament 71–2
    traumatic experiences
        77–9
Circle Approach 129
'class play' approach
    61–2
classroom
    management 160–1
    setting 110–12, 117
*Code of Practice on the
    Identification and
    Assessment of
    Special Educational
    Needs* 68
cognitive development
    14–15
conflicts between children
    126–7
consequences 87–103
    of anxiety 100
    of autism 101
    of depression 100–1
    long-term 91–103
    of 'neglected' status
        99
    of schizophrenia 101
    of selective mutism
        102
    short-term 88–91
    of shyness 98–9
    of social rejection
        98–100
'controversial' social
    status 41, 93, 99,
        127

counselling 107–8,
    130–1, 134–7, 158
    aims of 135
    effectiveness of 137
    group 136–7
    by peers 130–1
    strategies 136
    by teachers 107–8,
        134–5
    theoretical bases of
        135–6
cross-cultural studies 4,
    21
cultural diversity 20–1,
    26
    see also ethnic
        background;
        racism
curriculum issues
    113–19

delinquents 96
depression 8, 10, 44–5,
    59, 86, 88, 100–1,
    161
    assessment of
        *Kovacs Children's
        Depression
        Inventory* 59
        *Lang and Tisher
        Children's
        Depression Scale*
        59
        *Lefkowitz and Tesiny
        Peer Nomination
        Inventory of
        Depression* 61
    consequences of
        100–1
    maternal 73–4, 75
disability 11, 79–82,
    162–3
disadvantage 1, 19–20,
    22, 95

early childhood 4, 6–7,
    15, 16, 17, 22, 26,
    27, 28, 37, 38, 48,
    71, 74, 89, 95, 100,

114, 123, 124, 125–6,
    127, 128–30, 159
    and passim
educational psychologists
    133, 135, 140, 143,
    145, 158
educational welfare
    officers 158
emotional and behaviour
    difficulties (EBDs)
    2–9, 10, 20, 39–42,
    103, 50–60, 71, 90,
    92, 96, 100, 103, 161
    and passim
emotional development
    16–17
employment of children
    86
ethnic background 20,
    26, 27, 97
    and EBDs 20
    and friendship 26
    see also racism;
        cultural diversity

family problems 75–6,
    79, 81, 94, 122,
    151–2, 161
family therapy 151–2
fears, *see* anxiety; phobic
    behaviour
friendship 11, 25, 155
    and passim

gender differences 8,
    17–19, 96–7, 98, 124
general assessment 68
    *Scherer School Skills
        Checklist* 68
groups 84–5, 85–7, 90,
    155 *and passim*
    in middle childhood
        90
    neighbourhood 85

health visitors 6
'hovering' 32

Imaginary Audience Scale

(IAS) 34–5, 57
'incorporative classrooms'
105
individual differences
71, 94, 159
integration 162–3
intervention strategies
12, 98, 104–20,
121–32, 128–31,
133–50
interviewing 65–7
*Costello Diagnostic
Interview Schedule*
66
*Herjanic and Reich
Diagnostic
Interview for
Children and
Adolescents* 66
highly structured 65–6
*Hodges Child
Assessment
Schedule* 67
*Kovacs Interview
Schedule* 67
in school 65
semi-structured 66–7
*Richman Behaviour
Screening
Questionnaire* 66

language skills 145
learning difficulties 11,
12, 31, 80–5, 94,
104, 160
loneliness 9, 32, 38–9,
91
Asher Loneliness Scale
57–8
loss 78

maternal deprivation 22
middle childhood 4, 5,
7–8, 23, 25, 27, 33,
34, 35, 36, 37, 38,
40, 41, 42, 43, 44,
46, 63, 64, 73, 76,
80, 93, 95–6, 115,
126, 127, 144, 146,

157 *and passim*

National Curriculum 68,
114, 115–16, 120,
159, 160
neglectees 36–9, 99, 126
consequences of
social neglect 99
forms of social neglect
37–8
identification of 36–7
neuroticism 55, 72
new entrants to school
32–3

obesity 73, 80, 81
observation 62–4, 68
in experimental
situations 64
naturalistic 63–4
in school 62–3
see also behaviour
schedules/ checklists

pairing 129–30
parents 110, 121–7, 156,
157, 161–2 *and
passim*
collaboration with
school 107, 109–12,
122, 156, 157
contribution to social
development 156
supervision by 122–6
see also family
problems
parent–teacher
collaboration 107,
109–12, 122, 156,
157
peer counselling 130–1
peer-referenced
assessment 59–62,
63
see also sociometric
techniques
peers 12, 127–32 *and
passim*
collaboration between

12
in distress 128–9
role of 127–31
peer tutoring 12, 112
personal and social
education (PSE)
114–17, 118–19
models of 116
in primary schools
115–16
in secondary schools
116–17
phobic behaviour 43–4,
58–9, 64
assessment of 58–9
*Ollendick Fear
Survey Schedule*
58
*Reynolds and
Richmond Revised
Children's Manifest
Anxiety Scale* 58
*Taylor Children's
Manifest Anxiety
Scale* 58
see also anxiety; school
refusal
play 6, 20, 21, 27, 89,
124, 125, 127
playground
activities 112–13
behaviour 28, 80
prevalence of social
withdrawal 3–9
and passim
in adolescence 8–9
agreement about 5
in different countries
4
in early childhood 6–7
in middle childhood
7–8
problems in estimating
3–5
Project Aware 146
pro-social behaviour 52
protective factors 97–8
psychiatrists 133, 135,
158

psychotherapy 148–52
  cognitive 149–50
  family 151–2
  group 150–1
  individual 148

racism 26, 86, 97, 106
  see also ethnic
    background
refugees 86
rejected children 39–41,
  88, 99–100, 126, 127
  and passim
  consequences of
    rejected status
    99–100
  identification of 39
  types of 39–41
repertory grid techniques
  50
reserved children 31
Rutter Child Behaviour
  Scales 6–7, 8, 44,
  52–3, 54, 62

schizophrenia 8, 47, 96,
  101
school factors 11, 12,
  80–5, 94, 110–12,
  117, 160
  educational
    performance 82–3,
    87, 89, 112
  gifted pupils 83
  group approaches
    84–5
  learning difficulties
    11, 12, 31, 80–5, 94,
    104, 160
  see also classroom;
    school
    management;
    teachers; 'whole-
    school' approaches
school governors 107
school management
  109–13, 120, 160–1
school refusal 9, 43–4
selective mutism 47–8,

102
self-esteem 1, 11, 33, 84,
  85, 88, 90, 95, 105,
  116, 143, 155, 156
self-monitoring 67
  Zatz and Chassin
    Children's Cognitive
    Assessment
    Questionnaire 67
self-reports 5, 33, 34, 35,
  38, 45, 54–9
  Achenbach and
    Edelbrock Youth Self
    Report 56
  Cattell 16 Personality
    Factor Test 55–6
  Coopersmith Self-
    Esteem Inventory
    57
  Eysenck Personality
    Questionnaire
    55
  Harter Self-
    Perception Profile
    for Children 57
  Mooney Problem
    Check Lists 56
  Nowicki and
    Strickland Locus of
    Control Scale 57
  Rogers Personal
    Adjustment Inventory
    56
  see also depression;
    loneliness; phobic
    behaviour; shyness
shyness 6, 7, 9, 11, 33–6,
  57–61, 88, 96, 98–9,
  145 *and passim*
  assessment of
    Crozier Children's
    Shyness
    Questionnaire 57
    Elkind and Bowen
    Imaginary
    Audience Scale
    34–5, 57
  consequences of 98–9
  definitions of 33–4

forms of 34–5
peer assessment 61
prevalence of 35–6
sibling relationships 23,
  156–7
social class 19–20
social cognitive training
  144–7
  aims of 145
  effectiveness of 146,
    147
  implementation of
    145
social context 1–2, 29,
  49
social relationships 1–2,
  10–11, 14–29 *and*
  passim
  assessment of 10–11
  definition of 10
  development of 14–29
  factors affecting
    14–21
  importance of 1–2
social skills 4, 67–8,
  114, 141, 142, 143,
  144, 145, 146, 147,
  154, 159 *and passim*
social skills training (SST)
  67–8, 114, 140–4,
  147, 158–9
  aims of 142
  assessment of
    Spence Behaviour at
    School Questionnaire
    67
  effectiveness of
    143–4, 147, 158–9
  implementation of
    143
  principles of 142
  strategies 142–3
social workers 135, 158
socio-dramatic play 21,
  27
sociometric status 10,
  36–42, 48, 64, 93,
  98–100, 125–6 *and*
  passim

instability of   93
and parental supervision
    125
see also sociometric
    techniques
sociometric techniques
    36, 41–2, 60–2
    *Shapiro Sociometric
    Role Assignment Test*
    62
see also sociometric
    status
special educational needs
    104, 118, 122, 162–3
see also disability;
    learning difficulties
speech therapists   133,
    158
Stott Adjustment Pointers
    7
stress   75, 77–8, 79, 94,
    105, 107, 108, 161

in children   77–8, 79,
    117
in families   75, 79
in teachers   105, 108,
    161
substance abuse   86, 163
support services   133–52,
    158
collaboration with
    parents and teachers
    133–4
counsellors   134–37,
    158
Swann Report   20

teachers   2, 3, 5, 6–9, 44,
    49, 51–3, 62–3, 65,
    68, 83, 104–20, 135,
    137–9, 143, 145,
    153, 156, 157, 163
assessment by   6–9,
    44, 49, 51–3, 62–3,

68
collaboration with
    parents   107,
    109–10, 112, 122,
    156, 157
help from   104–20,
    137–9, 143, 145,
    160–1
interviewing by   65
stress in   105, 108, 161
temperament   16, 71–2,
    73, 92, 96
'Think Aloud' programme
    146

underachievement   82–3,
    87, 112
'unforthcomingness'
    33–4

'whole-school' approaches
    105–8, 120